NATURE'S CALENDAR

NATURE'S CALENDAR

The British Year in 72 Seasons

Kiera Chapman, Lulah Ellender,
Rowan Jaines and Rebecca Warren

With line drawings by Rebecca Warren

GRANTA

Granta Publications, 12 Addison Avenue, London W11 4QR

First published in Great Britain by Granta Books, 2023
This edition published by Granta Books, 2024

A CIP catalogue record for this book
is available from the British Library.

2   4   6   8   9   7   5   3   1

ISBN 978 1 78378 961 0
eISBN 978 1 78378 960 3

www.granta.com

Typeset in Miller by Patty Rennie

Printed and bound by CPI Group (UK) Ltd,
Croydon, CR0 4YY

To those who love nature everywhere,
and especially those who helped to develop this calendar.

Contents

Note on Illustrations

It has been a privilege and a pleasure to illustrate *Nature's Calendar* and I am deeply indebted to my co-authors for placing their trust in me to bring visual form to our collaborative project.

The essence of drawing is observation. An artist must understand the underlying structure of a subject in order to draw it successfully, even when much of the subject is hidden under petals, leaves or feathers. Illustrating this book has given me 'permission' to spend time really studying my subjects, noticing the intricacies of texture, colour and form, and observing details like the patterns of leaf veins, or how a flower connects to its stem, or the length of a bird's claws.

Among our essays we have suggested ways for our readers to actively participate in the practice of 'noticing nature', but nothing encourages us to look more carefully at something than when we draw it. It is not the quality of the picture that matters, but the process of close observation that really repays the time taken and I hope that my illustrations might inspire some of our readers to 'notice nature' through the medium of pencil, paper and paint.

REBECCA WARREN

Introduction

This book grew out of a chance encounter on social media involving four strangers and an unusual way of marking time. Our imaginations were captured by a traditional Japanese calendar, introduced from China in the seventeenth century, which divided the year into seventy-two brief microseasons. Each has its own poetic name: 15–20 May, for example, is 'Bamboo shoots sprout', 11–15 June is the season when 'Rotten grass becomes fireflies', 12–16 July is 'First lotus blossoms'. Intrigued by the idea, we wondered what ecological and meteorological phrases might encapsulate these fleeting periods in a British context.

This question quickly uncovered another: could dividing time differently sharpen the way in which we perceive the natural world around us? Our waking, sleeping and eating times may vary according to individual preferences and needs, but for most of us, everyday life coheres around clock time, its seconds, minutes and hours anchoring us in a shared routine that pivots around the working day. There is the same broad coherence in our measurement of wider time. There are lingering irregularities – longer and shorter months, leap years, the mobility of religious festivals still tied to lunar cycles – but our year is metered out by the unwavering succession of the twelve named months.

The ticking measure of standardised time also tells us when and how to observe change. We sense the distant coming of summer when the clocks go forward in spring and we suddenly have an extra hour of daylight. We 'know' autumn has arrived when the school term starts, no matter what we see around us in the changing environment. We notice abruptly that the days are drawing in when the clocks go back at the end of October, and for a few days we grumble about how dark and gloomy it all is. But as soon as we have accommodated ourselves to the bigger changes we tend to stop being curious, being observant, being open to local differences.

Could microseasons offer a way of seeing the natural world afresh? We decided to find out, and to make our project a collective endeavour. Our methodology was simple. On social media, we asked people to notice the changes around them, one short microseason at a time, and to share their observations with us. Every five to six days, we selected four of these observations and asked people to vote for whichever seemed most resonant. The winning observation became the name of that microseason. A year later, we had an entire microseason calendar, one based on noticing the passing of time in the natural environment around us.

In this book, we have taken a deeper look at each microseason, exploring and expanding on the original subject. Our approach is joyfully inclusive, mixing science, social science, economics, art, literature, history and politics. We all come from different backgrounds and have different specialisms, and we hope that this variety makes our book engaging, unexpected and informative.

Microseasonal changes are both temporal and spatial. Research undertaken at Coventry University suggests that spring moves at an average of 1.9 miles per hour across the UK, from south to north. Of course, some individual species respond to the passing of time more quickly, others more slowly. Hawthorn leaves, for example, open first in the south-west, and the timing of their unfurling travels in a north-easterly direction at a rate of 6.3 miles per hour. Sightings of the first flutterings of orange-tip butterflies travel at an average of 1.4 miles per hour. Frogspawn is slower, moving across the country at one mile per hour, which seems to suit its gelatinous state. Spring is not so much an event as a movement, and one that is subject to the vagaries of meteorological conditions in any given year.

Our project is not to try to create a placeless and timeless series of microseasons, applicable everywhere across the British Isles in any given year. We made a conscious decision not to smooth out the particularities of the year 2021–22 during which we collated our observations. Each year will necessarily have its own unique character, but much that we noticed during this time seems to accord with observations made by our contributors since. For this reason, we were less interested in the exceptional firsts – the return of the first pond-skimming swallow, the first skeletal tree of autumn, the first winter frost – because this competitive approach would inevitably lead to the over-representation of the warmer or cooler parts of the UK. Instead, we have chosen to highlight phenomena that are widely recognised, building a calendar that represents a collective act of observing and sharing.

A plant or animal can play a meaningful role in our everyday life without us knowing its Latin name or the details of its life cycle. One of the joys of the observations within this calendar is that they were made from the senses, rather than the textbook. However, as we looked more closely at the phenomena for each season, we found that scientific ways of understanding often hold their own stories, and that additional information about taxonomy or species behaviour can allow us to appreciate our observations more deeply.

It has been interesting to see how much our shifting understanding of the natural world over the centuries has been informed or complicated by our problematic colonial and imperial past. Our calendar is based in the British Isles, but it nevertheless recognises and celebrates the way that some plants have travelled across cultures. We understand, too, that in a multicultural community such as ours one plant can have different meanings and associations.

Of course, any current book charting seasonal change must reckon with the realities of climate change and habitat destruction. One year's observations cannot provide a record of these wider and worrying shifts, but the act of paying attention to small changes can nonetheless help us to avoid the problem of 'shifting baseline syndrome', where each generation accepts the environment that it inherits as normal, masking the enormity of ecological and environmental deterioration. As we gathered the microseasonal observations online and noted what we saw in nature around us, we found ourselves talking about what we were seeing with our children, our parents, our younger and older friends, realising the differences between the phenomena we remembered from the past and those we were seeing now. Through this kind of conversation, we can each tap into our own internal seasonal calendar and become more aware of the incremental changes, more alive to the ways in which human actions are affecting the natural world and, we hope, more inspired to do what we can to stem the damage.

Collectively, our book offers a calendar grounded in everyday, accessible, and much-loved natural events. We have tried to bring curiosity, attention and a sense of discovery to these events, to defamiliarise and re-enchant them. We hope that our essays will surprise you and make you see the natural world in a new light. We have tried to strike a balance between a celebration of the joy and wonder in nature, an awareness of the extent to which many species are under threat, and a need to tell histories that are sometimes emotionally complex. Above all, we invite you to compare the calendar of 2021 to the microseasons of your current year, to observe, to delight in and to develop your own practice of nature-noticing.

JANUARY

Noticing Exercise

The shortest and darkest days of the year are upon us, but this means that the light is growing quickly. On 1 January at Dunsop Bridge, Lancashire (roughly the centre point of Great Britain), the sun sets at around 15.58, yet by 1 February it will be light until 16.50.

This month, take a moment to watch the sky change colour as the sun dips beyond the horizon. Watch out for the way the hues of the sunset change with different weather conditions, and let the clouds form imaginary shapes as they are lit from shifting angles. Observe twilight creeping in, a few minutes later each day, and take note of the changing quality of the light that comes with the lengthening evenings.

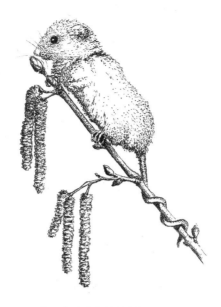

1–4 JANUARY

Catkins Dingle-dangle

In the dark and quiet early days of January, there is still brightness to be found: clusters of yellow flowers dangle from bare branches, as though bedecking the hedgerows for a festivity. Though spring might seem impossibly far away, at this moment in the year the common hazel tree (*Corylus avellana*) is readying itself for reproduction with an inflorescence of catkins.

These catkins actually start to form in mid-May and can be seen from June, but it is only now, in the period after the winter solstice, that they reach maturity as elongated, pendulous clusters of around 240 individual male-sex flowers arranged on dangling stems. While typical flowers are showy confections, brightly coloured, scented and richly sweet in order to attract pollinators, hazel catkins have an entirely different style and modus operandi. The hazel catkin does not rely on insects for pollination (it's still too early for that); instead, it just needs the wind to give it a shake. A shake strong enough for its pollen to reach another tree.

The hazel tree is a monoecious plant. This means that male and female flowers are present on a single individual. The hazel's female flower also emerges on its branches around this time in the seasonal year, too early to be pollinated by insects, which will not emerge until spring. These female flowers are reminiscent of sea anemones; their scaly green bud is crowned with a bundle of delicate red tendrils emerging from the top.

When you glimpse the hazel's catkins during this microseason, you should be aware that a spectacular feat is afoot. The pollen of a catkin cannot fertilise a female hazel flower from the same tree, and so the catkins become heavy with pollen, ready to be borne by the wind to another tree.

When a hazel catkin finally ripens, it only takes the slightest touch of the breeze to release a cloud of microscopic pollen grains. The flushed protrusions of the female flower begin to form at the end of June and can be seen on the hazel tree from around Halloween. Like their male counterparts, these female flowers are mature and ready to be fertilised in the earliest days of January.

When a male pollen grain is swept by the wind on to one of the red, anemone-like tufts of the female hazel flower on another tree, that female flower is fertilised. While a majority of flowers have an ovary containing ovules with egg cells primed for fertilisation, the flowers of the hazel tree have several pairs of long styles with stigmatic surfaces that are receptive to pollen. Like a Russian doll, inside the hazel's bud scales are the lower portions of between four and sixteen separate flowers, as well as a tiny bit of tissue at their base called the ovarian meristem.

Once an egg has formed, the pollen that stimulated the hazel flower's sexual maturation reawakens and fertilises the egg, forming a hazelnut. The female flowers bud in the early summer; they open the following January for pollination, which results in fertilisation around their first birthday. Finally they fruit, approximately nine months after this moment in the year when the catkins emerge, as little powder kegs of life to come. This long lapse between pollination and fertilisation is unusual in the plant world, where fertilisation usually follows pollination by a few days.

Corylus avellana is one of the earliest known cultivator crops, and as such it has moved with human populations over time and features regularly in folk tales. Along with other ancient plants such as the apple and the hawthorn, it is found at the border between the worlds where magical things may happen. The hazel appears as such in variations of the ancient Cinderella fairy tale, which also found their way into the version told by the Brothers Grimm. In this version of the tale Cinderella is called 'Ashputtel' and the magical role played by the fairy godmother instead belongs to the natural world, embodied in the form of a January hazel tree, adorned with catkins.

The tale begins in the familiar way with a young girl who is mourning for her mother and who has been reduced to a servant since her father remarried. Ashputtel's stepmother brings two daughters, and the three women force the bereaved girl to wear rags and perform demanding chores. But in this winter of discontent Ashputtel is saved by her care for nature. She is a friend of the birds, who help her with her tasks, and she tends to the hazel tree that she planted in her mother's memory, which she waters each day with her tears as she grieves. When Ashputtel is prevented from attending the king's feast, she visits the hazel and asks the little tree to shake its ripe catkins and to bedeck her in silver and gold.

Her wish is granted, and the prince of the kingdom falls in love with her.

Though her stepsisters have the privileges of money and power, they cannot rival the beauty that Ashputtel's relationship with nature has granted her. And when the prince comes searching for Ashputtel, it is the birds that alert him that he has been duped by the stepsisters, directing him to his true love and granting Ashputtel her escape from drudgery and servitude.

At this dark and cold moment of the year, as we see the catkins bedecking winter trees, we can consider the way in which myths, legends, and folk tales have advised us to form a relationship with nature and tend to it. And as we see the catkins being blown by the wind to a neighbouring tree, we might also remember nature's intention to blossom in the coming months and know a new burst of life is imminent.

ROWAN JAINES

5–9 JANUARY

The Light Steals Back

The days after the Christmas holidays and New Year festivities, when life resumes its normal routine, can feel flat and bleak. But the creeping increments of daylight bring solace and the promise of change.

By the end of this month we will have around one more hour of daylight than last month, depending on where you are in the British Isles, but it might not seem that way as the mornings feel darker than ever. Until 9 January the light *is* stealing back, but at sunset rather than sunrise. The days are stretching more at one end than the other. How can this be? The answer lies in astrophysics and horology.

These enduringly dark mornings are due to the 'Equation of Time', which describes the difference between solar time and clock time. Yes, there are different types of time. Solar time is measured according to Earth's position relative to the sun. It is affected by the tilt of the axis as it orbits, by the fact that the orbit is not circular and by the speed the sun travels. Clock time takes a mean measurement of where the Earth would be in relation to the sun if these movements were uniform, which results in disparities. A clock-time day is twenty-four hours long and noon and midnight fall at fixed times. A solar-time day runs from the highest point of the sun one day to the highest point the next day (including the dark in between). At this time of year in the northern hemisphere the Earth tilts closest to the sun and is spinning faster than clock time. This keeps our sunrises static for a few days.

As if this wasn't confounding enough, you might notice that twilights at this time of year seem to be shorter, giving us even less light. Twilight is the time after sunset when the sun is just below the horizon and the day blends slowly into night. And there are three phases of twilight, determined by the exact position of the sun in relation to the horizon. At dusk, civil twilight is the period between sunset and the sun dipping 6° below the horizon, nautical twilight is between 6° and 12°, and astronomical between 12° and 18°. At the start of January, the angle of the sun means that it passes through these phases more quickly, resulting in minimal twilight.

In this bare, cold month it is not surprising that we tune in to any increase in daylight and cling to what warmth we can feel from the weak winter sun. For those who suffer seasonal affective disorder this time of year can be especially difficult. This condition, also known as 'winter depression', is thought to be due to lower exposure to sunlight during the winter, which may impair the function of the hypothalamus. Light therapy involving sitting in front of a lightbox can be effective until the days get longer and the sun stronger.

Yet, before we wish away these quiet, inky days, perhaps it is worth thinking a little more deeply about darkness. We are used to it symbolising chaos and despair, but the potency of the dark sky has inspired artists across time, from an ancient Babylonian boundary stone depicting a starlit sky to the medieval illuminated manuscript *Scivias* by Hildegard von Bingen and Vincent van Gogh's *The Starry Night*. The painter Albert Bierstadt's work depicts North American landscapes at night or in twilight; and artist Katie Paterson collects astronomical photos showing voids in the darkest reaches of the sky. If we look closely at Gillian Carnegie's *Black Square* we see the outline of trees created by thick black brushstrokes. Perhaps darkness is not as empty as it first appears.

In fact, darkness is relative. NASA's black-marble images of the Earth at night contain pinpricks of city lights, showing that there is rarely true darkness. And, looking outwards, the Hubble Space Telescope reveals galaxies of stars invisible to the naked eye in parts of the sky that look like voids. If you find yourself somewhere with virtually no light pollution it is surprising how your eyes adjust and you make out the sense of objects even if you can't fully see them.

If you are in the right place at the right time after dusk in early January, you might see the sky lit up with the light trails and fireballs of the Quadrantid meteor showers, bringing a welcome burst of fire and light. But it is a fleeting show compared to the blazing summer sun, which is why we've developed our own rituals to bring light into the month. This microseason features the Christian feast of Epiphany on 6 January, and across Europe there are celebratory parades and fireworks, as well as rejuvenating cold-water swims which awaken the senses. The name Epiphany signifies illumination, but it is important for Christians, who believe that this was the day on which the Magi reached Bethlehem. Other celebrations, like the fireball-whirling ceremony in Stonehaven, Scotland or the old Distaff Day (6 January) ritual when men tried to set fire to their wives' flax-covered distaffs (rods for storing wool and flax) before the women could douse them with cold water, add a blaze of light to this period.

Epiphany also marks Twelfth Night, the end of the Christian Christmastide. This is the day for wassailing, a ritual dating back to the Middle Ages, possibly with pagan roots. Predominantly held in cider-producing parts of Britain, a wassail is a gathering of people in an orchard or around fruit trees, singing to the trees to bring a bountiful harvest later in the year. A wassail bowl of spiced cider or perry is shared round while people bang pots and pans to scare away evil spirits. Torches and bonfires are lit to welcome the incoming light, and wassailers pour cider over tree roots and hang toasted cider-soaked bread from the trees as a crop blessing. Historically, wassailing was also a way for poorer folk to make some money in the harsh winter months when there was little agricultural work. Women would go from house to house with cider to share, asking for money in return. Although it is an ancient custom there are now over seventy-three wassails in England alone – a sign that we are looking to the past for ways in which to connect with the land and cycles of nature (and that we are in need of distraction from the darkness).

As the light fills out, we begin to see signs of new growth. Yellow-maned dandelions, nodding hellebores, bright winter bramblings, berry-gobbling redwings and the delicate-looking yet surprisingly hardy cyclamen all add colour and hope to the landscape. The robin's red breast lights up the winter gloom, its song providing a soundtrack for garden chores and frosty walks. And the days are getting longer, however wonky the increments. After the frenzy and indulgence of the Christmas holidays, perhaps mid-January is a time to pause and observe, to look for light wherever we can find it and to remember that it is always held within the darkness.

LULAH ELLENDER

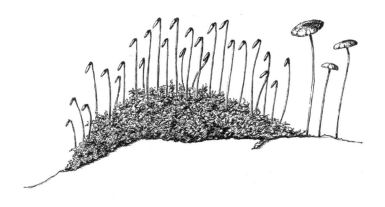

10–14 JANUARY

Mosses Glow Green

In the dank, grey light of January there's one group of plants that vibrates with a soft, vivid green. Inconspicuous amid the fresher leaves of the spring and summer, in deepest winter the mosses glow gently, calling our attention. It's tempting to describe their appearance in terms of more familiar ecosystems, as miniature forests or tiny ferneries. However, a closer look with a hand lens reveals a quiet riot of surprising textures: there are mosses that look like maggoty hummocks, tightly plaited hair, velvet pincushions, tufts of spiky grass. There are large rosettes, rounded hamster ears, Hawaiian flower necklaces, and even frozen firework displays of stars. Taking time to notice them, in detail, brings a new world into view.

Mosses are tiny because they don't contain any vascular tissue, which means they lack specialised tube-shaped cells that act as 'pipes' inside the plant, bringing up water from the soil and transporting fluids internally. This lack of internal structure also means that they cannot stand tall. As a result, they are often seen as ancestral plants, as if they had been frozen in time millions of years ago, relics of an era before more 'sophisticated' vascular plants evolved. But while some mosses retain certain aspects of a so-called primitive life cycle, evolution has nonetheless continued to act on these species, changing their traits over time. Rather than seeing them as living fossils, we should view them as remarkably well-adapted survivors. After all, how many organisms can grow on substrates as harsh as rock?

Many mosses survive by exploiting the different ways that air moves over surfaces. When an object like a rock or a tree interrupts air flow, the air immediately surrounding it slows down. The stratum of air above can be quite turbulent, but underneath there is a much calmer 'boundary layer'. This traps evaporating water vapour, creating a damper, cooler environment. The texture of the moss itself increases the thickness of the boundary layer by creating resistance to air movement. Obviously, other conditions affect this too: if the place is exposed to a lot of wind and sun, the boundary layer might get quite thin. Mosses wanting to live in such locations can't grow very high, and might have hairs or spines wafting above them to help them slow down the surrounding air. But in a forest, mosses can grow bigger, not least because trees act as a kind of large-scale boundary layer.

However, escaping the boundary layer can be advantageous, for example if you want to disperse spores into the environment. This is why so many wood mosses produce their spores on longer stalks, called setae: these act like stilts, lifting them into higher, more turbulent layers of air where wind vibration can assist dispersal.

Mosses are impressively adaptable. Some are resilient to drought: many can desiccate to the point that only 5–10 per cent of their dry weight is water, and still return to normal metabolism and growth when re-wetted. Yet they can also inhabit very soggy places. *Sphagnum* mosses, for instance, are the plant architects of peatlands (blanket bogs, raised bogs and fens). They typically form a carpet made of relatively long vertical shoots with lateral leaves, which become more closely spaced near the top of the plant, where they form a dense, spidery cluster called the 'capitulum'. Although they don't have roots to suck up moisture, water is moved up to the top of the plant by capillary action, the tiny spaces between the leaves wicking it upwards.

Sphagnum leaves also have a clever method for absorbing nutrients. A single cell thick, their walls are made from a sugary polymer that contains uronic acid and phenolic compounds. This helps the moss to find food: it releases positively charged hydrogen ions into the surrounding water, leaving a negatively charged group in the cell wall that can attract positively charged nutrient molecules. In the process, the moss also acidifies its surroundings, making it difficult for competing plants to grow. Effectively, these plants manipulate their environment to produce the harsh, acidic, cold, waterlogged and nutrient-poor conditions in which they thrive.

This property proved useful during the First World War, when fighting in Egypt led to a shortage of cotton, which was essential for making bandages. Sir Edward Ward, Director General of Voluntary Organisations, realised that *Sphagnum* offered an alternative and set up a drive to collect as much of it as possible. People headed out on to bogs, peatlands and moors, plunging their arms into rust-coloured water to pull out heavy, sodden mats of tangled growth. Many may have enjoyed the unusual experience of being permitted to walk on these then-private uplands.

By 1918, around a million bags of *Sphagnum* per month were being harvested, separated, dried, picked clean and packed in muslin for dispatch to British military hospitals at home and abroad. The best species for wound-dressing was *Sphagnum papillosum*, but others were also processed into dysentery pads and pillows. The absorbency of the new dressings proved to be superior to that of cotton, and they possessed an antimicrobial effect, perhaps thanks to the moss's ability to acidify its surrounding environment. This meant *Sphagnum* dressings could be left in place over a wound for longer.

But if extracted *Sphagnum* has been historically useful to us in wartime, then this plant's growth in situ may have an important role to play in our contemporary fight to mitigate climate change. Peatlands are an incredible carbon store: they occupy 3 per cent of the global land area, but contain around 25 per cent of soil carbon, much of it due to mosses. Yet since the eighteenth century, peatlands have been underappreciated, written off as aesthetically uninteresting, unproductive 'wastes', even derided as 'mamba' (short for 'miles and miles of bugger all'!).

Our inability to see the beauty and importance of moss means that we have taken poor care of our peatlands: across the world, drainage, horticultural extraction, deforestation, deliberate burning and inappropriate development are all releasing peat-locked carbon back into the atmosphere at an alarming rate. The impacts of this may amount to the release of more than two billion metric tonnes of carbon dioxide into the global atmosphere each year. If we don't look after our peatlands and keep our mossy landscapes wet (re-wetting some of those that have been dried and damaged), escaping carbon dioxide from them will account for an astonishing 12–40 per cent of the global carbon budget that we need to hit if we are to meet the Paris Agreement target of limiting warming to below 1.5°C.

Perhaps it's time we stopped relegating mosses to a curiosity of early evolution, and started appreciating not only their beauty but their current role in the health of our society and planet. After all, they may prove key in sustaining life on Earth in the future.

KIERA CHAPMAN

15–19 JANUARY

Snowdrops Emerge

'Blue Monday': this microseason often contains what has recently been identified as the most depressing day of the year. And yet, and yet . . . even at this bleakest of moments, there are signs that the year is turning. This is the season when snowdrops emerge, their white buds nestling in the grass like scattered pearls, delicate, perfect.

Of course, snowdrops are not the only flowers to appear in January. There are other species – the 'chancers' of the plant world – who will exploit any favourable microclimate or unseasonal spell of sunshine to race into flower. Herb Robert, common daisies and a raft of garden shrubs, for example, all employ this strategy. As climate change accelerates, they will undoubtedly be joined by others. But snowdrops are different: they are hardwired into our understanding of the progress of the year. They may flower a week earlier if the weather is mild, but they remain tied to that natural calendar we hold in our heads that tells us spring is just around the corner. This is why we care about their emergence; this is why seeing the 'first snowdrop' is news.

In Latin, the common snowdrop is *Galanthus nivalis* – 'milk flower of the snows' – a tribute both to its luscious whiteness and its winter flowering. If left to itself, this is the species that naturalises most freely into grassland. Yet while *Galanthus nivalis* is the commonest snowdrop species in Britain, it is only one of around twenty others so far identified worldwide, from the 'giant snowdrop', *Galanthus elwesii*, first recorded in 1875 and native to the Levant, to *Galanthus bursanus*, discovered as recently as 2019 in a single province of north-west Turkey. And from these twenty species, hundreds of cultivars have been bred, extending the flowering season from autumn into late spring. But snowdrops are essentially flowers designed to cope with hot, dry summers and harsh winters, and this explains their form. As bulbs, they can sit out punishing summer heat underground, dormant and in stasis, their leaves and flowers long gone. Then, as the climate softens in autumn, they spread their roots again, rebuilding their reserves and forming reinforced leaf-tips with which to push up even through frozen soil and snow in the winter sunshine to flower before they are shaded out by taller plants in spring.

Despite their adaptations for semi-arid conditions, however, snowdrops are, for us, flowers of wood and meadow, revelling in our temperate climate. Some of the best displays are found in graveyards, where the ground has been largely undisturbed and ungrazed for many years. This is an apt setting for a flower which has had long associations with Christianity. The pure white of the snowdrop's petals was thought to mirror the purity of the Virgin Mary herself, and the snowdrop season, which begins in this microseason, will reach its zenith in early February, around the feast of Candlemas, when the purification of the Virgin after the birth of Christ is observed. Snowdrops have long been central to the celebration of this feast, linked especially with the white-clad girls who traditionally processed into church to mark the festival. Indeed, one of the Italian names for snowdrop is *fiore della purificazione* (flower of the purification) and in France they are sometimes known as *violettes de la Chandeleur* (Candlemas violets).

Modern thought tentatively suggests that snowdrops arrived in Britain alongside the Romans, some two thousand years ago. They were probably already occurring in wild colonies by the time John Gerard wrote his 1597 *Herball or Generall Historie of Plants*, in which he called them *Leucojum bulbosum praecox*, or 'timely flowring Bulbus violet'. He almost certainly took this name from the *Historia Plantarum* of the Greek writer Theophrastus who, in the fourth century BCE, had referred to *Galanthus* as λευκοςιόν (*leukosion*), meaning 'white violet'. Seventeenth-century editions of Gerard's *Herball*, however, also recorded the folk-name of 'snowdrop'. It has been suggested that this word came from the German *Schneetropfen*, a term that was also used for the pearl-drop earrings popular in the sixteenth and seventeenth centuries, which were famously captured by the Dutch artist Johannes Vermeer in his 1665 painting *Girl with a Pearl Earring*. Whatever its origin, the English 'snowdrop' is a perfect name for *Galanthus*.

Snowdrops are not just pretty harbingers of spring –

they're useful too. Botanically, they fall within the sub-family *Amaryllidoideae*, which includes daffodils (*Narcissus*) and snowflakes (*Leucojum*). Like narcissi, snowdrops contain galantamine, an alkaloid that is being used to relieve the symptoms of Alzheimer's disease. Galantamine helps to counteract a deficiency in the important neurotransmitter acetylcholine, abnormally low levels of which are detected in Alzheimer's sufferers. In 1983 two neuroscientists, Andreas Plaitakis and Roger Duvoisin, suggested that the protective effect of galantamine on acetylcholine may also have provided some level of antidote towards a poison coming from *Datura stramonium*, a member of the toxic deadly nightshade family, long known to cause memory loss and amnesia. They went on to make an extraordinary suggestion: that snowdrops may have been the hitherto unidentified plant 'moly' mentioned in Homer's *Odyssey*. In this ancient Greek epic, the god Hermes was said to have given moly to Odysseus to protect him against the poisons of the witch Circe when he landed on Aeaea in the Mediterranean to rescue his friends. It was described as having a black root, while 'the flower was as white as milk; the gods call it Moly, and mortal men cannot uproot it'. Hypothesising that Circe might have used *Datura* to poison Odysseus' companions, Plaitakis and Duvoisin suggested that snowdrops may have been known even in the Homeric Bronze Age as a protection against such toxins. Well perhaps – although snowdrop bulbs are not black, and this theory does seem to hang upon on a rather tenuous chain of conditions . . .

Yet there is something magical, something slightly 'otherworldly' about the snowdrop. Perhaps it is the unusual three-petalled form of the flowers – rare in the botanical world – and their stark, drooping simplicity. Even the modern cultivars, selected for slight variations in colour or form, retain a singular stillness and precision that appeals to our aesthetic sense. It is little wonder that they inspire artists and designers, featuring on glass and ceramic ornaments, fabric patterns and wallpaper. So in this microseason we notice and celebrate the purity and simplicity of the snow-drop, emerging from the depths of the earth to signal that spring is on its way. At last.

REBECCA WARREN

20–24 JANUARY

Small Birds Fluffing

In the depths of the British winter, when temperatures regularly drop to within a degree or two of freezing, birds are often seen puffed up into fat little balls. This avian equivalent of pulling up your collar or hood against the cold is an act of self-preservation that opens up a complicated mystery regarding the evolution of the feathered creatures more generally.

Birds, like mammals, are a warm-blooded species, in scientific terms referred to as 'endotherms'. In order to survive in cold weather, endotherms have to prevent heat loss, particularly around the heart area. Heat transference can occur in three ways: through radiation, as happens with fire; through conduction, as happens when you touch a hot stove or a piece of ice; and convection, as happens when warm water or a cold wind passes over your body. Insulation slows down all of these processes of heat transfer. When we notice little birds fluffing up at this moment in the year, we are witnessing how birds increase the air space between their feathers into a honeycomb of insulation that keeps them warm.

Let us stop for a moment and think about what a feather actually is. In the most simple terms, a feather is a branched structure. Its trunk is a tube, called the rachis, which splays off into serial paired branches called barbs. These barbs stem into further branches, known as barbules, which are attached to one another by hooks that hold the structure together into the familiar flattened, curved 'vane'. The feathers that allow for insulation lack barbules and are fluffy rather than stiff along the vane. In many birds, some or all of the feathers lack the barbules or the hooks, creating the 'down' that birds use to insulate themselves.

Feathers are unique in their complex branching structure and enormous variation in colour, shape and texture, and they represent one of the most enduring and knotty problems in evolutionary science. It is well known that birds evolved from reptiles, but when we attempt to trace the evolution of feathers from reptilian scales we run into trouble. Early theories about how scaled reptiles evolved into feathered birds proposed that scales extended and grew fringed edges which developed into the hooked and grooved barbules that constitute feathers. However, this hypothesis is widely disputed since the two are so different in form. Scales are flat folds, whereas feathers are cylindrical sheaths (the rachis) from which a complex branching structure of gossamer filaments emerges.

So why did feathers develop? There are many competing answers. The most popular theory is that their effectiveness as a form of insulation conferred an adaptive advantage. Other researchers have argued that feathers evolved to act as a heat shield, to repel water, or to contour the body in order to move at greater speed on the ground. However, none of these suggestions manage to fully explain the evolutionary process behind the aerodynamic structure of feathers. Feathers continue to challenge our understanding of how and why flight fits into processes of natural selection.

In paying close attention to the feather, we realise we are less knowledgeable about the workings of the natural world than we'd like to believe. We are as baffled by these mysterious epidermal growths as were long-dead natural scientists from Aristotle to Darwin. We are as in awe of their beauty as the painters, writers and mystics who encoded this human fascination into proverbs, poetry, folklore, images and superstitions.

Birds and feathered anthropomorphic forms appear in myth, legend and religion the world over. The motif of the winged angel is consistently recognisable across many monotheistic religions as an allegorical figure who bridges the gap between earthly human life and the spiritual plane. Demons and devils also have wings, but angels alone have wings with feathers.

Feathered beings have historically held a more earthly symbolism too. Though today British people tend to identify more readily with mammals than with avian life, this was not always the case. During the Late Medieval period birds were often imagined as a mirror to the order within human society. We see this in Geoffrey Chaucer's poem *The Parlement of Foules*, in which he describes four groups of birds, each representing a different rank of social life, distinguished by their feeding habits. At the bottom are the 'worm fowls', in other words, the blackbirds, starlings and robins that we see fluffing at this moment in the year.

Little birds like the dunnock and the robin emerged as important symbols of the British labouring class. Both over-wintering birds and the labouring citizen were features of the seasonal landscape throughout the year, suffering through hunger and cold in the depths of winter: puffing, whistling and working without respite.

Through the metaphor of birds, writers could safely explore political issues such as enclosure, emparkment and forced migration. These images were later used and sub-verted by nineteenth-century working-class writers such as John Clare to talk about their lives – their social bonds, the spirit of creativity, as well as experiences such as privation, strife and independence – without fearing retribution from those above them.

The old saying goes that birds of a feather flock together. But at this moment in the seasonal year, when food is scarce, it is also common to see birds of different species gather-ing together to feed. This creates a fractal-like honeycomb of variegated feathers – every single one of them a reminder of the wonder to be found in the enduring mysteries of the natural world.

ROWAN JAINES

Bright Winter Aconites

In the spectre-grey days of late January, the winter aconite blooms in a heart-stopping display of bright yellow. This is a contrary plant; it resists the murky palette of the British winter landscape and has confused attempts at taxonomic classification since it first arrived in early modern Britain. The current scientific name for winter aconite, *Eranthis hyemalis*, is a Greek and Latin compound of a muddled nature. *Eranthis* stems from the Greek *er* and *anthos*, literally meaning 'spring flower'; *hyemalis* is the Latin for 'winter flowering'.

In the perplexing history of this winter-flowering spring flower, the strange construction of the British botanical landscape comes into focus. The winter aconite reminds us that when we notice nature, we are also catching sight of the history of culture as it is made, imported, cultivated and revised throughout time.

The winter aconite is native to France and Central Europe and was introduced to Britain by botanists in the late six-teenth century, though decades would pass before there was some consensus on exactly what the plant was and what to call it. The species was recorded in 1597 in Gerard's *Herball* as *Aconitum hyemale* under the common names 'winter woolfesbane' and 'winter aconite'. In this entry Gerard describes the similarity of the leaf shapes and fruit-ing bodies to the native species monk's hood *Aconitum*, also known as wolfsbane. Records from the Oxford University Physic Garden (established in 1621, and presently known as Oxford Botanic Garden) in the mid-seventeenth century show a January-flowering plant called 'winter wolfesbane' (*Aconitum hyemale*). Jacob Bobart the Younger and his father, the first two keepers of the Garden, kept meticulous herbarium specimens which allow us to positively identify this plant as the winter aconite.

In the late eighteenth century botanists reassessed the taxonomy of this winter plant and deduced that it was not in fact a member of the aconite family. Though they noted that some mistake had been made in the identification process, they used the same process of identification, namely look-ing for physical similarities with other species. Noting the similarity between the shape of these yellow blooms and the flowers of the hellebore (*Helleborus*), the winter aconite was renamed. Carl Linnaeus – known as the 'father of modern taxonomy' – labelled the plant *Helleborus hyemalis*, and it appears with this name in the first edition of *The Botanical Magazine* in 1787.

The winter aconite was given its final botanical name (to date) by Richard Salisbury in 1807, who classified it as *Eranthis hyemalis (L.) Salisbury*. Richard Salisbury had also had a change of name. Born Richard Markham, this clothmaker's son from Chapel Allerton, near Leeds, adopted the name Salisbury while studying medicine at Edinburgh University in order to inherit from a relative of his maternal grandmother. Salisbury became a significant force in British botany in the early part of the nineteenth century and spent a good deal of his career opposing Linnaeus's accepted system of plant identification. This unorthodoxy, as well as personality issues, led to Salisbury being ostracised by the botanical community, and his published plant names were ignored. However, posthumous re-examinations of Salisbury's research prompted by the *International Code of Botanical Nomenclature (from 1867 ff)* revealed the scrupulous nature of his work, and the world of botany now recognises many of his names for plants, including winter aconite, so *Eranthis hyemalis* now stands – albeit minus the *(L.) Salisbury*.

Although winter aconite began its life in Britain as the object of scientific study in physic gardens, nowadays it exists in a 'naturalised state' right across the country. The plant propagates in the landscape without any overt human assistance, but its present ubiquity can be traced back to one man: Lancelot 'Capability' Brown, the famous eighteenth-century landscape designer. Brown favoured planting this yellow flower in his 'sweeping landscapes' in order to ensure that there was something bright in sight, even early in the year.

But Capability Brown's landscaping wasn't just about creating attractive views: there was an ideological imperative too which had much in common with the imperial development of botanical taxonomy that led to two of winter aconite's name changes. The project of landscape improvement which introduced the winter aconite into the soil of the nation state was an exercise in 'place-making', a way of stating 'this is Britain'.

In this process, the naturalisation and taxonomic classification of plants such as aconite that had been brought from other parts of the world were inscribed within the physical and scientific landscape of Britain, effectively erasing their non-domestic roots. Indeed, we see this across Northern Europe, where Linnaeus's taxonomic process was part of an effort to impose a singular and logical order upon the huge variety of plant species that had been imported to Northern Europe as part of the colonial project. This meant the imposition of Greco-Roman official names on the wide diversity of monikers from various cultures, languages and dialects that came with the introduction of non-native species, embedding them within a carefully cultivated vision of a synthetic landscape.

In this moment of the year, before the fecundity of spring spreads colour right across the landscape, the familiar, bright winter aconite is a reminder that the authentically 'British' landscape is a cultural construction. The yellow sunshine of this plant in the depths of winter is a reminder of the place-making projects that shaped Britain's natural world.

ROWAN JAINES

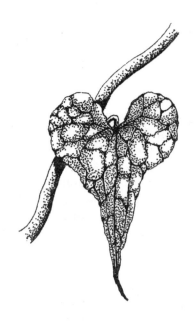

FEBRUARY

Noticing Exercise

Make a nature-inspired valentine. When you are outdoors, even in the cold and dark, keep your eyes peeled for heart shapes – pebbles, leaves, clouds or lichen, for example. Take inspiration from Andy Goldsworthy's nature art and assemble leaves into a heart shape on a pavement, in a woodland clearing or in your local park, sending love out into the world. Paint a heart on a pebble and give it to a loved one, or leave it on a friend's doorstep.

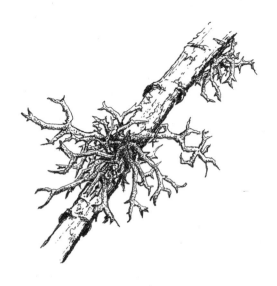

30 JANUARY–3 FEBRUARY

Lichens on Bare Branches

The first winter of our project saw the UK pounded by a series
of named storms, littering roads, pavements and gardens
with a flotsam of tangled debris torn from trees. Suddenly,
something that often retreats into the background was
brought into sharper focus: the strange, fractal geometries
and vivid colours of the lichens growing on these orphaned
twigs.

Our everyday lack of attentiveness to lichens is surprising,
because they are fascinatingly *weird*. There are 28,000 kinds
of lichen in the world, and over 2,300 in the UK. They vary in
size from tiny structures measuring less than one millimetre
to two-metre-long growths, and take a vast array of forms,
from crusts that seem to meld with their substrate to fringed
seaweed-like scabs to delicate three-dimensional, coral-like

configurations. They can live for a single season or for well over a thousand years, and they can grow in lush temperate rainforests or arid deserts.

What is more, they confound our idea of species as singular individuals because they involve at least two and sometimes three organisms, drawn from different taxonomic kingdoms. Lichens are an association between a fungal partner, called the mycobiont, and a photosynthetic partner that provides carbohydrate food, called the photobiont. The latter is usually a green alga, but sometimes a cyanobacterium.

The degree of lichenisation between these two partners can vary from a loose association to a well-integrated structure in which the fungus encloses the photobiont. In some species, the mycobiont penetrates the photobiont's cells with a specialist structure, termed a haustoria. The growth they form is called a thallus, and in most cases it looks nothing like its fungal and algal/bacterial components. Inside it the photobiont can be so deformed that it is impossible to recognise by sight alone. In other words, lichens are shape-shifters.

The nature of the relationship between the two partners in a lichen has long been a source of controversy. Even today, scientists can't work out if the organisms involved are working together in a mutually beneficial relationship or if the fungus is parasitising the alga or cyanobacterium. At first sight, the case for parasitism appears strong: the fungus seems to be in overall control and to get all the benefits, drawing carbohydrates from the photobiont, which often grows more slowly than it would when living freely. Yet there is also an argument for co-operation: becoming lichenised allows photobionts normally confined to aquatic environments to colonise dry land by reducing their exposure to light and providing them with water. In fact, some photobionts seem to exist predominantly in a lichenised state, and are seldom found living freely.

The scientific question of this relationship has inevitably been complicated by human politics and social questions. The idea that lichens involved a combination of a fungus and an alga was first mooted by the Swiss botanist Simon Schwendener in 1868, to a chorus of loud disapproval from lichenologists. In part, this was because Schwendener's 'dual hypothesis' challenged existing systems of biological classification, collapsing the professional expertise of lichenologists into areas already colonised by other biologists.

Another problem for nineteenth-century scientists was that Schwendener tried to explain his idea by comparing and contrasting lichenous relationships with those of predators and their prey. He described the mycobiont spinning a fine-meshed web around a 'captured' photobiont, just like a spider wraps its prey in silk. However, instead of killing its algal prisoner like a spider, the fungus exploited it with what Schwendener described as 'statesmanlike' prudence. 'Used to living off the work of others,' he wrote, the fungus held the alga in 'eternal captivity', even exciting it to more vigorous activity for the benefit of the lichen colony. This, Schwendener suggested, was the biological version of a master–slave relationship.

The idea flew in the face of the fungal science of the day. As one contemporary complained: 'In every known instance of parasitic fungi, the fungus lives at the expense of its host, which it injures and ultimately destroys.' What Schwendener was suggesting, by contrast, was a kind of parasitism that was less fatally one-directional in its costs and benefits, but in language that still emphasised the domination and oppression of one organism by another. The Scottish lichenologist J. M. Crombie was incensed, protesting that Schwendener had turned the discipline into a 'sensational "Romance of Lichenology", or the unnatural union between a captive Algal damsel and a tyrant Fungal master'. Not only had Schwendener created a trivial gothic tale out of serious science, he had turned lichens into a freakish story of female helplessness in the face of overwhelming male violence. So challenging was the idea of a more mutualistic relationship, and so unfortunate the metaphorical language that Schwendener had used to describe it, that it would be decades before the dual hypothesis was universally accepted.

While this complex and mysterious life form continues to bamboozle scientists, lichens have inspired several contemporary artists. Some street artists selectively remove them from walls and other structures, to create 'reverse lichen' paintings. At the Vouglans dam in France, Klaus Dauven has created a vast reverse mural using a team of climbers working with power washers. The work is sponsored by a leading power-washer company, and the living organisms that are not blasted from the walls depict a forestscape in silhouette, as if the shapes of the surrounding trees were shadowed on to the hard concrete surface.

Yet it's difficult not to feel unsettled by corporately sponsored art that relies on the destruction of so many delicate organisms from one ecosystem to create the representation of another. Why do we see the depiction of a forest as 'greener' and more ecologically conscious than the actual presence of a non-vascular ecosystem of mosses, liverworts and lichens? Has the tree become such a powerful icon of nature that it eclipses the importance of other organisms? Is this art as greenwashing, both literally and representationally?

A more positive artistic use of lichens can be seen in the work of Hubert Fenzl, who makes relief paintings and sculptures using sustainably harvested *Cladonia stellaris* (a species of lichen that is confusingly known as 'reindeer moss'). His *Rainforest* uses the lichen's resemblance to a miniature tree to build a bird's-eye relief of a forest, surrounded by a threatening area of flat red that represents the clearance of this critical habitat by human forces. Whereas the reverse lichen graffiti on the dam make destruction into a creative methodology, Fenzl's work turns it into a theme, using lichens to ask questions about our lack of care for forest landscapes.

Since his *Cladonia* material is specially treated to allow it to survive indoors for many years, a Fenzl relief is quite literally a living, respiring surface. The union of a natural material with a human artistic vision asks important environmental questions. It might also draw our attention back to the inherent textural beauty of these strange and challenging life forms. At this time of year, while the branches of the trees are still bare, the lichen on their surface offers up a world of colour and texture to the close observer.

KIERA CHAPMAN

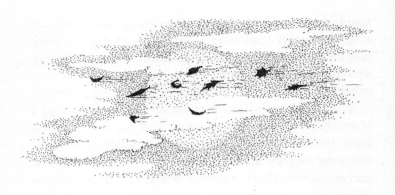

4–8 FEBRUARY

Winds Howling in the Night

It is a curious thing, the way that the sounds of place tend to be imagined in symphony with meteorological phenomena. Indeed, it often seems that weather acts as though it were a bow on the strings of place, stimulating an audible anima from leaves and grasses, streams and mountain passes with beating rain and gusty gales.

Fluctuations in air pressure at this moment in the year give rise to strong winds that last for days and nights on end. But when the wind howls in the night, it never howls in isolation. Rather it forms part of a 'soundscape' as it shakes trees, upends bins and whistles through alleys. We can understand a soundscape as an auditory landscape, all the sounds that make up a particular area at a given time.

Sound has been linked with the human perception of time since at least the fourth century, when the theologian and philosopher Augustine in his *Confessions* put forward a theory on the interconnected nature of acoustic and temporal experience. Sound, he tells us, is fleeting and transient; once heard, the moment has passed. What's more, sound unfolds over time rather than synchronically. For example, a song does not arrive all at once in our perception like a sculpture or a painting might; so too the drama of a soundscape unfolds in a different temporal register from that of a landscape.

As the wind whips a landscape, it seems to animate a band of rowdy players from a previously still scene. Like a Pied Piper, the liveliness of a gale enchants sounds so that they follow its journey through streets, across dales and down gorges and tors. There is a whole genre of composition, capturing the strange arrangements of soundscapes, that aims to discover musical alchemy as the motion of winds and tides, rain and birdsong interact in place and time. The World Soundscape Project has worked with artists and composers including Hildegard Westerkamp, Claude Schryer and Barry Truax to establish critical ecological-acoustic discourses.

The intensification of winter winds across the British Isles is one such ecological-acoustic concern. The soundscape of Britain's winters is likely to become more heavily defined by howling winds in years to come. But why is this?

The tempests that we experience at this time of year in the northern hemisphere are caused by large-scale weather systems carried on 'jet streams'. Jet streams are fast ribbons of air that form and are strongest where variable air temperature gradients are steepest. This is normally seen in two zones, firstly in the boundary between polar and mid-latitude air (which creates *the polar jet*); and secondly in the boundary between mid-latitude air and tropical air (which creates *the subtropical jet*). While the polar jet and the subtropical jet are separate entities, they sometimes join forces above particular areas of the Earth. The polar jet is usually the stronger of the two air streams because the temperature differential between the polar and mid-latitude regions is starker than that between the tropical and mid-latitude regions, particularly in the winter in the northern hemisphere, when temperatures have traditionally been further apart. The polar jet blows from west to east and was first brought to scientific attention by pilots in the Second World War, who noted shorter flight times from the US to the UK compared with the other way.

One way of understanding the polar jet system is to imagine the air flowing like a tide, with weather conditions pulled over the Earth below. When polar air from the north moves against a southward bulge of the jet, it forms a depression in which air flows fast, sucking air out of the top of the atmosphere and lowering the pressure system, which brings strong winds and stormy weather.

Rapidly rising Arctic temperatures are affecting not only the flow, but also the position of the polar jet stream. Climate models using data from the past 2,500 years have been used to simulate the jet stream in a hotter world. These models predict that if the planet continues warming at a high rate, the jet stream is likely to shift north over time and become more 'wavy', which will mean that storm systems move more slowly or become stuck in place, bringing more extreme weather for the countries below.

With this shift in weather, our UK winters will begin to sing different or more intense songs from those we have been accustomed to. The howling winds of this microseason perhaps mark a shift in the auditory texture of winters to come. This opens up a space of unknowing. What if we heard the movement of high winds as an anarchic Nature reclaiming, momentarily, the streets of the cities? As it tears through the urban fabric, setting off car alarms, throwing rubbish around and playing alleys like flutes, might we hear a song of rebellion? In this space of unknowing, what might our ears tell us that our eyes, in the dead of night, cannot perceive?

ROWAN JAINES

9–13 FEBRUARY

Birdsong Builds

Few things embody hope and gladness quite like birdsong. Something many of us noticed during the COVID-19 lockdowns was the sounds of birds, suddenly ringing out so clearly, without the muffles of traffic and aeroplane noise. It was a moment where the human presence was stripped back, revealing some of the wondrous life going on around us as our world stood still. While the man-made noise has now returned, this microseason is still filled with song as birds gear up for mating and staking their claims over territory. The growing dawn chorus is a sign that winter is drawing to a close.

At this time of year the bare trees offer us a better chance of spotting birds as they sing. If you can't tell who's who by their looks or if they're just too far away, perhaps you can try to pick out some individual songs within the crescendo-ing chorus. Starting with some of the common garden and urban birds keeps things manageable. In February we mostly hear resident species as their breeding season approaches. Listen out for dunnocks, blackbirds, wrens, blue and great tits, song thrushes, robins, collared doves, greenfinches and chaffinches. The RSPB guide to birdsong offers helpful trans-literations: the 'tea-cher tea-cher' of the great tit, the weary football chant-like 'united, united' of the collared dove, and the 'I don't want to go' of the wood pigeon (also described in my part of the world as 'my toe hurts, Betty').

A commonly heard sound is blue tit songs. These are varied, so it is hard to give one definitive identifier, but often you will hear 'sispi si-hi-hi-hi-hi' or a high-pitched 'tsee-tsee-tsee-chu-chu-chu'. Many of us will have noticed their particularly loud calls in our gardens or nearby parks as the males try to attract a mate by blasting out their best songs. Their other wooing strategies – beating their wings and making flamboyant dives towards a female's nest site – are rather reminiscent of boy racers skidding round town with music blaring.

Blackbirds (previously called ousels, woozels or wood thrushes) are also good birds to start noticing. Their song is much loved for its musicality and mellifluousness, and if you hear a loud flute-like trilling in your street or a nearby hedgerow (especially after it has rained) look for the glossy black feathers and yellow beak of a male blackbird. In February it is mainly the younger males we hear as they search for a mate, reassert the boundaries of their territory and see off rival males who are looking for their first patch. In March, older males will usually begin singing. Females also defend territory, but once they have paired up they join forces to protect their shared area. They don't use song as a warning or to assert territorial claims, but will listen out for a suitable mate nearby.

In some species a strong song indicates robust health and high levels of testosterone, so birdsong is an important part of the breeding process as females select the fittest partners. Once a male has found a mate he sings less frequently and less loudly, so we know that his primary motivation is procreation. But there may be another reason for birdsong besides romance and territorial defences. Amazingly, one study has shown that when birds sing without social interaction their brains release opioids and dopamine that make the act of singing pleasurable. They are singing for joy!

The timing of the dawn chorus gives us another clue to the function of birdsong. As the dreary end-of-winter February mornings are too dark and cold for foraging, birds use this time to seek out a mate. But the intensity of the chorus we hear at dawn is influenced by human behaviour. In rural areas there is less background noise, which means the birds' songs carry further through the early-morning air. Urban birds need to fight against the traffic noise, so they adjust their song to a higher pitch above the ambient drone frequency and increase the volume of their calls. At night or at sunrise there is less need to compensate for the muffling effects of human activity, making these less demanding times to make themselves heard. As well as changing the nature of their song, stress caused by human noise has been shown to lower the number of eggs laid, have a negative impact on development in young birds, disrupt hormones, and reduce general health.

But some human activities can be helpful, as lamp posts, fences and overhead wires become prime 'song posts'. Different species and individual birds have their own favourite spots from which to announce their presence. At this time of year there is little cover in the branches, so many sing from lower down, in the undergrowth or on bushes. It is thought some birds choose certain song posts because of the acoustics of surrounding buildings or structures, which amplify their calls. They make calculations about the impact of the environment on their song, working out the position that gives them the optimum range while not exposing themselves to danger. Males also avoid singing near nests as this could give away their location to predators. All these adjustments for place, safety and exposure are part of even the simplest-sounding melodies we hear as we wake from our slumber each day.

Yet we still don't know exactly what the tweets, warbles and trills actually mean. As Steven Lovatt writes, 'What the birds are "saying" science can conjecture, but what the birdsong means to us, what we feel in our blood, is that we're not alone.' Perhaps this is another reason why we noticed these songs in the pandemic – witnessing other creatures going about their daily business around us, despite the sudden halting of human life, reassured us that the natural cycles continued. Birdsong creates what Lovatt calls an 'emotional atmosphere', a sonic environment that humans perceive which evokes feelings of contemplation or happiness.

While human noise can be detrimental to birds, we actually benefit from hearing their song. Birdsong has a positive impact on wellbeing and shows that part of the idea of a 'nature cure' involves auditory input. It is thought that humans have learned over time that when birds are singing there is little danger nearby, and probably plentiful vegetation (which means food). One study also revealed that birdsong can increase levels of focus. When a group of schoolchildren listened to recordings of birdsong after their lunch break it was found they concentrated better and were more alert. This is thought to be due to the stochastic, i.e. non-repetitive, nature of birdsong – it doesn't take up space as an earworm or distract us, but is also not boring. At Alder Hey Hospital birdsong has been used to calm children's nerves before treatments and examinations; and speakers hidden inside model trees at Schiphol Airport in Amsterdam play birdsong to induce feelings of calm and relaxation among waiting passengers.

Of course, listening to birdsong is not just all about our needs. We are more likely to want to protect creatures and environments that we have direct knowledge of, so if we can identify the birds that share our neighbourhood we may be more inclined to create habitats and lifestyles that support them.

Hasidic teacher and writer Reb Nachman described listening to birdsong as a joy so great it becomes unbearable. It has inspired poets such as John Clare and Robert Frost, and musicians, with composers like Beethoven, Handel and Wagner (among many others) including songbird motifs in their work. From the mid-twentieth century musicians layered samples of recorded birdsong into their compositions. The French composer and keen ornithologist Olivier Messiaen tried to convey the freedom, improvisation and joy of birdsong in his music, basing one flute composition on the blackbird's song and later more holistic interpretations that incorporated not just the melody but the season and place in which the birds sang.

As we move slowly out of the winter darkness we too can find sustenance and inspiration in the simple songs around us, calling us forth to witness the coming spring and the wonders unfolding.

LULAH ELLENDER

14–18 FEBRUARY

Sparrows Squabble

Sparrows have long been a byword for a species so common as to be inconsequential. This goes back at least as far as the Bible. Matthew 10:29–31 famously uses God's concern for sparrows as an example of His omniscience and omnipotence, while emphasising the special place that humanity occupies in the Christian Creation:

Are not two sparrows sold for a farthing? and one of them shall not fall on the ground without your Father.

But the very hairs of your head are all numbered.

Fear ye not therefore, ye are of more value than many sparrows.

Yet in the dark, cold early months of the year, when our senses seem sharpened by our eagerness for the first, slow signs of spring, the sight and sound of male sparrows becoming territorial, cheeping continually to attract a mate, is a far from insignificant source of joy. Watch closely and you may see an interloper enter a newly established territory, causing an irate, fluttering fight. It's accompanied by a shrill avian slanging match, the language of which would certainly not be fit to print. If you are watching squabbling sparrows in your garden at this time of year, look out for the size of the black patch on a male's chest. It is a good indicator of his chances of winning a fight: more dominant birds develop larger patches, signalling their social standing.

The external, behavioural change in sparrows at this time of year reflects an internal, physiological shift. As the days grow longer, the testicles of a male sparrow get a hundred times larger, while the ovaries of females grow fifty times bigger. But how do sparrows sense what time of year it is, and when to get ready to breed? The answer may involve an extraordinary ability: they can detect light *through their skulls*.

To understand this, we have to disabuse ourselves of our common-sense assumption that changes in light levels are only detected visually, via the stimulation of the rod and cone cells in the retina of the eye. Some rather cruel scientific experiments that leave one feeling very sorry for their chirrupy subjects reveal that blind sparrows who lack visual cells still maintain both a daily and a seasonal rhythm, growing larger gonads in spring. This is because they can detect light using non-visual ganglion cells in their retina, which send signals to the deep brain (the hypothalamus). The mechanism acts like an internal clock, conveying information to the pineal gland, which responds by rhythmically releasing hormones. Removing a sparrow's pineal gland causes it to lose its sense of time. Putting the pineal gland of a bird attuned to one artificial day length into another bird attuned to a very different day length confers the donor bird's rhythm on to the recipient.

But here things become still stranger – because sparrows who have had their eyes removed, and therefore have no retinas and no non-visual light-detecting ganglion cells in them, can still detect light. They, too, grow gonads in spring. This means that they must be able to use photoreceptors that are located outside of the eye. Experiments suggest that their skulls allow light through to sensory receptors in the hypothalamus, deep inside their brains. The effect vanishes if a screen of ink is injected under the skin at the top of a sparrow's head, tattooing it black.

But the complexities of light detection in sparrows also warn us of a danger: artificial light at night. A growing body of research suggests that this is a stressor for songbirds: those exposed to nocturnal illumination are active earlier and later in the day, using up more energy. Their gut bacteria can also be disrupted, which may impact their ability to absorb nutrients and fight off disease.

This is important to us humans, because elsewhere in the world house sparrows are a reservoir for West Nile virus. Infected birds are bitten by mosquitoes, which then spread the virus to humans and other animals. West Nile virus is the leading mosquito-borne disease in the United States, and though many of those who contract it feel no symptoms, one in five will develop a mild flu-like illness, and one in 150 people will develop a serious, even fatal, infection. Scientists found that sparrows exposed to artificial light at night could transmit the virus for two days longer than birds kept in darker nocturnal conditions, making it more likely that a sick bird would spread the disease to a greater number of other birds.

So sparrows might lead us to a larger question, about the impacts of the stresses we humans are placing on ecosystems and their consequences for zoonotic diseases, which are transmitted from one species to another. Such infections have recently impacted all our lives: the COVID-19 pandemic may have been caused by a virus jumping from animals to humans. At the time of writing, the animal reservoir has yet to be determined, and there is certainly no evidence that the species in question will be the sparrow. But both West Nile virus and COVID-19 reveal that ecosystem health and human health are deeply entwined. The death of a sparrow is perhaps significant to all of us.

KIERA CHAPMAN

19–23 FEBRUARY

Daffodil Spears

The first thing you notice is a fan of tiny leaf-tips in the grass, like blue-green fingertips reaching up out of the ground, searching for a hold from which to pull themselves up and into the daylight. Within days, the fingertips have lengthened into fingers and then suddenly they have become leaves, standing in dense clusters, like stacks of little spears waiting for battle. The only fight here, however, is against time, because daffodils, like most bulbs, seek to flower and seed before the hot, dry weather of summer sends them back into dormancy underground. This eagerness to start growing is a blessing for us in the dark days of February, when the emergence of daffodil flowers drops little golden suns into our parks and gardens, sprinkling yellow stars across the grass.

Like so many of our garden plants, the daffodils we usually grow are 'jazzed up' versions of their more demure native cousins. Botanists have tamed, manipulated and reshaped the wild species (*Narcissus pseudonarcissus*) to provide us with bigger (or sometimes smaller), more colourful or more scented blooms. Some of the most extreme examples have flowers like yellow pom-poms, or petals reduced to whiskers, or have lost their trumpets altogether, replaced by tightly packed rosettes of interior petals. So the search for novelty has taken this cheerful flower a long way from the wild daffodil that still grows across Europe, North Africa and Central Asia. This species has a small, slightly drooping head, composed of pale-yellow petals around a central golden trumpet or corona. These were the daffodils that William Wordsworth made famous in the early nineteenth century, capturing their airy beauty as they danced and fluttered in the wind beside Lake Ullswater in Cumbria. And he was not alone in his admiration. Wild daffodils were so widespread across the country that during the nineteenth century they were picked in huge numbers by the poor and sold on in nearby towns and cities to help make ends meet.

Yet already by Wordsworth's day, a wide range of daffodils had been available to the keen gardener for several centuries. In 1629, the plantsman John Parkinson published one of the most influential horticultural books of the seventeenth century, *Paradisi in Sole Paradisus Terrestris*, in which he noted,

Of daffodils there are almost an hundred sorts ... some being eyther white, or yellow, or mixt, or else being small or great, single or double, and some having but one flower upon a stalke, others many, whereof many are so exceeding sweete, that a very few are sufficient to perfume a whole chamber, and besides, many of them be so faire and double, eyther one upon a stalke, or many upon a stalke, that one or two stalkes of flowers are in stead of a whole nose-gay, or bundell of flowers tyed together.

He added,

Many idle and ignorant Gardiners and others . . . doe call some of these daffodils Narcisses, when as all know that know any Latine, that Narcissus is the Latine name, and Daffodil the English, of one and the same thing . . .

For all the confidence of this pronouncement, the difference between a daffodil and a narcissus remains a source of confusion into the present day. And even Parkinson divided his narcissus into two categories: 'true' *narcissus* and 'bastard' *pseudonarcissus*, differentiating them by the size and length of the internal corona. He then divided these two groups again, noting four different forms within his 'true narcissus': '*latifolios* (broad-leafed), *angustifolios* (narrow-leafed), *iuncifolios* (rushe), *marinos* (sea)'. Faced with the sheer range of different daffodils already available to his readers in the early seventeenth century, however, he was forced to subdivide these categories yet again to try to make sense of the bewildering and burgeoning range of flower types. Indeed, a stroll through the daffodil entries of seventeenth- and eighteenth-century books on horticulture proves beyond doubt the true value of a standard plant taxonomy and the use of botanical Latin. In frustration, Parkinson begged his readers to use what he called the 'proper' English or Latin names to avoid 'mistaking'

the single English bastard daffodill <*sic*> . . . the double
English bastard daffodill; the French single white daffodill many vpon a stalke; the French double yellow
daffodill; the great, or the little, or the least Spanish
yellow bastard daffodill; or the great or little Spanish
white daffodill; the Turkie single white daffodill; or
the Turkie single or double white daffodill many vpon
a stalke . . .

One sympathises.

The common name, daffodil, comes from the Latin
plant name *Asphodelus* (itself from the Greek *asphodelos*)
a genus of lily-like plants, often with white star-shaped
flowers which perhaps resembled one of the white forms of
daffodil. From this, the Middle English name 'Affodill' was
derived, although it had numerous other names, including 'Lent Lily', which reflected its flowering season. Yet the
Latin name *Narcissus* also has ancient roots, entered under
this name by Pliny the Elder in his first-century CE *Naturalis
Historia*. Pliny refuted the claim, even then, that the beautiful but self-obsessed youth of Greek myth, Narcissus, gave
his name to the flower. In the myth, Narcissus was notorious
for hanging his head over a body of water to gaze longingly –
but fatally, as it turned out – at his own reflection, a drooping
pose that was also noticed in the wild daffodil. Rejecting this
theory, Pliny ascribed the name instead to the Greek verb
'*narkeo*', meaning 'to become numb', noting its causation of
headaches if ingested.

Daffodils are now known to be toxic, but for many centuries
they were widely believed to have useful medicinal qualities,
and indeed Pliny too recommended their use for external
complaints, such as cuts and bruises. Most pre-modern
herbals included them to alleviate a variety of ailments, and
in 1651 Leonard Sowerby's *Ladies' Dispensatory* suggested
that daffodil was good for aching sinews or as a diuretic,

and for gout, splinters, ulcers, burns, dislocations, facial moles, freckles and leprosy. In 1685, an English translation of *Modern Curiosities of Art & Nature Extracted out of the Cabinets of the Most Eminent Personages of the French Court* by Nicolas Lémery recommended that those who wished to make their hair curl should 'shave it off and then rub the skin with daffodil roots'. An alternative, he added, was to 'take Daffodil Water mixed with thick Juice of the Roots of white Mallows, as much of one as of the other'. Reading the advice of pre-modern herbalists, it seems there are very few ailments that daffodils were not at some time used to treat.

And yet, before we dismiss their advice entirely, it is worth remembering that daffodils are now recognised as the best natural source of galantamine, an alkaloid also present in snowdrops which provides one of the most hopeful new treatments for Alzheimer's disease.

Perhaps the daffodil spears that we welcome in spring may be weapons after all, but this time in the ongoing fight against dementia.

REBECCA WARREN

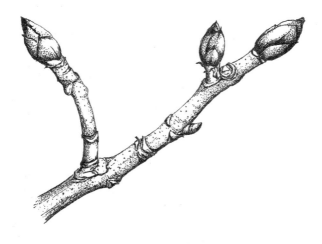

Leaf Buds Fattening

Named for the burgeoning buds appearing on trees all around us, this microseason is characterised by the miracle of growth, the mind-blowing mathematics of the natural world and the unfurling of spring. Right now you might see more advanced buds on magnolia, maple, cherry plum, willow, horse chestnut, elder, ash, beech and oak trees. Inside these tightly packed nodules leaves are waiting to unfold. But how do they grow, and what triggers them to open out?

The leaf inside a bud grows as its cells begin to divide and soak up more water. The form and appearance of these buds can help us to identify trees without needing to rely on leaf shapes. The arrangement of leaf buds along a stem is known as phyllotaxy. Some buds, like those you will find on the hornbeam, are 'terminal', with one bud growing at the end of a twig or branch; others, as on the elder, are 'opposite', with two buds growing at a right angle to the pairs above and below; some, as we see on the birch, are 'alternate', growing at alternating points along both sides with two leaves per 360°, sometimes in a zigzag pattern; some have 'whorls' with up to three buds per node; and others, like the oak, are 'clustered' at the end of a twig. You might also see 'lateral' buds which form just above a node point. In other species, like conifers, leaves grow in a spiral helix around a shoot.

You don't need to know the name of the tree or plant to marvel at the magic occurring within these tiny parcels. What we can't see until the leaves begin to emerge is the way they have fitted themselves into their bud. In some plants, like ferns, the leaves coil inside their buds, while others, like the beech or alder, have folded, rolled or pleated leaves. The packing method, or 'vernation', is determined by a tree's genetics rather than the shape of the bud. So a bud takes a particular form because that is how the leaf develops, rather than a leaf having to fit into a certain shape.

Look closely at the trees around you and watch as the leaves begin to unfurl. Can you see what shape they are emerging from? Are they spiralling out from a tight coil, or are they fanning out their pleats into full growth? Have they been neatly folded, waiting for the right temperature and light? Touch a bud and see how it feels. Horse chestnut, poplar and alder buds are coated in a sticky resin that is thought to deter pests and retain moisture within the bud. Hairy leaf buds indicate that the tree could be a pear, apple, rowan, hazel or star magnolia, among others.

Now, time for some maths! Remember the spiral leaves? In spiral phyllotaxy, the degrees between leaf positions follow a Fibonacci sequence (where each number is the sum of the previous two).

The distribution of these leaves fits a 'golden ratio' where they are separated at an angle of 137.5°. This ensures the leaves don't shade each other once they have come fully out, allowing the perfect filtration of light for each individual leaf. Fibonacci sequences are found throughout the natural world – in the number of branches on a tree, petals on a rose, leaves of a cabbage, in some tree trunk rings and on their bark, and in pine cones. Look out for spirals as you explore your neighbourhood.

So, why are these leaf buds emerging at this particular time? Trees need varying periods of chilling as they go dormant over the winter. When they get the ideal amount of chilling time they will have a plentiful harvest and good foliation. But if a winter is too warm, or there is a warm spell followed by a cold snap, leaf and fruit development could be delayed or insufficient. A really cold winter can, perhaps counter-intuitively, lead to bumper crops.

The timing of a bud breaking dormancy and the leaf becoming visible, known as 'bud burst', is determined by genetics as well as temperature, position and day length. Tree species respond in different ways to these triggers, with some needing warmer temperatures or longer days than others. They need to balance the additional time for photosynthesis that early leaf-out offers against the risk of a late frost. Those species with narrower vessel elements in their stems often come into leaf earlier because they are less prone to cold damage. A US study compared Henry David Thoreau's detailed notes on the leaf-out around Walden Pond in Massachusetts, 160 years ago, with current dates of leaves emerging. They found that leaf-out is on average eighteen days earlier now than in Thoreau's time. They also noted that for every 1°C temperature increase, leaves emerge five days earlier. Scientists, ecologists and foresters using satellite imaging and ground observations are adding to the body of research on leaf phenology in an attempt to understand what is happening and why. Data from the Thoreau study shows that in Northern Europe leaf-out is now occurring an average of one week earlier than fifty years ago.

What are the implications of earlier leaf-out? The myriad species depending on trees and leaves may not have adapted to this change quickly enough to survive. Caterpillars and insects will miss out on the fresh young leaves, which will in turn impact the birds that feed on them. The complex eco-systems that depend on trees may not synchronise with the earlier leaf-out. Young leaves can also be damaged by spring frosts. Changes in leaf-out times affect how much carbon dioxide trees take in, with longer periods in leaf resulting in greater carbon sequestration. There are also consequences for forest temperatures and water levels.

As our climate warms our traditional tree landscape will continue to change. We need to think about nurturing plants and seeds that can survive or thrive without proper winter chilling and with less water, and try to support plants that can fill in any gaps caused by early leaf-out. But we also risk losing our native trees to imported species which are better adapted to the shorter chilling times and warming spring temperatures. The leaf buds are not just a sign of the change of seasons, but a longer-term ecological shift too.

When you spot a leaf bud on a tree perhaps take a moment to reflect not only on the amazing mathematical secrets it contains, but also on the potential for radical growth that can inspire us as we emerge from winter's slower months.

LULAH ELLENDER

MARCH

Noticing Exercise

The world is beginning to wake up and brightly bloom. Now is the time to take a colour walk. Decide on three colours before you leave the house, and try to take a note or a photograph of every example of that colour that you see on your walk. This doesn't have to be limited to the natural world; in fact it is often exciting to notice how the colours that we humans use to decorate ourselves and our possessions echo the colours of the ecosystem around us.

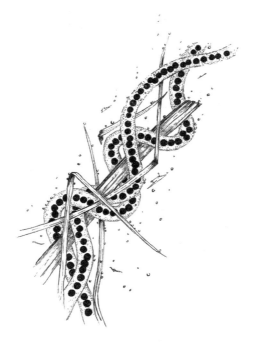

Frogspawn Wobbles

As schoolchildren many of us probably had a class jar of frog-spawn sitting on a shelf somewhere in springtime, our eager young eyes watching and waiting for tadpoles to emerge and start their fascinating growth into frogs. For many of us this was our first tangible interaction with an animal's life cycle, but we now know that it is not a good idea to move frogspawn from its natural habitat as it can spread disease and may mean the tadpoles end up in an unsuitable location. So for this microseason, let's observe the frogspawn exactly where it was laid, as we explore this intriguing annual occurrence.

The British Isles are home to two types of frog, the common and pool frog. The non-native marsh frog is also found in some parts of south-eastern England. Toads and frogs are in the *Anura* order – confusingly, all toads are frogs, but not all frogs are toads! Toads are browner than frogs, have rougher-looking skin and can live further from water. Common and natterjack toads are our native species. Over winter these creatures have been hunkering down in a muddy river bed, ditch, compost heap or burrow until spring returns and it is time to breed.

Their hibernation is facilitated by some pretty clever physical adaptations. Did you know that frogs don't drink water, they absorb it? This process of osmosis occurs through 'drinking patches' on their abdomen and thighs. Frogs also absorb oxygen this way, which keeps them alive over winter in deep water or below the river bed. Incredibly, in 2007 a team of researchers from MIT conducting a sonar survey of Loch Ness found a toad happily wandering along the lake bed, almost 100 metres below the surface.

Toad skin is fascinating – not only does it help them breathe and hydrate, in Surinam toads it also becomes a birthing chamber. These toads store their eggs beneath a layer of skin on their backs, and the baby toads (not tadpoles) break through this meniscus when it is time to hatch. Osmosis makes frogs vulnerable to toxins and pollutants in water, however, and they need well-oxygenated water to stay healthy. This sensitivity means they are what is known as 'bioindicators', detecting changes in water quality and levels of pesticides, herbicides, fungicides and heavy metals in water, all of which help us understand the health of their freshwater habitats.

Triggered by daylight and temperature changes, at this time of year frogs come out of hibernation for the breeding season, returning to the ponds where they were hatched. Frosts can kill spawn, which makes frogs vulnerable to early temperature rises that are followed by late cold snaps, so the timing of their breeding is crucial. The male common toad is usually the first to emerge from the winter slumber once evening temperatures hit 5–8°C, wiggling himself up and beginning the slow waddle back to his breeding pond. Toads can travel distances up to thirty miles, often making perilous road crossings – estimates by Froglife suggest that twenty tonnes of toads, or 250,000 individuals, are killed on British roads each year. As toad populations are in decline, current planning policy requires planners and road builders to mitigate any potential harm to biodiversity, which includes migrating or resident toads. In some places local residents have set up 'toad patrols' to carry toads to safety over busy roads.

Different types of toad are thought to use different navigational cues, but they all employ some combination of visual, olfactory and magnetic methods to find their route. Frogs and toads follow the scent of glycolic acid released by algae, but scientists believe the lunar cycle also plays a part, with larger groups massing and spawning around full moons. Sometimes the males encounter a female on the way, and jump on her back for the rest of the journey. This piggybacking is a way of pairing up with a mate rather than laziness.

Frogs tend to hibernate near their breeding ponds, avoiding the arduous and risky journey made by their toad relations. Once they've arrived at their home pond the solo males begin croaking. Females navigate using these calls, rather than the other cues used by male toads. The males try to out-croak their rivals but will also fight each other to win a mate. When a pair are mating the male climbs on the female's back and grips under her armpits, clinging on with special pads on his front feet and kicking off any rival males with his back legs. Hanging on for several hours, he fertilises the female's eggs as they are laid.

Female frogs lay clumps of spawn and can produce up to 4,000 eggs in one season. Toad spawn is laid in strings of three to five metres of gloopy pearls containing around 1,500 eggs, and is usually found in deeper water. You can identify which type of toad has laid it by looking at the structure – common toad spawn has double rows, and natterjack has single. Many tadpoles do not survive to adulthood, so these huge numbers are the frogs' way of hedging their bets. The eggs are protected by jelly because the adults don't stay to look after them, and it also helps them adhere and keeps them from drying out. As the eggs absorb water they expand, needing light and warmth to develop successfully.

After three to four weeks tadpoles hatch from the frog-spawn and it takes around fourteen weeks for them to fully develop. Toads hatch earlier (after just ten days), but they need around a fortnight longer to mature. If they are not eaten by newts, shrews, birds, fish and diving beetles, the adults are ready to live on land.

The eighteenth-century zoologist Thomas Pennant described toads as 'the most deformed and hideous of all animals – objects of detestation', and fairy tales are full of devilish amphibians. Given their incredible qualities and fascinating life cycle, why have frogs and toads traditionally been so reviled? Perhaps it is due to their warty-looking skin and nocturnal behaviours, giving them an otherworldly feel. Or maybe it is because toad skin contains toxins that are secreted from the parotid glands behind their ears. These secretions are hallucinogenic and can cause human hearts to stop beating, which is reason enough for people to recoil. Yet some people actively go looking for these psychoactive toxins and *lick toads* in an attempt to get high. This ill-advised and potentially harmful activity gives new meaning to the concept of kissing a frog and finding a prince. Perhaps this is even the source of the fairy tale trope?

Was it this poison, the bulbous eyes or the magical transformation of tadpole to toad that linked toads with the devil and witches? The toxins are released when the toad feels under threat, so if one were thrown into a vat (or cauldron, even) of boiling water the toxins would leach into the liquid and could cause severe illness if drunk. A woman with a score to settle and knowledge of herbs and animals had the power to do harm. During the sixteenth century the persecution of women accused of being witches was in part justified by any seemingly unnatural connection between the women and animals like toads. There was a long tradition of labelling innocent amphibians as 'familiars', or demonic spirits, helping witches do the devil's work. In 1582, Ursley Kemp admitted keeping 'foure spirits ... the third called Pigin ... like a blacke Toad,' while Margerie Sammon 'hath also two spirites like Toades, the one called Tom, and the other Robbyn'. Such 'confessions' cemented the demonic nature of toads in the popular imagination.

From witchy wrongdoers and unappealing princes to the rambunctious Toad of Toad Hall, it's time to rebrand the frog and toad. These fascinating creatures are a source of joy and wonder for all ages, and we can honour this by creating habitats that support them, adding ponds to our gardens and fighting to keep our rivers and lakes clean.

LULAH ELLENDER

6–10 MARCH

Woodpeckers Drumming

From *Bagpuss*'s Professor Yaffle and the cartoon Woody Woodpecker to indigenous stories and Roman myths, one bird has such a distinctive habit and appearance that it is deeply embedded in our culture. The woodpecker is shy but nonetheless widely loved for its beautiful appearance and extraordinary drumming. Indeed, you may hear them more often than you see them, as their percussive drilling high above our heads rings out across woodland and parks. At this time of year the drumming is particularly loud.

There are around 239 recognised woodpecker species worldwide. In the British Isles there are four species of woodpecker: the green, the great spotted, the lesser spotted and the wryneck. The green woodpecker is also known as a yaffle after its squeaky, laughter-like call. It forages mainly on the ground as it feeds predominantly on ants, and rarely drums. So the drumming we hear in British trees is caused by the great and lesser spotted species, which create crevices in wood to excavate for grubs and wood-boring insects. The other reason they drill at this time of year is to mark out their territory and try to attract a mate. Woodpeckers are the only type of bird to use another surface to make a sound, and this natural amplification of a mating call is a clever way to get attention. You might even find one tapping away on a fence, pipe, gutter or weathervane.

In order to withstand the impact and effects of regularly banging their bills against trees, woodpeckers' bodies feature some incredible adaptations and remarkable biomechanics. Let's start with how they manage not to have constant migraines or dislodge their eyes. For some time it was thought that tissue in their skulls, which consists of three layers (keratin, foam and bone), acted as a shock absorber, ensuring there was no damage or discomfort as they drum. This notion inspired the designer Anirudha Surabhi to create a cardboard helmet called the Kranium, which has cardboard shock-absorbing layers inside replicating the woodpecker's corrugated cartilage. Other designers considered woodpecker-inspired designs for US American Football players who, it was discovered, run at the same speed as a woodpecker drums (fourteen to sixteen miles per hour). But a recent study has thrown new light on how the woodpecker's skull actually protects its brain, discrediting this as an explanation.

In this new research scientists discovered that the internal skull tissues actually facilitate the birds to move quickly and use up minimal energy while still reaching deep into the wood. The impact of these swift, non-forceful blows is too soft to cause brain damage at the bird's normal drumming speed. So their skulls actually act like a refined, sturdy hammer rather than a shock-absorber.

Another amazing bit of evolutionary engineering is the woodpecker's tongue. Not only is this sticky and barbed, so it can easily trap insects (like an internal fly paper), it is also really, really long. This enables woodpeckers to poke deep into a crevice. But where does it go when it's retracted? The tongue is fixed to the skull by the hyoid bone at the base of the *upper* bill, in the nostril area. It then travels up and over the top of the skull, around the back and then into the lower bill, where we might expect to find a tongue. This wrap-around mechanism not only stores the tongue safely when not needed, it also provides extra cushioning for the skull.

If you've ever attempted some DIY you may have encountered the frustrations of a stuck drill bit. To avoid the same problem woodpeckers use some clever adaptations. With a slight turn of the head, they can drill at astonishing speeds with minimal risk of getting stuck. The top and bottom of their bills can also move in different directions, like an electric drill. They have a hinge-like bone at the front and a quadrate bone that joins with the skull, which helps ensure smooth drilling. That said, research has shown that they *do* actually get stuck as much as 36 per cent of the time. Without hands to free their bills, how do they extract them from the wood? Thanks to an ingenious adaptation woodpeckers are able to 'walk' their bills out of a hole in tiny increments, moving the top section back and the bottom up. This makes a small gap in the bill that they then close by tipping their heads. The walking action enables them to manoeuvre their bills safely out of a hole.

Drilling into wood inevitably results in dust and debris. Cue the woodpecker's protective eye membrane and tiny nasal feathers that filter out unwanted particles. And to prevent ant bites and insect stings, these birds have tough skin beneath their plumage. Then there are the super-strong tail feathers that create friction and the rear toes that act like crampons, allowing woodpeckers to cling on and balance against a tree as they drum and to descend tail-first (thus mopping up any surplus bugs other birds have missed). In sum, you've got an awe-inspiring feat of biomechanics going on beneath those stunning feathers.

If all this sounds like a lot of hard work just to extract dinner from a tree, woodpeckers also eat berries, seeds and nuts. Add peanuts and suet to your birdfeeder to try to lure some into your garden.

Long before we fully understood these wondrous adaptations, woodpeckers featured in myths, legends and stories across the globe. The ancient Romans told of a woodpecker named Picus (hence their family name, *Picidae*) who helped raise Romulus and Remus and achieved god-like status. Pliny wrote about the birds as being important in augury, and they held symbolic meaning in many diverse cultures. They are thought to represent luck, prosperity, strength, determination and protection. In Slavic tradition woodpeckers were associated with death, perhaps because they like foraging in dead wood. It could be that their drumming was seen as some kind of message from the deceased, an eerie signal resonating between worlds.

Their noisiness is matched only by their shyness, giving them an elusive magic as we traipse after the sound in vain, trying to spot a flash of their bright-red heads and chessboard feathers. But even if we only hear them in the canopy above, the woodpeckers' drumming reminds us that the Earth resounds and vibrates with pulses beyond our own anthropocentric world.

LULAH ELLENDER

11–15 MARCH

Chiffchaffs Return

Many of the signs of spring are subtle: the bedraggled flower of a rain-damp primrose, half hidden on a shady bank; a day of unexpected warmth, remarked upon by a stranger on the path . . . or a bird calling, a sound whose long absence has gone unnoticed until it is suddenly heard again. Such is the call of the chiffchaff, a little brown bird with a loud, repetitive song: 'chiff-chaff! chiff-chaff! chiff-chaff!'

Only the cuckoo has a name as perfectly reflective of its call as the chiffchaff's. However, unlike the cuckoo, a species in catastrophic decline, the chiffchaff is doing well – nearly two million pairs are estimated to breed annually in Britain and Ireland, yet they seem to arrive almost invisibly, migrating at night and hiding in dense undergrowth once here; only their distinctive song reveals their presence. Traditionally, chiff-chaffs have been seen as harbingers of spring, the advance guard of the summer visitors. But are they?

In recent years, small numbers of chiffchaffs have chosen to remain in Britain over winter. Feeding primarily on insects and, to a lesser extent, on seeds, these little warblers are usually forced to migrate to find sufficient food in winter. As climate change brings warmer, wetter winters to the British Isles, however, it seems that some birds are able to find enough food here to outweigh the risks of a long southerly migration. These hardy chancers are joined by a handful of others that have bred in more northerly regions of Europe and chosen to escape the bitter continental winters in Britain rather than face the rigours of migration to southern Europe or Africa. Yet staying put is a risky business too. Climate change may be bringing milder winters, enabling more insects to survive throughout the season, but chiffchaffs are not the only species that depends on this food source for part of their winter diet; competition for those insects will always be stiff. As ever, in uncertain times generalists do better than specialists. Perhaps chiffchaffs will broaden their dietary preferences to enable them to survive?

Yet climate change is not the only factor that is offering birds new options. Chiffchaffs are essentially birds of deciduous woodland, undergrowth and scrub, yet much of this habitat is being lost, or fragmented into small 'islands' within a sea of semi-sterile agricultural land. As our wild plants and insects are being decimated by chemical farming and pollution, many birds, including chiffchaffs, are finding better living conditions in our gardens. In the leafy habitats of our urban or semi-urban green spaces, they are able to take advantage of the food sources offered by a wide range of native and non-native plants and the insects that live among them. Perhaps there is hope in this? In 2018 around a third of the urban land in the United Kingdom was classified as 'functional green space', much of which is parks and gardens, offering possible, or sometimes ideal, living conditions for our native fauna.

So will more chiffchaffs choose to overwinter in the British Isles in the future? Will the 'chiff-chaff' call of these noisy little birds become widespread in early March or even February? Logically, this might be so. Permanent residents are able to monitor our variable weather conditions to their advantage, announcing their presence, searching for a mate and establishing a territory before the summer migrants even arrive. As a general rule it seems that, so long as adequate food is present and the weather favourable, earlier mating correlates with more successful outcomes for birds. Yet timing can be critical. The breeding success of the non-migratory blue tit, for example, is closely tied to the availability of large numbers of winter moth (*Operophtera brumata*) and green tortrix (*Tortrix viridana*) caterpillars on young oak leaves. The adult tits must time the hatching of their eggs to coincide with the leafing of the oak and the arrival of the caterpillars that feed upon it. Oak caterpillars are not the only foodstuff that blue tits feed their young, but there is a direct correlation between the proportion of these caterpillars in a blue tit chick's diet and the number of chicks raised: the greater the proportion of caterpillars consumed, the more chicks will reach maturity. So if the spring weather is mild, and enough caterpillars are available, the risk of early nesting can pay off, resulting in more surviving young and better chances of raising successive broods. Yet breeding early is a risky business. If late spring turns suddenly cold, leaf-burst may be delayed, resulting in insufficient food to feed the hungry chicks.

So where does this leave the chiffchaff? It is not known whether reproductive success is as closely tied to a specific food source for these species as it is for the blue tit, although this seems unlikely. Moreover, the start of the breeding season for birds depends not just on temperature, but also on the availability of adequate nutrition for female birds; it is, after all, upon this that their egg-laying capabilities depend.

Indeed, birds arriving from a well-fed winter in Africa may be in better physical condition for motherhood than those which overwintered on meagre fare in Britain. Still, if early nesting by overwintering chiffchaffs allows them to raise more young, either from one breeding cycle or from several, perhaps they will choose to overwinter in Britain in ever larger numbers. Overwintering birds may follow their parents' life choices and, by doing so, gradually change the migration habits of a whole species. This is unknown territory, but it is one possible scenario.

As our winters warm, we may need to move this micro-season back a week or two to keep up with this nimble little warbler's adaptation to our changing environment. In the meantime, the repetitive call of the chiffchaff in mid-March remains one of those welcome signs that spring is on its way.

REBECCA WARREN

16–20 MARCH

Butterflies Emerge

It's a day of early spring sunshine, and you are outside enjoying the unexpected warmth when a yellow sweet-wrapper blows into view, circles aimlessly for a moment, then flutters off into your neighbour's garden. Congratulations! Your day has been just photo bombed by a brimstone butterfly.

It's hard *not* to notice a brimstone on the wing. The males are a bright sulphur-yellow, the females a more demure buttermilk, but both have a wingspan of nearly six centimetres and seem to flap quite slowly as they search for nectar in the sunshine, lending them this 'wind-tossed sweet-wrapper' appearance. They really are 'flutter-by butterflies', and indeed it has been suggested that they were the original source of the word 'butterfly', the name reflecting their distinctive colour. Yet a brimstone at rest is far less obvious. After landing, they close up their wings and rely on the white-green coloration and prominent veining of their underwings to mimic surrounding leaves and thus provide camouflage from hungry predators.

Brimstone butterflies can live for up to twelve months, hibernating only during the coldest weeks of the winter, but, even so, it is possible to see them flying in every month of the year in periods of warmer weather. We tend to notice them most in February and March, perhaps because so few other butterflies are around. This is partly because brimstones have evolved to flourish in the early spring, when the primrose is in flower. Primroses have deep throats but brimstones have developed particularly long tongues which allow them to reach the nectar at the bottom of each flowerhead. This gives them an advantage over other butterflies that cannot access this food source; clearly it is a feast worth waking up for. And when that particular banquet is over, they will move on to feed on a much wider range of other flowers, before seeking out buckthorn or alder buckthorn bushes on which to lay their eggs.

Yet the brimstone is not the only butterfly to appear in early spring. Mid-March is also a good time for spotting the orange-tip butterfly, smaller than the brimstone but no less distinctive. The males sport the natty orange patches at the end of their wings from which they get their name; the females, which emerge a little later than the males, are a more demure white, with sooty black smudges where their mates are orange. Unlike the brimstone, the orange-tip does not overwinter as an adult. Instead, their emergence from chrysalis to butterfly is carefully timed to coincide with the growth and flowering of lady's smock (*Cardamine pratensis*) and other brassicas, especially garlic mustard (*Alliaria petiolata*), on which they feed and lay their eggs.

Recent records have shown that a variety of other butterflies may be seen on the wing in the early months of the year. Some of these, including peacocks and small tortoiseshells, overwinter in a form of dormancy called 'diapause' but sometimes emerge into activity during periods of winter warmth. Others, including small whites, commas and speckled woods, overwinter as caterpillars or chrysalises but hatch out in response, again, to warm conditions. The speckled wood, in fact, employs multiple strategies to get through the winter. This dapper little creature, its brown wings mottled with cream and black spots, only lives for about three weeks as an adult but during the summer several generations may be produced. Eggs laid early in the year can move from caterpillar to chrysalis to adult butterfly within a month. Later eggs will only reach chrysalis stage before going into dormancy over the winter, to hatch out in the spring. And some very late eggs that hatch into caterpillars in the autumn will continue to feed throughout the winter, only pupating in early spring. Timing, it seems, is everything.

The sight of a butterfly on the wing in early spring is a cheerful moment; it speaks of warm days to come, and of light and of colour. But it's also an opportunity to marvel at the extraordinary engineering that is the butterfly's wing. It seems so unlikely that such delicate structures can withstand the rigours of flight. Not surprisingly, the biomechanics of a butterfly's wing are beautiful and complex. Each wing is made of a very thin membrane of chitin, a biopolymer similar to the keratin that makes up our hair and fingernails. Both sides are covered with minute overlapping 'scales' which protect and insulate the chitin beneath. These scales also provide the intricate patterns that can hide the butterfly from would-be predators, as in the case of the brimstone, or scare off others, as the 'false eyes' on a peacock's wing are intended to do. Yet the scales are very delicate and easily brushed off if a butterfly is picked up, or hit by rain or hail.

Butterflies, moreover, are like reptiles in that they rely on external heat to provide the necessary warmth to activate their muscles. Ideally maintaining a body temperature of around 28°C, they require more energy to move when their muscles are cold than when warm. This is why hibernating butterflies that wake during the winter are at such risk; they can quickly become too cold to find food, escape predators or seek shelter again and are unlikely to find sufficient nectar to make up for the energy used to keep moving. In early spring, however, when overall temperatures are higher but may fluctuate and decrease rapidly, it is common to find butterflies basking with their wings outstretched, allowing the sun to reheat their muscles so that they can fly. Sometimes a butterfly may hold its wings half open, a pose that reflects sunlight down on to its body. Yet in periods of intense heat butterflies can overheat and may need to rest with closed wings to reduce heat gain or even seek out shelter and shade, as a mammal would do, to cool off.

So temperature plays a critical role in the life of the butterfly, and when we notice a vivid little orange-tip flitting over a patch of garlic mustard, or follow a 'sweet-wrapper' brimstone on its looping flight across the garden, it's worth remembering how fragile and complex these lovely creatures are. Careful observation of their behaviour can provide extraordinary insights into their brief lives, as well as marking the changing seasons in ours.

REBECCA WARREN

21–25 MARCH

The Thud of Dozy Bumblebees

As a society, we love depictions of bumblebees. They decorate crockery, cushions, babygrows, handbags and hundreds of items of jewellery. A breed apart from unfairly maligned 'creepy-crawlies', bumblebees are the acceptable face of the insect world: cute, rounded, fluffy and cartoon-like in their charisma. Even the word 'bumble' is soft and fuzzy: it means to hum or drone, with connotations of gently faltering incompetence. Perhaps we are also charmed by the fact that, like us, bumblebees are sociable creatures. Unlike solitary bees, who nest singly, bumblebees are a colonial species, living in social groups. Like honeybees, they operate a division of labour within a colony, producing a non-reproductive caste of bees who act as workers, foraging and helping to raise the young.

At this time of year, most of the really big bumblebees we see zooming around our gardens are queens, newly awakened from their winter hibernation. The exact species of these emerging bees can be difficult to distinguish, but the buff-tailed bumblebee (*Bombus terrestris*) has a slightly more beige rump and warmer yellow stripes than the lemon-coloured white-tailed bumblebee (*Bombus lucorum*). By March you might also see queens of the tree bumblebees (*Bombus hypnorum*), a species first recorded in the UK in 2001, and the unmistakable red-tailed bumblebees (*Bombus lapidarius*) with their rumps like glowing embers.

In autumn, as the other bees in their colonies wane and die, the young queens burrow down into the soil. They dig in areas where they can avoid winter flooding and maintain a reasonably constant temperature, like north-facing slopes. This is important because the queen will be dormant through the winter, surviving on the fat reserves that she has built up over the previous flying season. She therefore needs to avoid wasting vital energy in stirring on the kind of unseasonably warm winter day that is becoming ever more common as our climate changes.

When the queen emerges in early spring, she is ravenous. Completely reliant on early spring flowers, if she does not find an immediate source of nectar she will die. Zigzagging above the ground, she searches for food and for nesting sites, often colliding with our windows in the process – the characteristic thud that gives our microseason its name. Long, cold springs of the kind that climate change is producing mean that flowers bloom later, reducing her chances of survival.

Once she finds a suitable burrow, this time on a south-facing slope, she will construct a tiny pot and fill it with nectar. Beside this she will mould a mixture of wax and pollen into a lump, into which she will lay her eggs. Here she broods them, keeping them warm with her body heat. In just four to five weeks the larvae will have hatched, progressed through four stages (known as 'instars') and pupated. The worker bees that emerge are all female and pure white in the first instance, though they quickly develop the characteristic coloured furry coats of their species. Their job is to forage and help the queen increase the nest. If they succeed, male bees and new queens will be produced in further rounds of reproduction later in the season.

Their size and furry coats mean that bumblebees are surprisingly resilient to cold. Yet most species can only take to the air when their flight muscles hit at least 30°C (their thorax warms up, but not their abdomen, which remains 10–15°C cooler). To generate sufficient heat they bask in the sun, and also shiver rapidly, contracting both pairs of their flight muscles at once (the movement is so tiny that it can be difficult to detect visually, even in laboratory conditions). However, many species are not well adapted to very hot conditions: recent research suggests that they struggle at temperatures above 27°C, which means that they may be vulnerable to increasing summer heatwaves.

Dating back at least as far as Hesiod and Virgil, people have drawn analogies between the organisation of colonial bees and the political and economic workings of human society. Honeybees in particular, with their highly developed social organisation and intricate nests filled with neat rows of hexagonal cells, have been used to think about the balance between the pursuit of individual and collective goals in human society. Yet political writers have reached radically different conclusions about whether bees illustrate a monarchical system of subservience to a queen, a market organisation emerging spontaneously from private interests, or an altruistic, socially egalitarian society in pursuit of a common good.

Bumblebees are not entirely left behind in these debates. In his groundbreaking 1979 scientific study *Bumblebee Economics*, Bernd Heinrich studied the ways in which energy resources are managed in bumblebee colonies. In the process, he compared bumblebee organisation to that of a

human economy, though he reached very different conclusions about the possible lessons to be
learned at different points in the book. From a
reproductive angle, he argued, worker bumblebees are enslaved to the queen, with no choice
about their lot in life. From the perspective of foraging, however, he suggested that they resemble a market society like
that described by the neoclassical economist Adam Smith,
in which individual initiative in nectar-sourcing supposedly
acts as a force for collective good. The political instability
of these comparisons should warn readers that Heinrich
was not entirely serious about drawing human/bee analogies: indeed, at times he explicitly cautions against them.
Nonetheless, his work was taken up and used as a serious
endorsement of free-market capitalism; in a 2004 preface
to a second edition of his book, he expressed dismay at this
outcome.

By contrast, a number of economists draw another analogy, which relies on early scientific bemusement about the
ability of bumblebees to fly. In the 1930s, the entomologist
August Magnan mentioned in passing that he had discussed
bumblebee flight with his assistant, the mathematician
André Sainte-Laguë, and that the pair had concluded that
it ought to be scientifically impossible. This story has been
repeated countless times since, including in the opening of
the 2007 Hollywood film *Bee Movie*. It's often told in a way
that takes inordinate pleasure in the fact that science has
'failed' in the face of this problem, despite the fact that recent
research has actually been quite successful in explaining
bumblebee aerodynamics (spoiler: it's all about leading-edge
vortices produced by their wings).

In his opening address to the Congress of the Social
Democratic Party in March 2000, the Swedish Prime Minis-
ter Göran Persson gave Magnan's bemusement an economic
spin:

Think of a bumblebee. With its overly heavy body and little wings, supposedly it should not be able to fly – but it does. Every summer it comes back and makes the seemingly impossible possible en route from a forget-me-not to a daisy. This is how so-called analysts view the Swedish economy. We 'defy gravity'. We have high taxes and a large public sector, and yet Sweden reaches new heights.

The bumblebee's flight becomes a way of thinking about the economic inexplicability of Sweden itself within mainstream models, a cautionary tale about the limits of theoretical knowledge as we seek to describe a highly complex world. The metaphor of Scandinavia as a seemingly incomprehensible 'bumblebee social democracy' has since been adopted by a number of economists and financial journalists, though mostly as a preface to lengthy tomes that provide a complex variety of explanations for this Scandinavian success story.

Metaphor and analogy can be powerful ways of opening up the natural world, of noticing new aspects of its diversity. But analogies between the human and non-human are also fraught with peril. Perhaps, in order to see what is really happening to bumblebees, we need to stop treating them as characters in an economic fable, identifying them with our human society and drawing moral and economic conclusions from their behaviour. The life of bees *is* closely connected with our own, but the reality is that, far from being analogous to their way of life, the organisation of our economy and especially our food system is killing them.

We now have twenty-four species of bumblebee in the UK, but we used to have twenty-six: two have already been driven to extinction since the 1940s. Many of the remaining species are in deep trouble, with numbers nosediving. The systemic problems they face include the loss of floral diversity (especially flower-rich grasslands), the fragmentation of their habitat, the depredations of ever more intensive farming fuelled by public demand for the cheapest possible food, exposure to harmful pesticides (particularly neonicotinoids), and a changing climate. A burgeoning commercial industry in bumblebee-breeding, in which bees are raised to assist with pollination in the greenhouses of the soft fruit industry, adds an additional risk: the spread of novel diseases into wild populations.

Fortunately, many people are fighting back, planting pollinator-friendly plants that provide nectar early in the season, campaigning against unnecessary verge-cutting and use of pesticides in towns, installing bee habitats, and – perhaps most significantly of all – piling pressure on politicians to create a farming system that works for nature. Pollinators play a material role in our economy: estimates suggest that 5–8 per cent of global crop production depends on them, with an annual market value of between $160 billion and $689 billion. But while such calculations may be useful when trying to persuade policymakers, the wider value of this insect and its place within the ecosystem cannot be quantified in monetary terms. The buzz of a bumblebee pulls us out of the busyness of our own lives; it inspires wonder and affection. And isn't that why we put bumblebees on crockery, babygrows and cushions, after all?

KIERA CHAPMAN

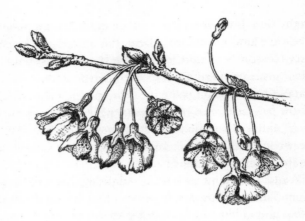

26–30 MARCH

Cherry Blossom Festival

There is a cherry blossom for everyone. You like your flowers delicate, unfussy? Then the wild cherries are for you: simple white petals, loosely cupping a diadem of golden anthers, fringing woodlands with clouds of diaphanous blooms. Or perhaps you prefer a hint of colour? Then the winter-flowering cherries are for you, coming out at the darkest time of the year, their tiny, papery flowers almost floating in a mist of palest pink against our damp, leaden skies. But for those of you who like your colours rich and vibrant, your petals full and blowsy, there are luscious swags of deep magenta or candy-pink blossom, double-flowered or single, clinging to an upright trunk or weeping down to the ground . . . Whatever your preference, ornamental cherries have been bred to suit every taste over the centuries, successfully crossing the divide between wild and tame, rural and urban, beautiful and kitsch.

Cherries are part of the *Prunus* family and grow in most temperate countries in the world, either naturally or by introduction, but perhaps it is in Japan that they have the deepest cultural resonance. There, the opening of the first cherry blossom – or *sakura* – is widely celebrated with the ancient practice of *hanami* or 'cherry blossom viewing'. The Japanese microseason calendar calls this moment 櫻始開 (*sakura hajimete saku*) and records it, like us, towards the end of March. For some, *hanami* means simply viewing the trees when the blossom is out, but for many people it is a time for families to gather beneath the trees, to share food, drink and entertainment while admiring the spectacular flowers. This tradition is so important that the appearance of the first cherry blossom is reported on the national news. As the warmth of spring makes its way north up the islands of Japan the cherry trees blossom in its wake, a slow tide of pink petals washing across the country, mapped and publicised as the 'Cherry Blossom Front' by the Japanese Meteorological Agency.

Hanami is an ancient practice, probably originating in China, where wild plum blossom was traditionally admired and celebrated. Chinese influence during the first millennium transferred this appreciation to aristocratic culture in Japan. By the Heian period in Japan (794–1185 CE) this influence was waning and the focus of Japanese *hanami* moved to cherry blossom. In 812, Emperor Saga held a celebration of *sakura* at the Shinsen-en Temple, and thereafter at his palace. The practice of *hanami* slowly spread throughout Japan, filtering down to every level of society and resulting in the widespread planting of cherry trees. Images of cherry blossom began to appear in art and literature. 'Everywhere I look,' wrote the poetess Kunaikyō at the turn of the thirteenth century, 'cherry trees are starting to bloom'.

Ironically, for such an enduring tradition, part of the appeal of cherry blossom in Japanese culture is its transience. At the same time that the cherry was replacing the plum as an object of devotion, Buddhism was spreading in

Japan, bringing with it the concept of *mono no aware*, an acceptance of the finite nature of existence. The beautiful but brief flowering of the cherry became symbolic of the concept of *mono no aware*, and it is this quality of fleeting beauty that continues to be prized as a reminder of the impermanence of life. It is not the beauty of the flowers alone that makes them precious, but the knowledge that this loveliness will soon be gone. The two qualities are inseparable; cherry blossom is more beautiful because of the haunting foreknowledge of its imminent loss. An anonymous haiku, written in the seventeenth century, lamented 'To learn how to die, watch cherry blossoms.'

Yet cherry blossom is also a traditional symbol of birth and renewal. In ancient Japan the new year began in spring, and the flowering of the cherries marked the beginning of the rice-planting season. The two events were so deeply intertwined that the word for cherry blossoms, *sakura*, in fact derives from two words: *sa*, the god of rice paddies, and *kura*, a place for a god. Cherry blossom thus played an integral role in the rituals and seasonal beliefs of early Japanese culture as part of the agricultural cycle upon which human life depended. The continued celebration of the arrival of *sakura* in Japan, despite the commercialisation of modern *hanami*, is a moment when, knowingly or not, Japanese people revisit the practices and values of their ancestors.

Cherry blossom carries none of those deep cultural connections in Britain. Perhaps the only gods who find themselves at home within our cherry trees are the gods of suburbia, jauntily perched among the frilly petals of neatly spaced trees along quiet residential roads. For a few weeks in spring the nation's parks, gardens and streets put on a frothy show of pink flowers. Ornamental cherries are usually small trees, and their correspondingly small root runs have made them ideal for roadsides and gardens. Offering a display of flamboyant flowers in spring and a brief blaze of red and orange leaves in autumn, they became a favourite tree for urban designers in the twentieth century, and it is rare to find a town that does not have ornamental cherries somewhere in its public spaces.

Yet the cherry native to the British Isles – *Prunus avium* – is a tree of greater refinement. Clouds of single white flowers are produced in abundance in early spring on tall trees that are often clustered along the edge of woodlands, where they can escape the shade of other trees. For a few weeks in April and May the countryside is lit up by a festival of white blossom, including that of hawthorn, sloe and cherry plum: towering above them all are the flowering branches of the wild cherry, lofty, elegant and ephemeral. In 1896 the writer A. E. Housman captured the spectacle of wild cherry blossom in a poem which echoes something of the Japanese recognition of the fleeting beauty of the flowers, and quietly acknowledges the inevitable transience of all human life:

> Loveliest of trees, the cherry now
> Is hung with bloom along the bough,
> And stands about the woodland ride
> Wearing white for Eastertide
>
> Now, of my threescore years and ten,
> Twenty will not come again,
> And take from seventy springs a score,
> It only leaves me fifty more.
>
> And since to look at things in bloom
> Fifty springs are little room,
> About the woodlands I will go
> To see the cherry hung with snow.

Cherry blossom time is truly a festival of lightness, a mark of the onset of spring and a time of new life. But it reminds us too that even youth and beauty will pass.

REBECCA WARREN

APRIL

Noticing Exercise

This month, we draw your attention to something that might at first sight appear unremarkable: the humble nettle. This is a moment in the year when young nettles are abundant in soil that is still richly wet from winter rain. Though they might at first sight seem less exciting than rarer and stranger plants in our neighbourhoods, paying attention to nettles can shed fresh light on our local history.

Since the sixteenth century, people have noticed that nettles tend to spring up around human habitation. This is because they enjoy the phosphate-rich conditions of human sites, which remain long after housing may have disappeared. Pay attention to where you see these common plants as you go about your business and ask yourself, what histories are hidden in their jagged-toothed presence?

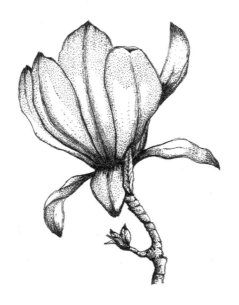

31 MARCH–4 APRIL

Hallucinogenic Magnolias

The graceful branches of beech trees may brush the sky, and fruit trees produce delicious bounties, but the magnolia's confection-like blooms capture our imagination in a distinct way. The blossoming of the magnolia is a sure sign that spring is here, and these first flowers cast a particular spell.

The strange allure of magnolia blossom has been documented throughout human history, but the tree itself pre-dates us. While our first human ancestors appeared between five million and seven million years ago, magnolias evolved during the Cretaceous period, when dinosaurs still roamed the Earth. Fossil records show that magnolias are one of the most primitive plants in evolutionary history.

Although today magnolias are native only in the southern United States and southern China, fossil records indicate that over 100 million years ago magnolias grew throughout what we now call Europe, North America and Asia.

The earliest Western record of the magnolia in cultivation is attributed to the Spanish naturalist Francisco Hernández de Toledo. Hernández is known as one of the fathers of natural history. He was one of the first European scientists to visit the Americas, and his observations reveal a great deal about Aztec history at the time of Montezuma, as well as descriptions and illustrations of thousands of species previously unknown to Europe, including the then rare *Magnolia dealbata*. The tree also features in translations of pre-conquest Aztec poetry. One verse in particular links the fleeting transience of the magical magnolia bloom to human mortality, stating 'Listen, I say! On earth we're known only briefly, like the magnolia. We only wither, O friend'.

The withered state of the magnolia flower is almost as striking as its brief bloom. Though the tree itself is hardy, its flowers are notably tender. As soon as its sweet-smelling petals are touched by cold or rain they turn brown and fall to the ground. The fragile and fleeting nature of the magnolia's flowers lend them a phosphorescent quirk, flashes of brilliance. And this transience is a link not only to human mortality but also to the nebulous dreams and mirages we associate with hallucinogenic states. They have a liminal quality that provokes a 'wandering in the mind', a movement between time and space that opens up a wider sphere of experience.

When the magnolia first opened its blossoms, the common pollinators that we think of today, such as bees, butterflies and moths, had not yet evolved. As a result, magnolias evolved to be pollinated by the flightless 'dumb' beetles, which were once the primary insect pollinators. These early insects could not perform the more specialised behaviours of later pollinators, such as flower identification and the manipulation of complex flowers to harvest pollen. However, these early beetles played a vital role in the co-evolution between insects and flowering plants which utterly changed the trajectory of the development of life on Earth.

Beetle-pollinated flowers tend to be large and coloured pink or white. In fact, most of the physical characteristics that we associate with the magnolia can be directly linked to their early relationship with beetles. The flower's reproductive structure is both striking and simple. The flower bud is enclosed in *bracts*, undifferentiated leaves, and the petals themselves are actually *tepals*, which are thicker and more leathery than what we tend to think of as petals. These tepals can handle beetle mouthparts, which are made for chewing rather than delicate pollen collection. Magnolia flowers also have tough *carpels*, female reproductive organs that look like *stamens*, the male reproductive organs. This aids pollination by encouraging beetles to spend more time on the flower, bumping into the stamens and covering themselves in pollen, before moving on.

The magnolia's inner tepals are remarkably responsive; they have the ability to open and shut in different circumstances. In addition, the magnolia is monoecious, meaning that, like the common hazel we explored in January, both male and female reproductive organs are present in individual flowers. In order to minimise the chance of self-pollination, the magnolia opens in the morning and exposes the receptive tip of its carpel to beetles who come and go during the day. When night falls the magnolia's tepals close and trap any beetle that was feeding within the bloom, first allowing it to distribute pollen and later covering it in fresh pollen. When the day breaks the tepals open and release the beetle, who ambles off to pollinate a different bloom.

*

Each spring, as these tender flowers capture and release their pollinators, they make manifest the prehistoric art of co-operation and co-evolution. The first 'modern' magnolia, *Magnolia virginiana*, was brought from the USA to the UK in 1688 by the missionary John Banister. Around a century later the Asian varieties *Magnolia denudata* and *Magnolia coco* were introduced to Britain. By 1800 a wide range of magnolia species were commercially available and being cultivated in gardens and parks across the British Isles, and they are the ancestors of the trees we see today. So these staples of our modern domesticated landscape have their roots in the wildness of deep time. Even if we don't inhale the intoxicating aroma of the fleeting magnolia blossom we might still experience the hallucinatory feeling of travelling back through the millennia, as this curious bloom connects us back to the long era on Earth before the arrival of our species and the flowering of cities, empires and geopolitical states.

ROWAN JAINES

5–9 APRIL

Hailstones and Sunshine

April is often cited as having 'four seasons in one day', shifting from rain to warm sunshine to hail and frost in the space of a few hours. In reality, these aren't really seasons, just *weather*. But it is true that the warmer spring temperatures combined with the cooler, unstable upper air can result in changeable weather at this time of year. This microseason is characterised by just such fickleness.

Weather-savvy Brits will know they should pack a coat and umbrella even if they leave the house in the morning in short sleeves. And perhaps it is this very capriciousness that fuels our apparent obsession with talking about the weather. Research by the social anthropologist Kate Fox in 2010 for an update to her book *Watching the English* revealed that 'at almost any moment in this country, at least a third of the population is either talking about the weather, has already done so or is about to do so'.

Why this constant fixation with meteorological developments? It is partly a cultural norm, a way of opening a conversation with something neutral but also shared. The weather is a social bond, a connection between strangers who find themselves in the same place at the same time. Author Bill Bryson famously noted that 'the most striking thing about the British weather is that there isn't very much of it,' going on to write: 'in a single sentence the British weather [is] captured to perfection: dry but rainy with some warm/cool spells'. For an American our piffling hailstorms and paltry heatwaves seem mild and unremarkable. But the point isn't the extremes, it's the possibility of change. And at this time of year there definitely is plenty of that.

This unpredictability is what makes our weather worthy of so much chat and attention. It is the result of our position at the end of an Atlantic storm track at the meeting point of six major air masses. The Gulf Stream and our coastline add further moisture to the air. In April rising temperatures and the still-cool air cause thunderstorms and rain showers, as well as spells of cloudless blue. Living with such frequently changing weather – particularly the pronounced changes, like the switch from sunshine to sudden hail – confounds our desire for certainty and fixedness and can make us feel unsettled, constantly braced for whatever the sky throws at us.

Perhaps we should be thankful that showers of frogs and locusts are not part of the British meteorological repertoire, as they were for biblical Egypt. Weather features prominently in the Bible, from the Flood in the Book of Genesis onwards. In Exodus we read of the ten plagues sent to Egypt. Verse 9:25 states that 'hail smote every herb of the field, and brake every tree', associating extreme weather events with apocalypse and punishment for humankind's sins. With little scientific knowledge it is easy to see how people sought explanations for devastating weather and the catastrophes that followed.

Writers and painters have long used the weather as a symbol for a state of mind, nature of a relationship or emotional condition. Turner, Constable and Whistler created majestic, accurate depictions of the sky, filled with gloomy clouds and turbulent storms and miraculous sunlight. Composers also incorporated weather into their work – from Vivaldi's *Four Seasons* to Beethoven's *Pastoral Symphony*, which portray the sublime energy and violence of storms alongside the calm majesty of sunshine.

The critic John Ruskin bemoaned the anthropomorphisation of weather in art in his 1843–60 work *Modern Painters*, and coined the term 'pathetic fallacy' to describe this imposition of subjective feelings on to natural occurrences, conjuring an emotional landscape through portrayals of storms or sunny pastoral scenes. Instead he called for artists to integrate 'pure fact' along with feelings in their work. This was rooted in his acute attentiveness to the natural world and interest in the weather – an interest that mapped the growing understanding and study of meteorology in the nineteenth century.

As we learned more about how weather occurs we developed a whole new lexicon to describe weather events and behaviours, and the ability to forecast meant that people could begin to mitigate the effects of, and prepare for, the weather.

So what about the hail that features in this microseason? We know that hail is not frozen raindrops, as is sometimes claimed, but in fact is formed when frozen water droplets form in the updrafts of thunderstorms and are thrown around in the winds within the storm. When the hailstones become too heavy for the updrafts to hold aloft they fall, sometimes in swathes of between ten and 100 miles wide.

The largest recorded hailstone was 20.3 centimetres in diameter and was found in South Dakota. That is around the same size as a football. Large hailstones are not uncommon in parts of the world where strong updrafts support them for longer, giving them time to amass more frozen droplets. Their size is dependent on a complex range of factors including their shape and the winds. Hailstones typically fall to the ground at speeds of twenty to fifty miles per hour, but large hailstones fall faster – some at over 100 miles per hour. They can cause significant damage as they land, denting cars, damaging buildings and even killing people and animals. A hailstorm near Moradabad, India in 1888 killed 246 people as cricket ball-sized stones rained down at speed, while during another in 1986 in Bangladesh forty people were killed and 400 injured.

As our climate warms, hailstorms are getting stronger and have bigger stones. Changes like this, which we can already see happening around us, can feel terrifying; they may not come as a punishment from the gods, but we know they are a consequence of our actions. And, at the same time as holding ourselves to account for the wholescale damage we are doing to our planet, perhaps we appreciate all the more the moments when the weather feels benign. In her poem 'Hailstorm' Kay Ryan describes the hailstones coming down like hornets and punches, with a strength that leaves us dumbfounded when they are gone.

In this microseason the changing weather works its magic on us. After the hectic pelting the arrival of sunshine feels especially welcome, bringing with it the relief of stillness and light.

LULAH ELLENDER

10–14 APRIL

Blackbirds Bicker

Perhaps the most familiar birdsong in all the British Isles belongs to the blackbird, whose adaptable nature has allowed it to thrive across various habitats. From coastal towns to urban centres and across peaks and valleys the blackbird appears wherever there are humans. And wherever the blackbird can be seen, it can also be heard. During autumn and winter this is a quiet, low sub-song. However, from March through to July – the breeding season – it erupts into a full operatic courtship performance.

Throughout February and March the male common blackbird reveals himself to be not only a singer but a dancer too, in the form of a striking courtship display. His routine involves running back and forth, bowing his head as the female common blackbird watches motionless. He holds his crown feathers partially erect, compressing his neck feathers and fluffing out his body feathers, depressing and fanning his tail in an artfully choreographed montage. From here the courting blackbird stretches and opens his beak, straining forward and staring at his potential mate as he emits low and stifled fragments of song interrupted by smatterings of alarm notes and warbles.

While this bodacious display is most often associated with pair formation in the earliest weeks of spring, male blackbirds often briefly repeat their performance in the days after copulation and before the female lays her clutch of eggs. By the second week of April, monogamous pairs will have formed, some involving juveniles and bereaved individuals of both sexes, while a few polyamorous males will continue to try their luck. While courtship and copulation continue, swathes of chicks will have already hatched and some of the first wave will have fledged, returning regularly to beg noisily for food. At this moment in the year, blackbird song season is in full swing.

In his 1901 book *Birds and Men* the naturalist, ornithologist and author William Henry Hudson spends some time pondering the strong resemblance between blackbird song and human voices. Hudson ruminates on a quote from the engineer and music scholar George Grove, who identified the shared repetitions, pauses, matching of tones and pace that make up the music of both human chat and blackbird song. Grove and Hudson recognised something important at work in the blackbird's vocalisation, namely that it is a 'song' rather than a 'call'.

But what is the difference? Recent work in the field of biosemiotics, which is concerned with the study of signs and meaning in living organisms and systems, elucidates the distinction: a 'call' represents a brief monosyllabic and innate sound pattern, aimed at attracting the attention of a specific other, in order to communicate a danger or a need. A 'song', on the other hand, is a prolonged and complex vocal performance that makes use of repetitions of tone and melody that have meaning for a wide range of species mates in a form of learned vocabulary. The only non-human species that display this characteristic are parrots, hummingbirds and the sub-order of common bird species known as 'songbirds'. This order includes buntings, sparrows, warblers and blackbirds, all of whom have complex vocal organs and forebrain neural circuits that result in the ability to learn 'songs' that have a detailed and locally meaningful form. So the bickering of blackbirds that can be heard throughout the British spring is really the bird equivalent of human chatter in a marketplace.

The blackbird's aptitude for both mimicry and learning creates a two-way stream of influence between their songmaking and ours. On the one hand their plastic neural networks and extraordinary vocal range mean that blackbirds and their songs have a particularly adaptive response to environmental noise. The blackbird is a skilled mimic and is renowned for attempting to copy almost everything it hears, from other birds to car alarms, ice cream van jingles and phone ringtones. On the other hand, as far back as the ancient Greeks we find evidence of birdsong as a model for poetic and rhetorical form: Homer's art of poetic variegation was reportedly modelled upon the many-toned voice of birdsong, Alcman claimed to have invented his poetic form by imitating partridge song, and Democritus takes this even further by specifying the swan and the nightingale as the true source of the human arts of song and imitation.

Scientists have noticed general patterns of birdsong modification that appear in response to noise, such as increasing the frequency and/or volume of song and changing its length and timing. It is the latter that is important for both blackbird song and human speech. Research is increasingly finding that in situations where there is an abundance of 'noise', which can include information, both humans and songbirds tend to make communications shorter and simpler and increase their frequency and volume.

Blackbird song can roughly be divided into two parts, the motif and the twitter. The twitter is a burst of high-frequency and low-amplitude notes that usually, though not always, follows the motif, which is composed of low-frequency and high-amplitude melodic tones. In urban environments (as well as during early breeding seasons), blackbirds have been found to both raise the frequency of their motifs and increase the proportion of stylised, emotive twitter.

We might see these adaptations as characterising a shift away from the lyrical and towards the rhetorical in blackbird communication. Another way of parsing this is that urban blackbirds seem to be forgoing the curious, improvisational shared song that Hudson and Grove spoke of with delight. In its place we have more of the twitter, the short, noisy bursts of self-promotion. In the age of social media, this bird behaviour feels rather familiar!

Legend tells that as a newborn, Homer, the father of Greek literature, sang in the voice of nine birds, one after the other, beginning with the swallow and ending with the blackbird. Today, I invite you to give a song back to the blackbirds: whistle as you hang the washing, hum, sing, or simply turn up the radio. Revel in the joy of communication beyond the meaning of the words.

ROWAN JAINES

Blackthorn Spring

The old phrase a 'blackthorn winter' refers to unseasonably wintry weather in spring. Our take on the name, blackthorn spring, notes the blackthorn as a tentative herald of spring; a signifier of change that still contains the chill of winter.

A shrubby tree that grows in low-ish tangled, thorny thickets, blackthorn is associated with death and violence but also with the difficult transition from darkness into light. In spring a foam of milky-white blossoms blankets the hedgerows like drifts of snow, illuminating the still-sparse vegetation. The flush of softly starred blossoms, with their fuzz of yellow or white anthers, contrasts with the almost-black, spiky branches to create a sense of both beauty and danger. The blackthorn (*Prunus spinosa*) is complex and contradictory, just like the seasons it spans. It is monoecious (like the hazel and magnolia we have described in earlier microseasons), having both male and female reproductive parts, and so contains its own duality.

The pretty blossoms offer nectar and pollen for bumble-bees; yellow-tail, magpie, swallow-tailed and lackey moths; and brown hairstreak butterflies. And yet beneath the froth of petals there are long, sharp thorns. The tree has been used as a weapon, but also – over the centuries – as protection and medicine.

Traditionally, the flowers, bark and fruit have been made into a blood-cleansing tonic, to help ease rheumatism, reduce cholesterol and soothe indigestion, and as an astringent, laxative, diuretic, diaphoretic and detoxifier. But the leaves, once used to bulk out tea leaves when prices were high, actually contain prussic acid, which breaks down into hydrogen cyanide on contact with saliva. The thorns too have hidden dangers. Not only incredibly painful if touched, they also contain toxins that can result in a synovial fluid reaction, causing serious sepsis, granuloma, joint pain or abscesses if they break off under the skin. The fruits are the sloes that appear in early autumn, clustered like small plums or rounder blueberries among the spines. Examinations of a preserved 5,300-year-old body discovered on the icy slopes of the Öztal Alps revealed that the man was carrying, and had digested, sloes; and excavations at Glastonbury exposed a Neolithic pit full of sloe stones. We can assume that these berries formed part of the hunter-gatherer diet and were easily foraged. We may baulk at eating sloes, which are sour and bitter, on their own, but when added to gin and then strained and made into boozy jam, they are delicious.

Our relationship with the wood from the blackthorn is also full of contradictions. Perhaps because of its magical associations, blackthorn was said to be protected by fairies, to whom you must ask permission before cutting or harvesting any part of the tree. In druidic lore it is unlucky to cut the wood or pick sloes on Samhain or Beltane.

Blackthorn was traditionally used to make Irish shillelagh, or cudgels, thanks to its strength and durability. To enhance these properties people would cure the wood by burying it in manure or daubing it with butter and placing it inside a chimney. These weapons can both attack and defend. But blackthorn contains darker stories too.

It has long been associated with witchcraft, being the witch's material of choice for wands or spiky instruments used to inflict pain and even cause miscarriage. The wood was thought to be imbued with evil spirits and to curse people – in Scottish folklore it is said to be 'crossed' and is connected with the Crone of Death, Cailleach, who walks in winter causing storms and taking life. Blackthorn was also used on pyres to burn women accused of witchcraft, as well as being one of several materials suggested to have been used to make Christ's crown.

In contrast, the wood makes excellent walking sticks, and can be used in hedging around a boundary. Blackthorn also provides protection and security. It plays a part in our democratic tradition – in the House of Commons in Westminster, the Usher of the Black Rod carries a staff made from the wood. Black Rod's role is to oversee parliamentary proceedings and maintain order, and the staff holds great ceremonial significance at the opening of Parliament. Before the Queen's or King's Speech, the Commons door is slammed in Black Rod's face, forcing them to bang three times with their staff before the MPs follow them to the House of Lords to hear the speech. Along with the ceremonial mace, the blackthorn rod is deeply rooted in our parliamentary rituals and history.

Blackthorn often grows alongside its sister tree, the gentler hawthorn. You can distinguish it from this and from the cherry plum by looking (carefully!) for its fierce spines and darker bark. These trees mark the boundaries between fields, line the edges of roads and rivers, and populate the fringes of our woodlands, providing sustenance and protection for a range of species. They also put on a very welcome springtime show.

It may only be photo-worthy for a fleeting moment before returning to being what the academic and writer Robert Macfarlane refers to as its 'un-Instagrammable nature', but there is such rich history tangled up with this enchanted tree. The blackthorn is a symbol of death but also of wonder and transformation. And whether we are cutting branches as an offering to the moon fairy or merely admiring the foam of its flowers, this microseason encourages us to think about duality in the natural world, as well as in ourselves.

LULAH ELLENDER

Llygad Ebrill
(April's Eye – the Celandine)

There are two types of celandine in Britain – and, confusingly, they're not even from the same plant family. This microseason is named for the lesser celandine, *Ficaria verna* or *Ranunculus ficaria*, a low-growing plant from the buttercup family. With its glossy heart-shaped leaves and bright-yellow flowers it has long been seen as a symbol of the returning sun, flowering from March and spreading into spangled carpets of yellow stars by April. It prefers shady, damp areas, so look out for it in woodland, beside paths and on riverbanks. The other type, greater celandine (*Chelidonium majus*) is part of the poppy family.

To identify lesser celandine look for ground-level glossy green leaves, which are completely different from the greater celandine's more upright blue-green pinnate leaves. Depending on the lesser celandine variety, there will be between six and twenty-six yellow petals, but there are usually around eight to twelve. As well as the commonly seen yellow flowers there are different cultivars with white or green flowers. These shiny petals both absorb and radiate light, signalling their presence to pollinators (for more on this, see the 26–30 May microseason on buttercup meadows). They close overnight or during rainfall and open again between 9 a.m. and 5 p.m. Once its short flowering season is over, a few seeds are released, the foliage dies back and the plant disappears into the ground – which means we need to appreciate it while it is still around.

The plant is a prolific spreader, leading some countries to classify it as an invasive weed that threatens woodland and native habitats. Its success in self-propagating is due to its ability to reproduce both asexually and sexually. Fertilised seeds are spread by birds, offering a wide-ranging dispersal. But it mainly reproduces via clonal tubers and bulbils and by sending out rhizomes to spread over a closer range. With these different options, celandine may be better able to adapt to changing environments than other plants.

Lesser celandine is also known as cheesecups, butter and cheese, golden guineas, brighteye and llygad Ebrill ('April's eye' in Welsh). In Gaelic it is named *grian*, meaning sun. The Victorians assigned it the symbolic meaning 'joy to come', which reflects another common name, spring messenger. You can't help but feel cheery just reading this list.

Both lesser and greater celandine have long been harvested for medicinal purposes. Because the two distinct plants come from different families, they also have different effects and dangers, so herbalists need to differentiate wisely. Lesser celandine was traditionally seen as a cure-all, and the roots, leaves and petals were used for a range of ailments and conditions. Perhaps its most widely known medicinal usage is the treatment of piles (haemorrhoids). The Latin name *Ficaria* is thought to originate from the fig-like lesser celandine roots – piles are also known as 'figs' – and gives rise to the folk name figwort. The leaves or ground-up roots are mixed with lard as a topical salve and applied to these painful protrusions, or taken internally. The young leaves were once used as a treatment for scurvy thanks to their high levels of vitamin C. They can also be eaten in salads, applied to wounds and scratches, and have even been used to clean teeth. Medicinal or culinary use is risky, however, because as well as useful saponins, astringent tannins and fungicidal and antibacterial compounds the plant also contains protoanemonin, a toxin. This is neutralised by cooking or drying, but the plant must still be used with caution – lesser celandine has been known to cause liver damage, and the orange sap can irritate skin.

Greater celandine, meanwhile, has been used in herbal medicine to treat eye problems. Its common name, swallow wort, is thought to have stemmed either from the flowers coinciding with the return of the swallows, or from the belief that the birds applied the leaves to their offspring's eyes to restore impaired vision. This entry in Gerard's *Herball* explains further: 'The juice of the herbe is good to sharpen the sight, for it cleanseth and consumeth away slimie things that cleave about the ball of the eye.' The book also recommends greater celandine root to treat various diseases found in hawks.

At this time of year, lesser celandine and greater celandine are just two of the plants that dot our landscape with yellow, alongside primroses, daffodils, colt's foot, cowslips, aconites and oxalis. Why are so many spring flowers yellow? And why do so many more yellow flowers appear in spring than in any other season? The reasons may lie with pollinators.

In spring the main pollinators are flies, which have limited colour vision. In order for a flower to successfully attract them in these low light levels it needs to be highly visible and distinct from the surrounding foliage. Open or cup shapes also help guide flies to the pollen and nectar and don't require specialised pollen-extracting features, so the lesser celandine is perfectly adapted with its splayed, glossy petals. If you've ever worn a yellow item of clothing outdoors in warm weather you will probably have been assailed by flying insects, experiencing the colour's magnetic charms. Yellow also absorbs heat so these flowers can make the most of the sun's weak springtime warmth. However, although this theory has a sound basis in what we know about insect colour vision, pollinator interactions are complex so we need to be careful about generalising across species.

This quiet, fleeting flower may not be a show-stopper, but its sunny appearance is a welcome harbinger of spring and it has been celebrated by many writers and artists, including Wordsworth. Although most famous for his poem about daffodils, Wordsworth also wrote several poems praising lesser celandine. Indeed, he was so fond of the plant that he requested a sprig of it be engraved on his tombstone. The flower was duly depicted on the poet's memorial plaque in St Oswald's Church, Grasmere – however, the artist used the wrong kind of celandine.

The potential for confusion aside, the lesser celandine is the quintessential springtime flower. Its appeal lies not just in its cheerful bright-yellow petals, but in its ephemerality. Now the year has turned, life is accelerating, with new growth, new flowers and new spots of brightness to notice.

LULAH ELLENDER

25-29 APRIL

Bluebells Blanketing Woods

Blue is a colour we don't often associate with the land. Give a child a blue crayon and they will inevitably use it to represent the vast 'nothing' of sky-space when illuminated by a sun-like star. Or perhaps they will draw the sea. Blue seems to be the colour of the less earthly elements, and of purity. Perhaps this is why in Christian paintings both the Virgin Mary and Christ wear blue robes. But during this microseason blue is the colour of the ground, as the rich, deep violet-blue of the bluebell carpets the glades of our woodland.

The botanical name of the British bluebell is *Hyacinthoides non-scripta*. (This is not to be confused with the larger, paler, more upright Spanish bluebell, *Hyacinthoides hispanica*.) According to the nature writer Richard Mabey, the name – which translates as 'unlettered hyacinth' – contains a nod to

Greek literature. Mythology had it that when Hyacinthus, the mortal lover of the god Apollo, was dying in his arms a flower sprang from his spilled blood and Apollo marked its petals with the letters of lamentation 'AI AI' (meaning 'alas'). The bluebell was thus differentiated from the hyacinth by being 'unlettered'.

Despite being found in other parts of Europe, half of all the world's *Hyacinthoides non-scripta* reside here in the British Isles. They thrive in areas where the soil has not been disturbed, and are a clear marker of the presence, or the disappearance, of ancient woodlands.

As spring begins to gather pace and the overground world erupts in secret covens of cobalt corollas, it is easy to forget that the living world does not end at ground level. Beyond the bluebells' terrestrial beauty, their lives and communities in the subterranean realm are also extraordinary, particularly the way in which they relate to their botanical neighbours.

The bluebell is the homebody of the flower world. Mostly they do not spread their seed far and wide, preferring instead to germinate near the base of their parent within the leaf litter of the autumn and generally putting down their initial contractile roots (which pull the bulb deeper into the ground) prior to the first frosts.

It takes between four and five years from this first burrowing of bluebell roots into the autumn soil to the bright blue inflorescence of flowering. During this time, their contractile roots grow further into the soil, away from the dangers of frost, drought and predators. These roots do not branch, and they do not have enough surface area for adequate nutrient uptake, but the bluebell does not work alone.

Like many (non-leguminous) plants, bluebells work in partnership with a group of microorganisms. These fungi are called 'arbuscular mycorrhiza' (AM) and they colonise plant roots, expanding the rooting zone of the plant in exchange for the carbohydrates produced during photosynthesis. In short, AM provide bluebells with access to more nutrients than they could access otherwise, and the bluebells share the raw fuel that is carbohydrate.

Plants are generally most reliant on AM while they are seedlings, becoming self-sufficient as they develop. For bluebells, however, the opposite is true. As their coarse root systems continue to descend to depths of around twenty centimetres below ground level, they move further away from the nutrient-rich topsoil and depend more heavily upon the AM fungi for food.

This particular relationship between bluebells and AM has cast new light on the different ways in which plants and their mycorrhizal associations can work together, and has allowed scientists to learn more about how ancient symbiosis may have been instrumental in enabling plants to colonise terrestrial habitats.

Perhaps the most culturally significant of the mycorrhizal symbionts working alongside the bluebell is *Scutellospora dipurpurescens*, which attaches to the root area during the autumn and winter when the plant is almost entirely subterranean. This particular fungus transfers phosphorus to the bluebell root in exchange for the carbohydrates generated by the bluebell bulb.

In 2014, the necessity of *Scutellospora dipurpurescens* to the rich displays of bluebells in the ancient woodlands of the Scottish Highlands was publicly recognised. This fungus was nominated as one of eighty species synonymous with the ecosystem there, alongside more iconic species such as the golden eagle, the red squirrel and juniper. As part of this project, *Scutellospora dipurpurescens* was acknowledged as crucial, not only to the bluebell but to the much wider range of flora and fauna that depend on undisturbed soils.

In Britain today it might seem that there is very little landscape that is undisturbed by human activity, but the presence of bluebells shows that it does still exist. In folk-lore across the British Isles the bluebell is associated with the fairy folk, who are said to hang their spells on these nodding cobalt blooms. To pick a bluebell, to dig the area around it, to trample these blossoms is to break a spell. Perhaps it is easy enough to respect the bluebell's territory while we can bathe in the intensity of its blue from a distance, but the challenge is to leave the earth undisturbed when the flower has faded for another year, to resist the urge to force the earth to become 'useful'. This microseason we invite you to ask yourself what you can leave alone. Can you trust the processes going on beyond your perception?

ROWAN JAINES

MAY

Noticing Exercise

May is a month of bustling busyness in the natural world, and yet this increased activity can be easy to miss in the midst of the frenzy of our human lives. Make sure you look after yourself by finding a different way to interact with the natural world around you this month, and by noticing with *all* your senses.

Why not undertake a spot of forest bathing? Find a comfortable spot under trees and tune into the woodland around you. Turn off your phone and be still, even if it's only for a few minutes. Watch for movement – you may be surprised by how many small rustlings and flutterings you start to hear and see. Notice and smell the fresh greens around you.

Take in deep breaths of forest air. Tune into your senses. Let this state of 'soft fascination' be a moment of restorative relaxation.

30 APRIL–4 MAY

May Day Gorse Crowns

Common gorse (*Ulex europaeus*) gilds the British country-side across grasslands, fells, heaths, wastelands, rough hills and gardens. This needle-leaved, coconut-scented plant generally flowers from January until June, bringing glints of yellow to dark days. Despite its ubiquitous presence through-out the first half of the year, within the Celtic tradition gorse is especially associated with one particular day.

The festival of Beltane is celebrated on the eve of the first of May and marks the beginning of summer. It is also referred to as *Cétshamhain*, which translates as 'first of sum-mer', and is mentioned in even the earliest of Irish literature as a date not only for ritual but also for carrying out practi-cal tasks. Beltane and Samhain, the latter of which we now celebrate as Halloween on 31 October, mark two halves of the year for the Celts. The Scottish social anthropologist and folklorist James George Frazer noted that while the seasonal moment in which Beltane occurs has little significance for crop-growing communities, it is a period of great significance for herdsmen and represents a shift in their pastoral rhythm.

Similarly, the traditional Welsh calendar marks two turning points in the year. Calan-gaeaf falls in the autumn on the first of November, and Calan-mai falls on the first of May. In fact, right across Gaelic and Celtic communities in the British Isles and into France where these festivals are celebrated the stories may differ, but many of the essential elements are the same.

For the Celts, both Beltane and Samhain were thought to be moments in the year that adhere to the pure definition of a carnival, in which all rules, both physical and metaphysical, are lost for a short duration. They were moments when the boundaries between the tactile, phenomenal world of nature and its supernatural drivers were conceivably thin, when witches, faeries and other sentient 'more-than-human' beings could emerge from beyond the veil. They might appear as beguiling members of the community one moment and transform into animal forms the next. Though we remember this in our present-day Halloween customs, we have forgotten it in our contemporary understandings of the first of May. As a result, we have also lost our collective memory of the symbolic power of the gorse.

In volume one of *Celtic Folklore: Welsh and Manx* the Celticist scholar John Rhys tells us that at daybreak on the first of May the gorse bushes would be set alight in order to excise witches, who were inclined to take the form of a hare. Gorse also had a protective role. Because of its yellow flowers that bloom from darkest January through to midsummer in June, the gorse was associated with the Celtic sun god, Lugh, and was believed to have special powers of protection for herds of sheep and cattle as well as territory against any 'dark' or malignant forces of nature, which might be abroad during this liminal moment in the year. And so, traditionally, a sacred heath of the gorse was set alight and cattle adorned with the sweet-smelling yellow flowers were driven between the fires to offer the herd protection from the perils of disease, thirst and famine that could occur throughout the summer months.

The burning of the gorse on the first of May was, however, not only a superstitious practice. The gorse is a highly invasive plant that can easily dominate the ecological balance of an area. In *The Battle of the Trees*, which describes the sentient power of the arboreal world, the sixth-century Welsh bard Taliesin documents that the Furze (Gorse) is badly behaved 'until he is subdued' by the fires of Beltane, allowing new tender growth to emerge that could be grazed by sheep.

Taliesin is not the only one to have thought about the agency and will of gorse. Fourteen centuries later, the early-twentieth-century Welsh philosopher Henry Habberley Price used the gorse in his argument concerning the existence of more-than-human minds, stating that '[i]f the rustling of the leaves of an oak formed intelligible words conveying new information to me, and if gorse bushes made intelligible gestures, I should have evidence that the oak or the gorse-bush was animated by an intelligence like my own.' This invocation of the gorse was later called on by the philosopher Malcolm Norman, who makes the case that the gorse bush cannot produce information that is tangible to the human intellect because it would be filtered through a human conception of meaning.

Both philosophers, whether unconsciously or deliberately, recall the ancient Celtic customs of Beltane, in which humans are made to reflect on the untamable elements of nature that shape our lives. As you check the weather to see if it is wise to put on a load of washing, or wonder about the well-being of the bulbs you planted in the garden earlier in the spring, take a moment to think about the yellow of the gorse. Let yourself revel in your own inability to know what nature has in store next, and enjoy what is sweet-smelling and bright around you now, in this moment.

ROWAN JAINES

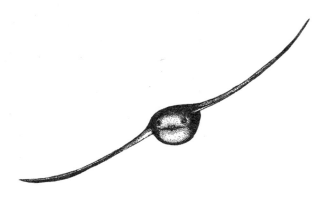

5–9 MAY

First Swifts

The return of swifts from their overwintering grounds in Africa is anticipated more keenly by our Twitter followers than any other spring event. When I asked people why these birds – more than other migrants like the blackcap, chiff-chaff or cuckoo – captured their imagination, I received a host of answers. Intensity: the swift's concentrated, animal joy in the present moment. Movement: that thrilling, hurtling flight, trailing searing cries from which we catch a spark of an alien way of being. Connection to the past and future: the promise that a balmy summer is imminent, and an echo of so many other returns, stretching back through hundreds of years. Resilience: the indomitable nature of a bird that spends its life on the wing. Proximity: the way this magical aerial being stops briefly to nest under the eaves of our very own houses.

Few people mention more negative emotions. And yet, for modern swift watchers, it's easy to detect something darker in the eagerness of our collective upward gaze, scouring the clouds for the first of these screaming summer sky-scythes.

We know swifts are struggling, and this brings unarticulated questions: how many fewer will return this year? Will this be the first summer that our own patch of sky is empty of these birds? The first sighting is accompanied by an unmistakable sense of reprieve. We know that the effects of carbon emissions, habitat destruction and intensive farming are coming home to us, and yet in the return of the swifts there is temporary respite. They are back! This marker of unravelling has not been reached. This joy is not yet curtailed.

It's easy to judge this response, like all others that occur against a background of our twin climate and habitat disasters, as in some way wanting. The play of anxiety and relief that surrounds swifts can seem like a privileged form of denial. It ignores the unfairness and unevenness of the global situation: the way that climate change is still often understood as something 'yet to come' in the global north, while ecological and human disasters unfold in the present of the global south.

But there is another way of looking at it. Swifts can connect us to wider webs of life, to larger geographies, and even to the climate itself.

According to recent research, if we want to understand why swifts are struggling we have to look far beyond our own borders and even beyond land itself, to vast global movements of water and air. In the scientific literature these rhythms are known by the rather unromantic acronym 'ENSO', short for 'El Niño Southern Oscillation'.

To understand ENSO, we must first grasp that both our oceans and our atmosphere have currents, influential patterns of water and air circulation that affect a large part of our planet. Under 'normal' or neutral conditions, trade winds blow east to west across the Pacific, from the west coast of the Americas towards Asia. In the east Pacific, the wind pulls up water from the deep ocean, creating a cold, nutrient-rich pool that sustains marine life. This is carried in a westerly direction, across the ocean, where it is gradually heated by the sun, eventually forming a warmer pool of water off the coast of Asia. The higher temperature of the sea's surface here gets transferred into the atmosphere, driving convection and forming clouds that bring predictable seasonal rainfall to certain areas of the planet. Meanwhile, the cold pool of water in the eastern Pacific inhibits cloud formation, creating dry conditions along the west coast of South America.

But these conditions can vary from neutral, in two opposite ways. In an 'El Niño' year, the east-to-west trade winds weaken. The upwelling of cold water from the deep sea slows down or even stops altogether, so that there are fewer nutrients available for marine life. When this happens, the warm westerly pool of water moves eastwards. In a 'La Niña' year the opposite happens: east-to-west trade winds strengthen, increasing upwelling and cooling down the sea in the east, so that the pool of warm water moves westwards. Both El Niño and La Niña change atmospheric convection and cloud formation, which alters where rain falls, resulting in unusual patterns of drought and flooding.

ENSO currents affect huge areas of our globe, including parts of south-eastern Africa where our swifts overwinter. These birds are nomadic, and their strong flight should theoretically allow them to escape bad weather, moving away from drought, avoiding rainstorms and capitalising on the insect life that a downpour generates. Yet emerging data suggests that La Niña years are particularly bad for swift survival, meaning that they may be vulnerable to something that we don't yet fully understand in the way these changes to our seas and atmosphere impact their overwintering grounds. Some scientists think that La Niña conditions will become more frequent as climate change alters the flow of ocean currents, though others, including the IPCC, believe that this will lead to more El Niño years.

When we care about the return of swifts, then, we are led down a path that forces us to think quite literally on a larger scale than the patch of land, air and sky that we inhabit. Worrying about these birds can be a way of recognising the interconnectedness of our globe, and of hearing a call for justice, restitution and political and economic change. In the plight of the swifts there is a wrong that we need to right: that the consequences of climate change fall most heavily on the vulnerable communities (human and non-human) who are least to 'blame' for carbon emissions.

But there are nonetheless things we can do to help swifts at a more local scale. Providing nest boxes (and ensuring existing nest sites are accessible to birds) can mitigate the smoothness of our modern homes, where construction leaves few nooks and crannies for wildlife. Protecting insect life by planting wildflowers, and supporting sustainable farming, can help to ensure a supply of summer food and a healthy ecosystem. You can even volunteer to be part of a local swift group, surveying nest sites and rehabilitating young and injured birds. These might seem like small actions in the face of global crisis, but they are important and powerful ways of building solidarity with humans and non-humans alike.

As I write this in the summer of 2022, my own patch of sky is mostly empty. A few swifts have returned, veering occasionally across the cliff-bounded bowl outside my house in suburban Sheffield. But they are not the constant presence that they were ten years ago, and my day is no longer punctuated by regular, excitable screaming parties as they chase one another around the roofscape. What is more, this is another La Niña year, the second in a row. I wonder how people will mark this microseason in the future, when our skies are perhaps empty of these birds. How will we explain to new generations what it felt like to have a sky full of swifts?

KIERA CHAPMAN

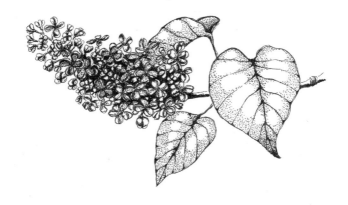

10–14 MAY

Lilac Time

How would you capture the fragrance of lilac?

I sneak out to a lilac shrub on a patch of ground that belongs to no one in particular and steal back guiltily with a few panicles of flowers. The theft seems worse because I am taking something that belongs to everyone. This lilac wafts its fragrance over all the nearby houses, quietly reminding us for a few brief weeks that we all breathe the same air.

On the plant, the flowers smell fresh. Hyacinths, lily of the valley, marzipan, with a note – this is strange – of the rubberised smell of a new car. Once cut, the weight of the scent seems to increase dramatically, becoming sweeter, dirtier, almost headache-inducing. I'm suddenly aware that this is one of the many plants that it is considered unlucky to bring indoors, with white varieties being particularly ill-omened.

Scientists tell us that the fragrance of *Syringa vulgaris* comes from dozens of different lightweight molecules that readily vaporise into the air. One study found that, with some species, the scent varies with the time of day. The number of volatile compounds released by *Syringa pekinesis* is around forty-four at 6 a.m., but rises to seventy-two by 3 p.m., decreasing again towards early evening. The proportion of different fragrant molecules also changes with the time of day, subtly shifting the smell. I wonder whether I am imagining it when I think I detect a fresher, more floral smell from *Syringa vulgaris* in the morning, and a more sickly perfume later in the day?

If there's something about the fragrance of lilac that is mobile and difficult to pin down, then the plant's material presence in our landscape is also testament to the way that plants travel. Lilac is not a British native: it is a plant of scrubland in the Balkans. In Britain it has gone from being a notable exotic novelty of the fashionable wealthy garden in the sixteenth century to a taken-for-granted part of our suburban landscape today.

Syringa species probably arrived in the UK via plant collectors, but from Ottoman gardens rather than their native habitat in eastern Europe. The provenance of the plant consequently became confused, with botanists like William Curtis and Carl Linnaeus describing it as Persian in origin. It was only at the very end of the eighteenth century, when John Sibthorp rediscovered it growing in what is now Bulgaria, that botanists began to reconnect *Syringa vulgaris* with its native place.

In his diary for 13 May 1794 Sibthorp recounted his awe at the Balkan scenery: 'immense groves of oak, the noise of waterfalls, the projecting rocks, the torrent rolling along its bed', though 'a most violent bilious cholic' and fear of bandits prevented him from fully enjoying the botany. He did, however, have time for lilac: 'From the rock hanging over the torrent bed we gath'd specimens of lilac *Syringa vulgaris* now in full flower.' It is thought that two lilac bushes still flowering in the garden of St Hilda's College, Oxford may have been planted from the seeds Sibthorp gathered on this trip.

Lilac reached the American colonies in the eighteenth century. A young Thomas Jefferson planted some in the garden of his family home in Shadwell, Virginia on 2 April 1767, and recorded the presence of lilacs in the shrubbery of his slave plantation at Monticello (also Virginia) in 1771. An obsessive microseason noticer, Jefferson frequently wrote to friends and family recording the time and place of lilac's first flowers, exploring how his marker of the season varied with geography. He records blossom on 30 April in 1791 in Philadelphia, but earlier, on 3 April, in 1794, in the more southerly Monticello.

Like Henry David Thoreau (see our microseason on leaf buds fattening, 24–28 February), Jefferson also noted the timing of the first lilac leaves. They appeared on 25 March 1791 in Philadelphia, but in 1809 there were no lilac leaves as late as 17 March further south in Monticello. That spring, he complained, was 'remarkably backward'. He may have been noticing the local effects of a global event: we now know that in late 1808 a large volcanic eruption, the location of which is still a mystery, threw huge volumes of aerosols into the atmosphere. This caused a period of global cooling that lasted several years.

Writing a century later than Jefferson, the poet Amy Lowell associates lilacs with northerly New England in May. Repeating the story of the plant's Persian origins, she describes lilac entering the US through 'the wide doors of Custom Houses' with other global commodities like sandalwood and tea. Her description of its domestication is at once redolent of an exoticising, sexually charged orientalism and a critique of the tameness of contemporary American life:

You have forgotten your Eastern origin,
The veiled women with eyes like panthers,
The swollen, aggressive turbans of jewelled pashas.
Now you are a very decent flower,
A reticent flower,
A curiously clear-cut, candid flower,
Standing beside clean doorways,
Friendly to a house-cat and a pair of spectacles,
Making poetry out of a bit of moonlight
And a hundred or two sharp blossoms.

If lilac's intoxicating scent brings out the poet in those with house cats and spectacles, it also unsettles the clerks who sit at their desks cataloguing the warehouses full of merchandise:

You called to them: 'Goose-quill men, goose-quill men,
May is a month for flitting.'
Until they writhed on their high stools
And wrote poetry on their letter-sheets behind the
    propped-up ledgers.

The irresistibility of the scent comes loaded with the creative thrust of late spring, an invitation to step outside the domain of counting and calculation. Fleeting, fugitive, fragrant – lilac is a call to wandering ways!

KIERA CHAPMAN

15–20 MAY

Ferns Unfurl

A woodland walk in May is a sensory feast: sapphire seas of bluebells exuding an intense and heady scent; sunlight filtering in fragile beams through tiny new leaves; pungent carpets of wild garlic, speckled with starry white flowers; and ferns, gracefully unrolling their stems upwards and outwards into crowns of delicate green, each one an exercise in natural symmetry.

Ferns lend an air of the exotic to wherever they grow. They may have no flowers and no scent, bear no fruit, carry no dramatic seed pods, but there is, instead, something otherworldly about them. Some produce knots of tightly curled stems nestling under last year's foliage, from which feather-like fronds uncoil into the light. Others produce leaves like glossy green tongues, held stiffly aloft on narrow stalks. Some are delicate fans of the finest lace; others bear leaves like wide-toothed combs. But whatever their form they are always striking, always distinctive, always evocative of another time. Ferns bring rumours of rainforest to our woodlands; they whisper of dinosaurs and giant dragonflies.

There is justification for this, for ferns are ancient plants. Their ancestors appeared during the Devonian period, around 350–400 million years ago, peeling off from the evolutionary development of vascular plants well before the flowering plants emerged. They continued to evolve and multiply during the Jurassic and Cretaceous periods when the dinosaurs flourished, and some species from those primeval periods were so successful that they remain with us, largely unchanged, today. Yet they have never been able to escape entirely from the chains of their primordial past. Like all plants, ferns originally evolved from aquatic algae, which needed water for their spores to reproduce. Over those millions of years of evolution they developed into complex, land-living plants, but they held on to their ancestral 'water habit' when it came to reproduction. Ferns produce billions of minuscule spores on the underside of their leaves, which germinate into minute, heart-shaped plants called prothalli. In these prothalli, the fern's sex cells or gametes develop and then disperse, depending on water through which they can swim to find and fertilise other gametes, just as their aquatic ancestors did. So ferns, which have successfully made the leap on to land, nevertheless remain tied to damp areas, where they can rely on rain and humidity to provide the ambient moisture needed for their lovesick gametes to find each other and pair up.

There are, of course, exceptions. The most widely recognised fern in the British Isles is bracken (*Pteridium aquilinum*), believed to be the commonest single plant species in the world. Bracken produces spores, like other ferns, but it also develops networks of underground rhizomes which can extend over vast areas. This has enabled it to escape the requirement for damp conditions in order to spread, besides making it one of the most difficult plants to eradicate once established. Yet bracken is beautiful too. In May, the new shoots uncurl from underneath last year's dead brown fronds and, as they grow, the little pinnule leaves that line the ribs unfurl too, relaxing their own tiny spirals of green until they are open and flat. When the main stem – the rachis – of bracken and other ferns is still coiled it is called a crozier, taking the name of the distinctive bishop's staff, which itself took the shape of the traditional shepherd's crook. In the fern world, these croziers are a sign that spring is well on its way; reaching up from the woodland floor, they are heralds of the splendour to come, as the leaves spread out into their full majesty.

Does any other group of native plants have such poetic names? Lady fern and shield fern, filmy fern and buckler fern, hart's tongue, adder's tongue, spleenwort and pillwort . . . this list needs no explanation, no detailed botanical key; the joy is in the images conjured up by the names alone. And we are by no means the first to find these plants so enchanting. In the late eighteenth and early nineteenth century the Romantic movement took hold in Britain, exerting a profound influence over writers, artists, musicians and landscape designers. A central pillar of romanticism was the finding of magnificence and awe in the natural world, emotions to be captured and translated into the arts. Suddenly wild, rocky landscapes, ruined castles and gushing waterfalls became fashionable subjects, and the exotic-looking fern, which so often grew in such places, became an object of admiration and desire.

This revolution in appreciation of the natural world coincided with the development of the Wardian case in the 1830s, a small, portable 'greenhouse' which enabled delicate plants to be transported across the world. It also meant that delicate, moisture-loving ferns could be collected and grown inside even in the polluted cities of industrialising Britain. Very rapidly a craze for finding, gathering and growing ferns took hold, especially among women, for whom botany was seen as an acceptable hobby. The wealthy constructed outdoor ferneries, filled with stone and logs to replicate the wild, romantic landscapes that had become so fashionable, or they brought ferns into the warmth of conservatories, greenhouses and indoor terraria. Fern-collecting became so popular that numerous books were written for every level of enthusiast, and ferns were quickly assimilated into the vocabulary of artistic motifs, appearing on fabrics, wallpaper, ceramics, stained glass and canvas. Plant nurseries capitalised on the booming market. James Backhouse's fern and orchid catalogue of 1857 contained eighteen pages of available British and imported ferns, including so-called 'tree ferns', offering over 135 different species; of just one of these species, *Polypody*, fifty-one varieties were available. Sadly, the explosion in fern-collecting – snidely nicknamed 'pteridomania' by the author Charles Kingsley in 1855 in reference to its popularity with women, whose 'weaker constitutions' were believed to make them vulnerable to unnatural levels of passion – led to some areas, especially those in popular beauty spots or close to cities, becoming virtually denuded of ferns.

One or two species, including the already scarce Killarney fern, were brought to the brink of extinction.

The Victorian fern craze did not long outlive the death of its queen, but a less frenzied appreciation of the beauty of ferns endures. The sight of unfurling fronds, picked out in a shaft of sunlight or emerging from the gloom of a shady bank, still catches the attention, still speaks of other worlds just out of reach. This is the season for marvelling at these ancient plants and the complex biology that creates them.

REBECCA WARREN

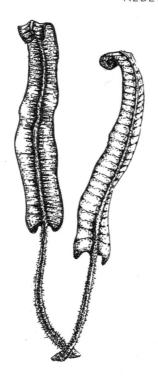

21–25 MAY

Frothy Hawthorn

From maypoles to medieval sex allegories, few British plants are as steeped in folklore and myth as the hawthorn. So ubiquitous is the spindrift of white blossom at this time of year that it even shares a name with the month – hawthorn is sometimes called Queen of the May and sometimes simply 'may'. Other folk names include fairy thorn, mayflower (another plant shares this nickname, the *Epigaea repens*), bread and cheese (not to be confused with 'butter and cheese', which is a name for lesser celandine), whitethorn, thornapples, hagthorn, may-tree and quickthorn. The name hawthorn comes from the Anglo-Saxon *hagedorn*, meaning hedge thorn. In Britain we have two species: *Crataegus monogyna* (common hawthorn) and *Crataegus laevigata* (Midland hawthorn), whose botanical name comes from the Greek word *kràtys*, meaning hard or strong. Their strength is manifest in the oldest known living hawthorn in Britain, the Hethel Old Thorn in Norfolk, which is an astonishing 700 years old.

What stories this grand old tree could tell! Its past intertwines with ours – with agriculture, medicine, legends and art. When this Norfolk tree was a mere 300 years old, William Shakespeare wrote *As You Like It*, one of several of his works that feature the hawthorn. In the play Orlando 'hangs odes upon hawthorns', verses written to his love, Rosalind. Twenty-one years after Shakespeare's play a ship bearing the name *Mayflower* set sail from Southampton for the new colonies of North America, though the vessel could also be named after lily of the valley, which shares a common name. This famous voyage transported Puritan migrants across the Atlantic to escape religious persecution. Many of the passengers on the *Mayflower* started their voyage in Holland, coming to England on another flora-inspired ship, *Speedwell*. When they arrived in Cape Cod, on land owned by the Wampanoag peoples, they drew up the 'Mayflower Compact', etching the name of this unassuming tree (if indeed that was the inspiration for the ship's name) into American history.

As the Hethel Old Thorn grew into its seventh century of winds, sun, springtime and frosts, another writer, Edward Thomas, set off on a bicycle trip across the south of England in 1913, hoping to capture the essence of spring. He was enchanted by the magnificent hedgerows awash with hawthorn flowers: 'I had found the Spring in that bush of green, white, and crimson.' In this same year Marcel Proust published *Swann's Way*, a novel that attempts to step back in time, to unpick and recapture memories. One of these is a boyhood memory of finding 'the whole path throbbing with the fragrance of hawthorn-blossom. The hedge resembled a series of chapels, whose walls were no longer visible under the mountains of flowers that were heaped upon their altars . . . spread out into pools of fleshy white, like strawberry-beds in spring.' He describes looking through the branches and blossoms and catching a glimpse of a young girl with whom he falls immediately in love.

As another century turned and the ancient Hethel hawthorn stood firm beside a stone church, the artist David Hockney returned to Yorkshire from California. He relished witnessing the changing seasons again after LA's bland sunniness. He began painting the seasonal cycles of the countryside, notably the great hawthorn hedges covered in unctuous blooms that he describes looking 'as if a thick, white cream had been poured over everything'. The vibrant globules of whites and greens of his hawthorn paintings capture the sheer frothy ebullience of a hawthorn hedge.

What was it about the hawthorn that captured the imagination of these writers and artists? There is the beauty of its blossom, of course. But it could also be its mystical and folkloric connections which lend it an otherworldly air. For all its gnarly rootedness, superstitions, fairy stories and myths swirl about its branches.

In May the hawthorn burst into flower, filling the hedgerows and fields with a cascade of white clouds. Tempting as it is to cut some blossom for the house, it is seen as bad luck to bring hawthorn indoors, and sitting under a hawthorn tree is also meant to be inauspicious. These superstitions stem from a long-held belief that hawthorns were thresholds between the human and fairy worlds. In some rural areas it is still seen as unlucky to cut or dig them up. But on one night of the year, and with the fairies' permission, hawthorn blossoms were cut and used in May Day (or Beltane) celebrations across Britain. On the last night in April people went out to gather hawthorn flowers for wreaths, garlands and maypole dancing – and, it seems fair to assume, some *al fresco* sex while they were at it. Hawthorn is associated with fertility and features in medieval love allegories as a symbol of erotic rather than spiritual love. It was thought to have other powers too. Women bathed their faces in dew collected on the blossom's leaves to enhance their beauty, and men washed their hands in the dew to give them extra skill and power.

Yet for all its sensuous appeal, many people find the scent of hawthorn repugnant. In earlier times it was described as smelling like the plague, and we now know this is because the flowers contain trimethylamine, an insect-attracting compound that forms in decaying tissue.

It has played a part in a darker period of history too. The poet Robert Burns frequently depicted hawthorn in his work, but if we look more closely at what was going on at the time he was writing, this is more than just a decorative feature. During the Highland Clearances landowners evicted rural tenant farmers, enclosing what had been common grazing land and transforming the landscape. They planted hawthorn extensively as it made a fast-growing and effective boundary. Burns's poems are imbued with a sense of loss and absence that links back to the displacement of the rural poor, kept off their homeland by hedges of may. Here the hawthorn marks another threshold, albeit a disenchanted one.

The old phrase, 'Ne'r cast a clout til May be out' is thought to pertain to the hawthorn (though it could equally be referring to the month of May) and advises us not to shed any clothing until the blossoms emerge. Unlike the 'blackthorn winter', the flowering of the hawthorn was seen as a reliable marker of warm weather returning. The timing of this flowering is interesting. May blossom usually comes out around the middle of the month, not on May Day, so how could hawthorn have been used in traditional celebrations? The answer lies in the switch from the Julian to the Gregorian calendar in 1752, which cut eleven days from the year and brought the feast days forward. Before 1752 May Day would have coincided with the explosion of white.

Hopefully the Hethel Old Thorn will stand for centuries longer, casting its spume of flowers like a springtime spell.

Wherever we are at this time of year, we can look out for the hawthorn's blossom along roadsides and in hedgerows. Beneath the pungent blooms and within its knotty limbs there is a rich, beguiling and twisted history that sheds new light on the effervescent brilliance of its May display.

LULAH ELLENDER

26–30 MAY

Buttercup Meadows

The past few months of spring have brought a succession of yellows: we have already met green-ruffed aconites, the miniature turbines of golden daffodils, the earthbound stars of celandines and the bishop's mitre flowers of gorse. But this first month of summer brings a richer yellow still, in the shining bowls of the meadow buttercup (*Ranunculus acris*). As the seventeenth-century English botanist Nicholas Culpeper noted: 'I do not remember that ever I saw anything yellower ... unless you run your Head into a Hedge, you cannot but see them as you walk.'

The yellow of buttercups is so strong that it is transmittable. Maybe you played the childhood game of holding one of the flowers under someone's chin to see if they like butter, and seeing the glimmering reflection of the colour back from the skin? But why does the buttercup have this ability, more than any other spring flower?

Studies suggest that the effect comes from special properties in the flower's cells. To understand this, we have to imagine the top layers of a buttercup petal as a three-dimensional sandwich. The upper layer contains a concentrated pigment that strongly absorbs blue-green light. This gives the flowers their characteristic yellow colour. However, the cells here are also unusually flat on top, forming a thin film over the petal. By comparison, the petals of most other flowers are a bit bumpy or 'papillate' on the upper surface, which makes them feel velvety. It is these plate-like cells that give the buttercup its glossy, shiny appearance.

Meanwhile, the middle of the petal sandwich contains a layer of bumpy cells made of colourless starch and an air gap. This structure is very unusual in petals. The air gap reflects back light like a mirror, while the starch cells diffuse and scatter the light. Together, they enhance the intensity of the buttercup's yellow and give the light hitting the flower a strong direction. This allows the flower to create a yellow spot when held beneath someone's chin.

Yet the flat shininess of buttercups is perplexing, because in other plants it is flowers with bumpy epidermal cells that get attention from pollinators. This may be because a soft, unreflective surface makes them more vibrantly colourful. So why is the buttercup glossy?

One explanation is that its lustrousness acts as a long-distance signal. Under normal incident light (i.e. when the ray of light is perpendicular to the flower), the reflectance of the buttercup does not increase much. At a more oblique angle, however, the flower flashes, almost like a mirror reflecting sunlight. This means that pollinators close to the flower may be attracted mainly by its yellow colour, while those further away see its glassy sheen.

An alternative explanation, which may comfortably coexist with the first, is that glossiness enhances the amount of light around the buttercup's reproductive organs, which also increases the temperature there. This may help seed and pollen to mature, combined with the fact that the flowers are heliotropic, turning to face the sun as it passes through the sky.

We might think of buttercups as emblematic of cheerfulness and childhood play, but one writer imagined a darker side to their yellowness. Alfred Döblin's 1910 'The Murder of a Buttercup' follows the story of Michael Fischer, an obsessive bully of a businessman. His fragile mental health topples into psychosis after he decapitates a buttercup in a moment of rage while out walking in woodland. Overcome by a sense of guilt, and feeling that he has committed a kind of murder, he is tormented (and perhaps also a little thrilled) by the idea that a vengeful forest is hunting him down in search of atonement. He finds particular torture in the thought that the flower's pristine colour and glossiness will be ruined as it rots: he imagines the blooms 'crushed, dissolved by the rain, putrefied . . . a yellow, stinking sludge; greenish, yellowish-iridescent, slimy like vomit'.

Fischer's life begins to revolve around attempts to expiate his guilt via a series of tormented exchanges. He first personifies the dead buttercup, naming her 'Ellen', then resentfully begins to leave her a plate of food at every meal, and finally opens a savings account in her name. When none of this works he digs up another flower and brings it home in Ellen's place, planting it in a pot on which he has written a legal paragraph about debt. It is only when Fischer's housekeeper knocks over the new pot and throws out the broken flower that Fischer finally feels free of his 'crime'. His first action, however, is to head back to the forest. Fired by a feeling of impunity, he is ready to murder more of its plants and animals: 'flowers, poletads, toads too better watch out'!

Unable to accept nature's otherness, Fischer tries to subject the buttercup to a logic of reparative exchange, in which he translates all of the world's many different kinds of value into the narrow practices of property, credit and debt. For Döblin, this is clearly a sign of a developing mental illness. Yet increasingly, policymakers are doing something similar: reducing the multifaceted wonders of nature to a matter of economics, calculating the added value provided by a park, a tree or a buttercup in pounds and pence. Putting a price on biodiversity, figuring how much natural goods and services are 'worth', and establishing mechanisms for trading in new types of natural capital, like carbon, might provide a justification for nature that speaks to those who can only think in terms of balance sheets. But it is also so reductive that it risks missing the point. The value of a child's delight in the yellow reflection of a buttercup on a chin, and the importance of that buttercup for a whole wider network of being, including our own, surely cannot be reduced to numbers on a spreadsheet.

KIERA CHAPMAN

JUNE

Noticing Exercise

Even if you feel like you do not have green fingers, germinating and planting seeds can be a magical experience and it doesn't have to cost anything. Next time you eat an apple or a tomato, save the seeds, rinse them and put them on some wet kitchen paper on a warm windowsill.

Take time each day to check in on your seeds and notice new life starting as the shoots begin to push past the kernel of the seed. Once this has happened put some soil in a container and plant your seeds. Watch as they change and grow day by day.

If you plant a citrus pip you may get two or three shoots from it. One of these will be a true 'daughter' plant, combining genetic material from both parents, but the others will be clones of the original pip, producing identical fruit to the one you ate – if you are lucky. But beware! You'll have to keep them all for several years before you know which is which!

31 MAY–5 JUNE

Poppies Popping

When we think of poppies, two quite different images may spring to mind. The first is of the common poppy (*Papaver rhoeas*): the red bloom that springs up on our verges or in rich agricultural soil, which is why it is also sometimes known as the corn poppy. This is the poppy that flowered in the no man's land of the First World War known as the Western Front, and which is now used as a symbol of remembrance – worn on lapels to honour members of the armed forces who have died in the line of duty. The second is the opium poppy (*Papaver somniferum*), which flourishes in warm, dry climates and produces the seeds that have been used throughout human history to relieve pain and induce sleep.

This poppy is still intensively grown throughout the world, both legally for pharmaceutical morphine and codeine and illegally for the production of the street drug heroin.

As May gives way to June, however, there is a less notorious poppy popping open on the shingle shales and sand dunes of Britain's shore. The yellow horned-poppy (*Glaucium flavum*), also known as the sea poppy, is a highly distinctive species with infolded leaves that ruffle into rosettes of silver-green. It has yolk-yellow flowers that burst open at this moment in the seasonal calendar and bloom until September. Its common name refers to the very long, distinctive horn-shaped capsules in which its seeds nestle. Its restrictive habitat means that the yellow horned-poppy is a rare plant, and although it may be locally abundant in the right conditions, it is protected under the Wildlife and Countryside Act (1981), meaning it is illegal to pick it without the landowner's permission.

Robert Bridges, poet laureate from 1913 to 1930, dedicated a poem to the strange, neglected, beach-bound poppy:

> A poppy grows upon the shore
> Bursts her twin cup in summer late:
> Her leaves are glaucous green and hoar,
> Her petals yellow, delicate.
>
> Oft to her cousins turns her thought,
> In wonder if they care that she
> Is fed with spray for dew, and caught
> By every gale that sweeps the sea.
>
> She has no lovers like the Red
> That dances with the noble Corn:
> Her blossoms on the waves are shed,
> Where she sits shivering and forlorn.

The yellow horned-poppy, however, is much more than a poor relation of the fabled corn poppy. The topical application of its foetid, anti-inflammatory, narcotic milk was once common as a treatment for wounds and contusions as well as ulcers of horses and cattle. Nicholas Culpeper claimed that the plant's sap is good for digestion and for cleansing of the liver, for curing jaundice and scurvy, as well as the plague. The Scilly Isles were considered to have the best specimens, and apothecaries would send for them to be delivered by boat to the mainland. Other coastal communities made use of their home-grown poppies. In Cornwall, the yellow horned-poppy was known as a powerful pain-killer and cough suppressant. Modern medicine recognises that the plant's sap contains glaucine, which does suppress coughs but comes with a caveat: glaucine also causes powerful hallucinations.

Research has shown that glaucine increases in the yellow horned-poppy throughout the summer months, before a sharp reduction as the weather cools. Those who lived on the coast had folkloric knowledge of this seasonal waxing and waning of potency. The early-twentieth-century pharmacist and bacteriologist John Wycliffe Peck describes the gathering of the golden flowers and tusk-like seed pods by people in Devonshire in the months of August and September, specifically for the plant's sedative properties as well its ability to clear up wound infections.

The yellow horned-poppy's coastal habitat and its hallucinogenic qualities give rise to fantastical origin stories in Victorian botanical writing. Perhaps the most evocative appears in W. T. Fernie's 1895 *Herbal Simples*. Fernie links the yellow horned-poppy's botanical name *Glaucium flavum* to the mythical Greek fisherman Glaucus of Bœotia. Glaucus, Fernie tells us, noticed that all of the fish that he caught received fresh vigour when laid upon the ground where this flower grew, and decided to try some for himself. On eating the leaves of the yellow horned-poppy, Glaucus found himself suddenly filled with an intense desire to live in the sea. His wish was granted by the Titan god Oceanus, who made Glaucus a sea god, and Glaucus in turn gave his name to the flower.

There are other equally memorable accounts of the potent effects of consuming the yellow horned-poppy. In his book *The Englishman's Flora*, Geoffrey Grigson recites a peculiar tale, taken from a 1698 report to the Royal Society, regarding a man who made a pie with the roots of sea poppy, having mistaken them for the edible roots of sea holly. The psycho-active and purgative effects of the plant acted on the man's system simultaneously and he 'voided a stool in a white chamber pot, fancied it to be gold, breaking the pot in pieces, and desiring what he imagined as gold might be preserved as such. Also his man and maid servant eating of the same pye, fancied of what they saw to be gold.'

Indeed, glaucine has been found to have an effect on the same neuronal receptors that are stimulated by 'classical' psychedelics such as LSD and psilocybin (magic) mush-rooms. Clinical trials and recreational users of glaucine have reported lethargy and bright, colourful visual hallucinations, and a dissociative effect where the environment is still per-ceived accurately but the ability to take action is suppressed temporarily.

The flare of the bright-gold flowers of the yellow horned-poppy, as well the wider array of more familiar poppies at this moment in the year, reminds us of the complex physical relationships that human culture has with the vegetal world. Plants of all kinds have not only nourished our bodies, but changed and continue to change our minds and senses of perception of who, where – and even what – we are.

ROWAN JAINES

6–10 JUNE

Dancing Dragonflies

There is perhaps no scene that captures summer's glinting jig so fully as that of the dragonfly, tripping the light fantastic over its watery stage. The dragonfly is a deft dancer. With each glide and stroke these flying insects perform swift internal calculations about the placement of their bodies in space, like miniature ballerinas.

The dragonfly uses an improvised choreography of structured turns that allow it to keep the image of its prey in steady focus as it hunts. These mesmerising movements are linked to the mysterious etymology of the dragonfly's name.

The dragonfly's scientific designation places it in the *Odonata* order, a Greek reference to the strong mandibles and serrated teeth of this class of insects. It is of the infraorder

Anisoptera, which can be translated, once again from Greek, as 'unequal-winged' and describes the uneven proportions of the dragonfly's broad hindwing in relation to its narrow forewing.

It is commonly thought that the dragonfly received its common name from the seventeenth-century scholar Francis Bacon. The British Dragonfly Society asserts that the earliest reference to dragonflies in literature appears in Bacon's 1626 *Sylva Sylvarum: or a Naturall Historie in Ten Centuries*. This, however, seems to be a modification of early folk names for this insect, whose writhing and twisting movements gave rise to allusions to snakes, in particular the adder. A large portion of the ninety-five English and twenty-three Celtic colloquial names for the dragonfly, compiled by the philologist Elmwood Montgomery, make this serpentine connection and include flying adder, adderbolt, snake doctor, snake feeder, adderspear and snake waiter.

Thus Bacon's 'dragonfly' appears as an iteration of long-standing names for this insect rather than a novel moniker. The word 'dragon' emerges from the Latin *draco*, which in turn comes from the Greek *drakon*. The lexicographer John Ayto states that this word originally signified 'snake', and that 'the form is usually connected with words for "look at, glance, flash, gleam" . . . as if its underlying meaning were "creature that looks at you (with a deadly glance)"'.

However we refer to this insect, the Greek root of the dragonfly's common name has been revealed by contemporary entomologists to be startlingly apt. Studies of the dragonfly's steering strategy during hunting behaviour have shown that dragonflies literally do fix their prey in a deadly glare.

Dragonflies have large compound eyes comprising up to 30,000 tiny lenses, bisected into an upper (dorsal) region and a lower (ventral) one. The dragonfly is a diurnal creature, and the dorsal section of these extraordinarily sensitive eyes is expert in perceiving light from the sky above, while the ventral region registers reflections from below. Both eyes work together in a continuous panorama of reflected and refracted light which turns the dragonfly's optical experience into a propagating prism, a gleam of perception in which it can accurately locate its own body in space, as well as that of its prey. This is more than vision as we understand it; rather it is a whole-body experience of a multifaceted field.

For vertebrates the ability to control movement – for example, the act of extending an arm to reach for something – relies on internal models. These representative maps of the external environment are formed in the brain through sensory inputs and used to predict the movement of our bodies in relation to the target of our actions. Until recently, scientists have been unclear whether invertebrates such as the dragonfly use similar strategies of 'targeted reaching' to navigate the world.

A 2014 study of dragonfly movement found that dragonflies continually track the angle of their prey's position by rotating their heads. These head rotations provide information about the location of the mosquitoes, midges and flies that they hunt and form internal maps, or models, that guide systematic rotations of their bodies in relation to their prey. This method of movement control is both similar to and yet totally distinct from how we humans move our bodies. And it is the mechanism behind the complex flight patterns, or dances, that we associate with dragonflies at this point in the seasonal calendar.

The strange intricacy of these movements has been associated not only with snakes but also with needles, horses and the devil. A common folklore name for these deft creatures was 'devil's darning needles', and it was warned that they could sew up the mouths of impertinent women and children.

As well as being a reflection of social expectations in the past, it is possible that such fears have an evolutionary basis. The species that we now call the dragonfly was one of the earliest orders of winged insects that evolved around 300 million years ago. While contemporary dragonflies have wingspans of around five to twelve centimetres, fossil evidence has been discovered of dragonflies with wings that span up to sixty centimetres.

Research has found that humans evolved mechanisms in our brains that enable them to identify the movements of insects and snakes and to react to them rapidly. This perhaps explains early stories that link the dragonfly with snakes and with evil. An early Christian legend recounts a battle of the angels where St George led the mounted forces of God on a beautiful horse, which abruptly began to rear and buck. St George, informed by the Lord that the horse was possessed by the devil, dismounted and renounced ownership of the horse, asserting: 'Then, be it the devil's own.' At once the horse transformed into the insect that we know now as the dragonfly and flew away. This story gave rise to some of the insect's most colourful common names, such as 'the devil's horse' and 'St George's steed'.

In this microseason, as we see dragonflies dancing, let us be reminded of Shakespeare's assertion in *The Tempest* that 'Hell is empty, and all the devils are here.' Though we have nothing to fear from dragonflies, they have much to fear from human society. As the climate crisis deepens, temperatures rise and pollution and habitat loss intensify across the British Isles, research shows that dragonflies have shifted their habitats north, and are experiencing significant declines in population.

Now is the time to interrogate the historic ambivalence that accompanies our fascination with the natural world that we have come to dominate. Today, even if you don't spy a dragonfly, can you overcome your aversion: rescue a spider, or let a fly out of your window? During this microseason, perhaps we can all take a moment to realise our responsibility to the species that we once feared.

ROWAN JAINES

11–15 JUNE

Oxeye Daisies Turn in the Sun

In summer, our verges, field edges and waste grounds are strewn with the bright faces of oxeye daisies basking in the sunshine. These flowers conjure nostalgic visions of vast meadowlands buzzing with insects, symbolising a long-gone era when our countryside looked less tamed and was teeming with wildlife. In Britain over the past sixty years we have lost over 97 per cent of our meadows thanks to changes in agriculture and land use, fertilisers and herbicides. As we reckon with this huge loss of habitat and rich biodiversity, many gardeners are leaving areas of lawn to grow long and councils are planting wildflower mixes along roadside verges and traffic islands. Encouraged by stewardship schemes and agriculture policy, farmers also are keeping field margins for native wildflowers and grasses to grow. Often these new places, as well as some old meadows, feature the sunny, petal-frilled orbs of oxeye daisies. And at this time of year they treat us to a final floral display before the grasses and seedheads take over.

Oxeye daisies close their petals at night and open them again in the morning, a habit that gives the daisy its name: from the Old English *daeyes eage*, or 'day's eye'. The saying 'fresh as a daisy' is also thought to come from this daily unfurling, as if the flower greets every morning with a dew-kissed, open-hearted smile. But the plant has gone by many other names denoting either its appearance, uses or associations. There is a lovely poetry to these names: moon daisy (because it glows in the evening light), moon penny, horse daisy, golden, thunder flower, bruisewort, St John's flower, maudlin daisy, dog daisy and marguerite. The *'leuc'* part of its Latin name, *Leucanthemum vulgare*, is from the Greek *leukós*, meaning 'white'.

Interestingly, the name marguerite comes from Margaret of Anjou, who married King Henry VI and used an oxeye daisy as her emblem. It is also, confusingly, a shared name with another flower, the *Argyranthemum frutescens*. According to the Doctrine of Signatures (a method of identifying plant properties according to the body parts they resemble and that they should therefore be used to treat, hailing from the Middle Ages), because an oxeye daisy looks like an eye it is a suitable remedy for eye problems. Other uses include the treatment of coughs, nervous conditions, jaundice, bruises, cuts and respiratory diseases. They are also edible – the flowers and buds can be made into tea, and you can eat the leaves in salads. But they are not always seen as useful. In some countries they are classed as an invasive weed, thanks to the success with which they reproduce. Oxeye daisies spread via seeds and rhizomes, and one mature plant alone can produce 26,000 seeds.

For insects, such abundance is very welcome. Each flower is a landing pad for a wide range of invertebrates which enjoy this prolific pollen producer. They are actually *composite flowerheads*, meaning that every oxeye daisy flower is made up of disc florets (the yellow parts) and ray florets, which each have one white petal. The nectar is contained within the disc florets.

It is this uniting of two parts in one harmonious whole that gives oxeye daisies their association with love. In Norse mythology the daisy is the sacred flower of Freya, goddess of love, new beginnings and fertility. Daisies – including the common daisy, *Bellis perennis* – are some of the first flowers we might recognise as children. They are distinct and within easy reach, dotting lawns and playgrounds. As we grow older we might learn to make daisy chains or to strip the petals off one by one saying, 'He (or she) loves me, he loves me not.' This chant and the rhyme 'Tinker, tailor' (also recited while plucking daisy petals) were fashionable in Victorian times, when flowers became laden with hidden meanings.

The notion of a 'language of flowers' gained popularity at a time when many people were not able to openly pursue romances. Women were supposed to wait for love to appear and transform their lives, rescuing them from a future of spinsterhood and eternal outsider status. Finding a love match was a matter of urgency and these rhymes helped them turn this waiting into a game, to look to the natural world for answers and patterns. Oxeye daisies were also used to predict how many children a woman would have. She would take the yellow disc florets and throw them into the air, then catch them on the back of her hand. The number of pieces that landed on it indicated the number of children she would bear.

The Victorian era was a time of great interest in the supernatural: people paid for tea leaf and palm readings, crystal ball consultations and meetings with mediums.

From working-class city streets to stately homes, people held seances and dabbled in the occult. Practitioners of these 'dark arts' risked imprisonment under the 1824 Vagrancy Act, but creating spells and auguries as parlour games or singing divination rhymes using daisies was a less controversial, and much more ladylike, way of making predictions.

The great Victorian novels by the Brontës, Eliot, Hardy and Flaubert all centred around love – and around women waiting for love to find them. It wasn't until later and the modernist movement that female characters gained more agency – and in *The Great Gatsby*, Daisy Buchanan gives a destructive spin to the name of a flower which had previously embodied the feminine ideal. This Daisy turns out to be headstrong, manipulative and dangerous. She would have had little patience for the Victorian lovesick woman wistfully plucking petals and waiting to be swept away.

Even before Fitzgerald's novel, daisies cropped up frequently in literature and culture. Early Christians associated the flower with Mary Magdalene (hence 'maudlin daisy'). In Goethe's *Faust* Margaret pulls petals from a flower to determine whether Faust truly loves her, with the Devil looking slyly on in the background. This plays on the image of daisies as representing innocence and youth, particularly in contrast to the terrible fate that awaits her; the childish game can be interpreted as a naive, futile frippery, powerless to stop the evil plan the Devil has for her. But the divination can also be seen as a way in which Margaret has agency over her future and expresses her desire.

From queens to milkmaids, the oxeye daisy is a leveller. Love reduces us all, at some point, to wish-making and dream-hatching. As we watch the daisies follow the summer sun, we could be forgiven for plucking one flowerhead and asking it a question we cannot ourselves answer.

LULAH ELLENDER

16–20 JUNE

Rain-soaked Roses

In June the light comes early, filtering through the curtains, imperceptible, ethereal. It is a gentle way to wake, a slow emergence into consciousness. And with the outflowing tide of sleep comes an incoming flood of birdsong, fluting, warbling, trilling, a tapestry of sound, a beckoning.

Some mornings are not to be ignored, not to be put off, and so you steal downstairs and outside, out into the rain-soaked garden, out on to the wet grass and under the dripping leaves, out into the lush jungle of rain-damp June. And every sense is alive, aware, filled with a June morning, filled with a moment so fresh it could be the first morning of the world. The taste of wet earth is on your lips, the blackbird's song cascades in liquid notes, the grass is cold under your feet, sunlight scatters diamonds on to every leaf. And then there are the roses; on mornings like this they release a smell so sweet it takes your breath away. And you bend your face into the wet petals and lose yourself in the scent, and for a moment the world stands still, the birds fall silent, and all that exists is the taste of wet roses and the scent catching in your throat.

Heaven is a rain-soaked rose on a June morning.

Why do roses speak to us of love? Surely it must be the seductive quality of their scent, which has perfumed our skin and our food, our baths and our homes since the unrecorded days of our distant past. Roses are native to a wide swathe of Eurasia and even the Americas, where the earliest fossil rose has been found, dating back forty million years. They are sewn into our collective histories, valued and loved by civilisations that flourished and died, just as the flowers themselves bloom and decay. In the middle of the third millennium BCE, Sargon I, King of Akkadia, an empire that extended from the Red Sea to Turkey, recorded his acquisition of rose bushes while on military campaign. Assyrian cuneiform tablets of the same period list numerous medicinal uses of roses and rose water, suggesting a long-established familiarity with the plant and its properties. Thereafter roses appear consistently in records from across the ancient Near and Middle East: on the walls of the tomb of the Pharaoh Thutmose IV in Eighteenth Dynasty Egypt; at the Minoan palace of Knossos in Crete; in the trade lists of the Mycenaeans at Pylos; and in the writings of Greek and Roman authors, including Theothrastus, Dioscorides and Pliny the Elder. In 810 BCE, records show the Persian province of Faristan, one of the most important centres of rose cultivation, sending a forced tribute of 30,000 bottles of rose water to Baghdad, but the region also exported it commercially across the Middle East, North Africa, Europe and even into China, where roses had long been grown and valued. In the middle of the first millennium BCE the imperial Chinese library already contained over 600 books on roses. It seems that the flower that, to us, is quintessentially English has haunted the cultures and cuisines of the world down to the present day.

But still – why do roses speak to us of love? Why do we give red roses to a valentine, throw roses on a coffin before it is buried in the earth, use them as a metaphor for passion and romance? Why did Robert Burns write 'My luve is like a red, red rose?' when it might have been 'a white, white daisy'?

Early Christianity may have hesitated about embracing the iconography of the rose, uneasy about its long association with pagan deities, especially the Greek goddess of love, Aphrodite, and her forebears, the Sumerian and Egyptian goddesses Inanna and Isis. Yet the rose crept into the Christian Church anyway, not least through the gradual fusion of the biblical garden of Eden with the Persian – and later Arabic – concept of Paradise, in its earthly form of a garden filled with water and sweet-smelling flowers, including the rose. And in CE 431, a Christian Council held at Ephesus officially recognised the Virgin Mary as the 'Mother of God'. As her cult developed, so did her association with the rose, an almost inevitable transfer of the flower long associated with other mother goddesses. The red petals of the rose rapidly came to symbolise the martyrdom of her son, while the white petals represented her own virginity. Mary became the 'rose without thorns', and a focus of intense spiritual love.

The biblical Song of Songs helped to foster the association of love and roses through its confusing but vivid phraseology, including the literally, if incorrectly, interpreted 'Rose of Sharon' and the passionate descriptions of a woman as a sealed garden:

> A garden inclosed is my sister, my spouse;
> A spring shut up, a fountain sealed.
> . . .
> Let my beloved come into his garden,
> And eat his pleasant fruits.

Despite its overt sexual references, theologians chose to interpret the Song of Songs as an allegory of devotion to the Virgin Mary and the kingdom of heaven – but whichever way the text was read, these images were highly influential in reinforcing the connection between Virgin, rose and love.

By the eleventh century, however, the complex metaphors surrounding the rose and love had escaped the purely religious context and were being assimilated into the developing tradition of chivalry and courtly love, which began in France but rapidly spread out across Europe. Here it became possible for men to communicate love and desire for a woman through the allegorical device of Marian devotion. As the line blurred between earthly and religious love, the association between Mary, the idealised virgin forever out of reach within her enclosed garden, and the rose, her flower, with its multilayered symbolism of perfection, purity, love and the secret delights of passion, found its apogee in the thirteenth-century French romance, the *Roman de la Rose*. The *Roman* was an epic of chivalric love, but here it had slipped the leash of religious devotion altogether, focusing instead on the rose as a metaphor for a lady, enclosed within a guarded garden, yet offering the pleasures of sexual love:

> Through the magic power
> Of Venus, in that self-same hour,
> A wondrous miracle befell.
> The Rose became a damosel
> Of form and beauty past compare.

Perhaps more than any other single work it was the *Roman de la Rose*, which was the equivalent of a modern bestseller, that cemented the connection of roses with the emotion of love in European culture. And yet, as we've seen, roses and love have been intertwined since antiquity and feature in stories and myths from many different places and cultures.

Something in the scent and delicate beauty of the rose has been whispering lovingly to us for millennia and looks set to do so for many years to come.

Back in the garden, on an early June morning, rain-washed roses remain a metaphor for the pleasures of love, at once sensual and beautiful, seductive and consuming. Only the thorns that scratch your skin as you reach for the flowers and the raindrops that fall from their petals like tears offer a reminder that, even in the depths of passionate love, there is no pleasure without the possibility of pain.

REBECCA WARREN

21–26 JUNE

Thunderbugs on Fizzing Elderflower

If you're passing an elder tree in June, take a moment. Pause. Inhale the honied, heady scent of the elderflowers that brighten the hedges and parks like a galaxy of delicate stars. Look closely at the tiny inflorescences (flowerheads) made from up to 1,000 tiny, stalked flowers. Amid the frills and fizz you might see hundreds of barely visible black creatures crawling around the flowers. These are thrips, or thunderbugs, also known as cornflies, storm bugs, harvest flies, freckle bugs and thunderflies.

On a hot summer's day, have you ever suddenly found yourself dotted with these minuscule insects, especially when wearing yellow or another bright colour? If you had sunscreen on you will inevitably have ended up with several stuck to your skin. You might even have spotted them inside your computer, stuck between the screen and display like disconcertingly mobile pixels. Many of us associate them with a coming storm, hence their popular name, but in fact thrips (from the *Thysanoptera* order) are not actually predictors of weather patterns. It is just that they are mostly seen in hot, humid weather, which is often the time storms brew.

There are an astonishing 6,000 different species of thrips. If you look at them under a microscope you might be able to identify different features; for example, some have wings. Due to their size, however, these winged thrips are not very good at flying. In the absence of muscle power or feathers they use a 'clap and fling' flight mechanism first modelled by the Danish zoologist Torkel Weis-Fogh, which involves the thrips (their name is the same in singular or plural) touching its wing edges together, like a clap, on an upstroke, creating a vortex that results in vertical lift. It then rotates its wings open on the downstroke in a 'fling' movement that also creates a vertical force. Because its wings are so fragile the clap motion could cause wear, so it won't usually completely touch them together. It is the same movement made by pigeons on take-off, but far less noisy.

Thrips appear in summer around harvest time in agricultural areas, feeding off crops, pollen, fungal spores and flowers. They are regarded as a pest because they carry viruses that cause diseases and can damage plants. But there is more to this story than a simple case of small nuisances. Research has shown that some thrips species are actually valuable pollinators, despite their size and lack of visible pollinating anatomy.

In fact, the biologist Irene Terry argues thrips were among the first pollinating creatures, and fossil evidence dates their ancestors back as far as *c*.250 million years. Terry believes that thunderbugs have been overlooked as they were not considered able to fly far enough or carry sufficient amounts of pollen to be useful pollinators. She argues that because they can make frequent trips between flowers and in such large numbers, they actually contribute substantially to plant reproduction.

Evidence bears this out: in one study elderflowers were covered to prevent any insect pollinators accessing them, others were covered to permit only tiny creatures like thrips and the rest were left open to wind and pollinators of all sizes. The flowers that were completely covered failed to produce any fruit, while those accessed by thrips did produce berries.

Some types of thrips predate codling moths, mite eggs or paper wasp eggs, but the kind we are concerned with for this microseason are the flower thrips, Thrips major. Back to Irene Terry: 'Flowers that tend to be associated with "thripophily" . . . are medium-sized, with white to yellow colour, they are sweetly scented . . . and their pollen grains are small and dry.' Hello, elderflowers!

Elder trees are found in parks, fields and gardens across Britain. The common elder, *Sambucus nigra L.*, is one of our most prolific and recognisable trees. In folklore the elder is both a protector and a possible malevolent force. According to tradition you must ask permission of the 'Elder Mother' before you harvest its fruits or flowers, and burning the wood is thought to bring bad luck.

As well as making delicious jellies, fritters and sorbets, the flowers have been used for centuries as herbal medicines to treat chest infections and relieve joint pain. In 1671 the German physician Martin Blochwitz wrote *The Anatomy of the Elder*, a 300-page tome containing remedies from different parts of this one tree that were used to treat 'most and chiefest maladies'. There is also a story about a young soldier blinded at Dunkirk in 1940 who was advised by a Romany woman to place elder blossom over his eyes in order to restore his sight. The story goes that initially his eyes got worse, but after some time using the blossom he saw a flash (his mother's wedding ring) and his vision came back. Others say that in years of strong viruses the elder will produce larger quantities of berries, as if Nature knows what needs healing.

In June, the elder's open flowers are heavily dotted with thunderbugs. They are attracted by the flowers' scent, which contains volatile organic compounds (VOCs) like linalool and citronellol. Research has shown that this scent is most potent in the mornings, which is when you will notice the largest congregations of thrips. These morning visitors are predominantly female thrips, suggesting they are particularly responsive to changes in VOC levels. Interestingly, as the flowers age their chemistry alters and their scent changes, causing the thrips to leave the plant and go elsewhere. And as they leave, they take pollen with them to a new host.

In return for pollinating the elder the thrips get a safe place to breed and plenty of food. Although other thrips species have destructive habits, these flower thrips are beneficial to the ecosystem. Their relationship with the elder is an example of 'mutualism', where two organisms or creatures benefit each other, and if we are able to understand more about how this relationship works it could help avoid the unnecessary use of pesticides. It also helps us look at these apparently insignificant, occasionally pesky, crawling hyphens in a different way. Though you might still want to wait until they disembark from your elderflowers before you start making cordial or sparkling wine and create your own distillation of summer's sweetness to savour in the darker months.

LULAH ELLENDER

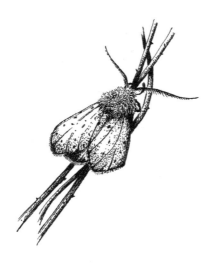

JULY

Noticing Exercise

The abundance of life in bloom and abuzz at this moment in the seasonal year makes for a perfect time to look out for moths. You can buy specialist equipment to trap moths, keeping them temporarily overnight and releasing them unharmed in the morning. However, these kits can be quite expensive, and a simple white sheet combined with a bright light source like a torch can work just as well at attracting these nocturnal insects. (You may have discovered this yourself if you've accidentally left a window open and the light on overnight!) Why not sit out on a balmy summer evening and watch them flying around you?

If you can, take a picture of the individuals you see. There are nearly 2,500 species of moth in the UK and many of them look very alike, which can make identification a challenge. Fortunately, there are some friendly and helpful social media groups who will be more than willing to show off their skills and help you to identify a species from a good photo. If you're lucky, you might spot one of our stunning hawk moths: the elephant hawk-moth is a shade of vivid pink that can rival any of our day-flying butterflies!

27 JUNE–1 JULY

A Messy Riot

As the month of June wanes and gives way to July, the vegetal kingdom enters into a phase of chaos. In even the most meticulously maintained gardens, an anarchy of unbridled fecundity swells and breaks in tides of floral drama, choreographed and soundtracked by birds, bees and butterflies.

For anyone who looks after a plot of land, however big or small, this is a moment in the year when the strongly held belief that humans have the ability to order nature is thrown into question. Our carefully planted seed arrangements and neatly ordered borders are overthrown by a carnivalesque welter of wildness, and normal hierarchies are subverted in favour of a polyphony of abundance. This occurs not only in the perceptible world above ground but also in the soil below, where microorganisms including bacteria and fungi go through their own period of rampant proliferation.

The moment of flowering holds great cultural and philosophical importance. It marks a florid midpoint between the potential of spring's verdant beginning and the death and decay of autumn. For Hildegard von Bingen (also known as St Hildegard and the Sibyl of the Rhine), the surfeit/profusion of flowers during this period carried a symbolic weight. Hildegard was a German Benedictine abbess, scholar, philosopher and visionary who wrote in the early twelfth century during the High Middle Ages. Her writing has recently been used by ecological humanities scholars to explore the relationship between European Christian philosophy and the natural world. The proliferation of flowers during this microseason appears to her as the dark foreshadowing of the fruits to come, which themselves are intimately implicated in/part of the Fall of humankind. The apple that tempts Eve in the Garden of Eden illustrates Hildegard's link between fruiting and destruction; beyond fecundity lies darkness and decay.

Within Hildegard's symbolic interpretation of the seasonal year, the Virgin Mary plays an important role. Traditionally, the Virgin Mary was associated in theological terms with the ripe fruit of summer which harbours its concealed follicles. In contrast, Hildegard looks at the Christian story from a botanical perspective and makes the case that summer is the *end* of a cycle, and thus synonymous with death rather than conception. For Hildegard, Mary's relationship with ripe fruits, full of seeds, locates her temporally upon the green branch of spring, on which the potential of the flower of salvation exists. In this framework, the Christian figure of Mary appears as intimately bound up with the image of Persephone, the ancient Greek goddess of spring, who is pure potential. This is another story where fruit and destruction are bound together, this time in Persephone's consumption of the seed-laden pomegranate that binds her to the realm of the dead. Persephone, Mary and Eve in this vegetal imagination form a triad, their feminine fertility unfolding along a trajectory from potential to mortality. While these feminine figures are associated with spring, by the height of summer their potential is realised in an augury of decline and destruction.

The theme of flowering as a harbinger of death and decay was taken up and given a fresh twist in twentieth-century French literature and philosophy. In *Les Fleurs du mal* (*Flowers of Evil*), Charles Baudelaire identifies the moment of flowering as a chasm between the poetics of potential and the vulgarity of material life. This moment, in which vegetal life realises its potential in an abundance of blooms, also marks the crossing of a boundary between becoming and decaying. In a similar mode, the short essay 'The Language of Flowers' by the philosopher Georges Bataille highlights the smells of decay that are neglected in traditional flower symbolism. Bataille sees flowering as failure, a flash of splendour followed by vulgar decay. Viewed through Bataille's eyes, 'most flowers are badly developed and are barely distinguishable from foliage; some of them are even unpleasant, if not hideous . . . spoiled in their centers by hairy sexual organs and where on close inspection the elegance of flowers appears as satanic and perverse'. This is the season in which beauty and the spirit are fully bound up in material form, unable to resist the march of time. This messy riot of flowers is a harbinger of their inevitable physical death.

Falling within this microseason, on 27 June, is 'Seven Sleepers Day', a feast day that commemorates a tale told in Jewish, Catholic and Islamic traditions. The story echoes the death and resurrection cycle seen in the myth of Persephone, as well as other rebirth tales. Regardless of the faith in which the story is set, it takes the same form. A group of wealthy young men who worship a monotheistic god find themselves under persecution by a pagan state. The young men are presented with an opportunity to renounce their faith and bow to the polytheistic god, but refuse. Instead, they distribute their possessions among the poor and together retreat to a mountain cave to hide and pray. While there, they are overcome by significant sleepiness. The entrance of the cave is then blocked, sometimes by a natural disaster and sometimes by local pagans. More than a century passes and the young men awake, believing they have slept for only one night. They venture outside and find that they have been asleep for many years, and that their faith is now accepted.

This legend echoes the sequence we see in nature during this midsummer season in which flowers bloom, jostle for space and drop their seeds within the dying days of the seasonal cycle. Like the young men in the tale, the seeds are sealed in the earth, out of sight, where they sleep. In spring they emerge into a world of potential in which the conditions are favourable for them to thrive.

This microseason gives us pause to think about the seasonal patterns of the botanical world and the ways in which they have led, over the centuries, to a flourishing of theories, essays, poems and legends that try to make sense of these transitional moments. The messy riot of this point in the year may hold within it the inevitability of death and decay, but deeper still there is rebirth and new potential.

ROWAN JAINES

2–6 JULY

Purple Knapweed Against
Thunderous Skies

There is something about the light at this time of year that exaggerates everything. The strong sun bleaches out colours and gives the landscape an overexposed feel. But when the skies darken with swelling storm clouds, suddenly the hues around us seem brighter and stronger. Like the vivid purples of knapweed silhouetted against thundery skies that characterise this microseason.

With their raggedy rays these thistle-like flowers inhabit a range of spaces, particularly chalkland meadows, verges, field edges and clifftops. They are part of the abundant *Centaurea* family, and although common knapweeds look like thistles, they don't have prickles. Their flowerheads are inflorescences made up of tiny florets and a crown of bracts. Knapweed flowers are great for pollinators and butterflies – you might see them dotted with bees, hoverflies, marbled whites, six-spot burnets, meadow browns, common blues, ringlets and chalkhill blues. A 2014 survey found that knapweed was one of the top five nectar-producing plants in its habitat, with a notably high nectar-sugar production per floral unit. It continues flowering into early autumn, which further benefits insects as other flowers fade, and the seeds are enjoyed by finches, robins, warblers and wrens.

As well as helping insects and providing welcome pops of late-summer colour, knapweed has a rich etymological history. The word 'knap' comes from the Old Norse *knappr*, meaning bud or knob. Beautifully evocative folk names for the plant include hardheads, bachelor's buttons, loggerheads, black soap, blue bottles, iron knobs and chimney sweeps. Common knapweed (*Centaurea nigra*) and greater knapweed (*Centaurea scabiosa*) are part of the extensive *Astercerae* family. Their genus, *Centaurea*, was named after the wise Thessalaian centaur Chiron, who used a poultice made from knapweed after he was accidentally injured by one of Hercules' poisoned arrows. For centuries the plant has been used as a salve, applied to wounds, sores and bruises.

Knapweed flowers are also edible and in the Middle Ages were eaten with pepper as an appetiser. In Wales they were traditionally combined with field scabious and birthwort as an antidote to adder bites. However, caution is required as the plant contains pyrrolizidine alkaloids which can cause liver damage in humans and are toxic for some animals.

Like the oxeye daisies in our earlier microseason, knapweed was also used in divination games. In his poem *May* John Clare describes how a girl would pull off the rays and place the bare flower inside her blouse for one hour:

> They pull the little blossom threads
> From out the knapweed' button heads
> And put the husk wi many a smile
> In their white bosoms for awhile

When she took it out, if any new florets were blooming her true love was near.

But in some places knapweed is not regarded so kindly. In North America, spotted knapweed (originally from eastern Europe and not found in Britain) is considered a major problem due to its invasive habit. It is interesting to consider what makes us see some plants as weeds and others as beautiful or useful. Perhaps it is connected to the way in which native plants interact with them, with introduced plants being more acceptable if they don't harm existing habitats. Where spotted knapweed has been introduced it dominates native plants. The means by which one plant overpowers others are not fully understood, but a suggestion is that they use an allelochemical mechanism. It is thought that the new plants release chemicals that are toxic to nearby plants that have not evolved alongside the introduced species, but research into this is so far inconclusive.

There is ambivalence about knapweed in British agriculture and horticulture too, but given its benefits to pollinators and nectar-seeking insects, plus its cheering, bright shaving-brush flowers, it can be a welcome sight in wildflower patches, meadows and downlands.

This purple flower is connected to the dark skies of an incoming storm by one shared factor: summer. Not only is this the time of year when knapweed flowers, it is also the season in which there are more storms than any other. Bringing lightning strikes and flash floods, storms are more prevalent in the summer due to high humidity and rising warm air. We also see a peak in lightning-strike deaths, partly because there are more storms but also because people spend greater amounts of time outside in the summer, and may be more likely to be on water.

Our instinct tells us that when we hear thunder we should take shelter; by the time we hear those ominous rumbles and cracks the storm is usually within ten miles of us. Research into the acoustics of thunder reveals that it is at its loudest when the lightning bolt hits the ground. One project in 2015 captured photographs of the energy radiated from a lightning bolt as it struck, creating an acoustic image of thunder. Yes, we can *see* thunder! And the colours chosen to represent thunder in the research imaging were, rather wonderfully, green and purple. Just like the knapweed.

LULAH ELLENDER

7–11 JULY

Yellow Wagtails Courting

The western yellow wagtail (*Motacilla flava*) is a migrant species that summers in the UK and winters in West Africa. Their arrival in the British Isles begins in early April, with the spring sunshine, and peaks in early May. By early July the communal roosts are host to a flurry of courtship activity.

The yellow wagtail belongs to a family of passerines that is home to many other wagtails, as well as longclaws and pipits. All are slender, small- to medium-sized insectivores which eat a diverse range of invertebrate prey dependent on local availability. The yellow wagtail nests on the ground of wetlands, particularly favouring the east of England's water-logged, low-lying land. There they roost in monogamous pairs throughout the long, warm days of the British summer, when each year females lay up to two broods of five to six prettily speckled eggs.

At this period in the year you will often see these busy birds running around the meadows, farmland and marshes where they make their summer homes – chasing after insects that have been disturbed by the footfall of animals. The movement of the wagtail is perhaps best evoked by John Clare, who in an eponymous poem referred to this bird as the 'little trotty wagtail'. As in many species, it is the male who does most of the trotting, and at this time of year it is in the form of a courtship dance composed of fluttering flights and songs.

The mating season for yellow wagtails and other members of the wider *Motacillidae* family is not all roses. This time of year is not only the moment for courtship but also for stunning displays of aggression. Wagtails have communal areas where they spend time with the flock, but they also have solitary nests. This allows them to share resources when food is abundant and protect their own offspring when food is scarce. They are fierce defenders of their territory and resources against other species. Yellow wagtails can be seen foraging individually on a patch of ground, and coming together to defend this ground against avian outsiders. They peck, claw and shriek at intruders to assert their claim. There is also another form of fighting seen at this point in the year, known as 'reproductive fighting' between rival males, usually at territorial boundaries.

While wagtails are a monogamous species, this does not mean that these relationships are lifelong. In the fluid social environment of post-migratory nesting space, 'divorce' (the termination of a co-operative pair bond) and 'partner-switching' (when new mating bonds are formed) are both common. Research on passerines has shown that in sites where a higher proportion of 'bachelor birds' arrive from abroad there is a higher divorce rate between less well-established mating pairs. For both the bachelor birds and the precariously mated males there is a lot at stake, and the scenes of competitive sparring are spectacular. The movements performed in reproductive fighting displays are also subtly different from those in any other territorial behaviour. The courting male wagtail will raise his bill, puff out his breast feathers and vibrate his wings, fluttering and strutting.

In the yellow wagtail's behaviour we see in action what the twentieth-century father of psychoanalysis, Sigmund Freud, called 'the drives'. For Freud there are two 'drives' or internal forces that motivate behaviour: the drive towards life (sex) and the drive towards death (aggression). Although Freud's work explicitly deals with the human mind, his theories cast a light on the overlap between the sexual and the aggressive in the yellow wagtail's performance.

Freud believed that drives are reactions to stimuli, and this idea has been used by later thinkers to consider the pressures on the individual of the social world in combination with the material environment. Again, we can see how this might apply to the yellow wagtail as it migrates across many thousands of miles in flock formation, comes to settle in a group within a completely different habitat, and has to compete both to find a reliable food source and to form a pair bond in order to propagate the species – all of which are playing out within the context of climate change.

Research has found that as the effects of climate change intensify, the aggressive behaviours of male birds escalate. This affects the yellow wagtail and its courtship rituals in specific ways. In the yellow wagtail's favoured environment of eastern England, arable fields and furrows are becoming increasingly intensively managed. This affects the timings of draining and grazing in particular and makes the food supply unreliable, with the result that the birds often end up leaving the area in the middle of the breeding season. Strong fidelity between breeding pairs has been documented despite these small-scale migrations, but the stress upon the yellow wagtail should not be underestimated. The 'courting' behaviour that we see in this pretty bird's mid-season mating period is not a romcom. It is a battle for survival.

At this point in the seasonal year, the elaborate performances of the yellow wagtails remind us that we should not be beguiled by romantic aspects of nature. Indeed, when we see them fight for their territory or their mate, perhaps we can also reflect on our desire to conquer territory and feed our families and the damaging repercussions this can have for other species.

ROWAN JAINES

12–16 JULY

Puffs of Meadowsweet

The English name for meadowsweet has a straightforward derivation: it comes from the Anglo-Saxon *meodu-swete*, meaning 'mead sweetener'. The taste of the flowers is light and grassy, with vanilla notes adding richness. The leaves, however, have a dual flavour that is not entirely pleasant:

part cucumber, part antiseptic. The aroma of the foliage is changeable too: when carefully cut, meadowsweet smells pleasant, but when crushed its fragrance becomes pungently medicinal. This is the source of one of its most bittersweet common names, 'courtship and matrimony'.

Meadowsweet has also played an important recent role in the development of one of the world's most used drugs: aspirin. This pharmacological tale, however, is complicated, because there are two competing versions which cannot both be true. Just as the plant has two aspects, so do the stories: one is sweet, light and celebratory, the other astringently tragic.

The first tale goes like this: on 10 August 1897, Dr Felix Hoffman was working in a lab at Bayer in Germany, trying to make the world's first synthetic drug. Hoffman was a gifted chemist, but the motivation behind his research was personal. His father suffered from chronically painful rheumatism and, like many other patients of the time, he could not tolerate the bitter taste, the stomach pains and the tinnitus associated with contemporary anti-rheumatic drugs.

These were mostly made from salicylic acid, the anti-inflammatory effects of which had been known for thousands of years. In 1763, the Reverend Edward Stone of Chipping Norton, Oxfordshire published an account detailing how he had successfully treated ague (fever) in his parishioners with a preparation made from local willow trees, a good source of the chemical. Stone assumed that the drug worked because there was a natural sympathy between willow, which grows in wet places, and fever, which was associated with 'miasma', or marshy, damp air. By 1874, a more modern approach to the chemical manipulation of matter led to the discovery of a production process for synthetic salicylic acid, but the strong side-effects remained a problem.

On that August day, Hoffman had been adding acetyl groups (CH_3CO) to a whole range of molecules. This was an established strategy that Bayer used to generate new drugs. One of his targets was salicin, which he had obtained not from willow but from the leaves of meadowsweet. He heated it with acetic anhydride for three hours and then distilled off the acetic acid, to discover needle-like crystals. They still tasted sour, but were much easier on the stomach than earlier remedies. Hoffman had discovered a way of making acetylsalicylic acid, a new substance that showed powerful analgesic and anti-inflammatory effects.

Naturally, the question arose about how to name this new drug. The current Latin name for meadowsweet is *Filipendula ulmaria*, but at the time Hoffman was working it was called *Spiraea ulmaria* (an older name for salicylic acid was 'Spirsäure'). Bayer's drug was named after this: 'a' for acetyl, 'spir' for spiraea, and 'in' to indicate a chemical give the brand name: aspirin. It has since become one of the world's most successful drugs: estimates suggest that at least fifty billion pills are consumed globally every year.

We know about Hoffman's involvement in the discovery of aspirin from three sources: a few lab notes, a footnote to a history of chemical engineering written by Albrecht Schmidt in 1934, and the fact that he is named on the US patent for the drug in 1900. However, this somewhat scattered evidence is placed in question by the second version of the story, which is considerably darker.

Another of Bayer's employees, a man named Arthur Eichengrün, contended that it was he, and not Hoffman, who had discovered the drug. Writing in a paper published in 1949, he argued that Hoffman was a low-ranking laboratory assistant who was simply working to direction. What is more, Eichengrün described an uphill battle to get Bayer's managerial team to recognise the medical significance of the discovery. A particular roadblock was a more senior scientist named Heinrich Dreser, who was so convinced that acetylsalicylic acid would cause heart damage that he wrote the drug off before it had even been tested. Eichengrün maintained that it was only by quietly testing aspirin on himself and a number of discreet medical colleagues that he was able to prove Dreser wrong.

So why would Bayer want to present a different story in Schmidt's 1934 account? One plausible explanation is that Eichengrün was Jewish. In the period since the 1890s work, he had left Bayer to become a high-profile industrialist in his own right. His vulnerability in the increasingly anti-semitic climate of the 1930s may have significantly limited his ability to rebut the company's official account in Schmidt's history when it appeared, meaning that he had to wait until 1949 to set the record straight. The context of the German pharmaceutical industry is relevant here: in 1925 Bayer merged into IG Farben, and the company rapidly Nazified in the 1930s, eventually becoming one of the major donors and contractors to Hitler's Third Reich.

We can perhaps gain an insight into the reasons behind Eichengrün's silence in his later description of a 1941 visit to Munich. Inside the city's German Museum was a case filled with white crystals. Its inscription read: 'Aspirin: inventors Dreser and Hoffman'. Eichengrün had not only been written out of the drug's history, he wasn't even officially allowed to enter the building. A large sign hanging outside flatly forbade the entry of all 'non-Aryans'.

Eichengrün's caution did not spare him from persecution, however. He was imprisoned in the Theresienstadt concentration camp for fourteen months while in his seventies. During his internment he wrote a letter pleading for his release, in which he cited his scientific discoveries with Bayer, including aspirin, as a reason for mercy. Sadly, his request failed and he remained trapped in Theresienstadt until its liberation by the Soviet army in 1945.

Eichengrün died just a month after publishing his 1949 claim to be aspirin's inventor. Years later, when the pharmacological historian Walter Sneader gave a conference presentation outlining Eichengrün's claim to recognition as the drug's discoverer, Bayer took the unusual step of issuing a lengthy press release maintaining Hoffman's title as its inventor. While it may never be possible to know definitively which scientist was responsible, whenever I see the innocent candyfloss puffs of meadowsweet I can't help but remember Eichengrün. And with him, the many millions of less famous and less powerful people who had their contributions erased, and their lives destroyed, by the fascist forces of ethnic hate.

The story of this analgesic turns out to be surprisingly painful after all.

KIERA CHAPMAN

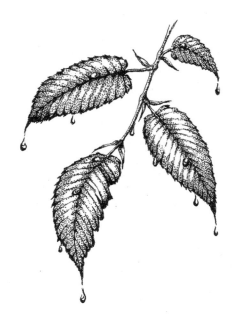

The Smell of Cool Woodlands in Summer Heat

July 2021 was confirmed as the hottest month since records began in 1853. During this microseason it was also extraordinarily wet. The heat of the ground evaporated moisture into the atmosphere and the rising water droplets congealed and condensed into the crystalline crust of cumulus clouds. Cumulus is a Latin word meaning 'little heap', and it is easy to see it in action as water *accumulates* in the clouds, filling them to the brim until their hordes of crystals fall to Earth once more as rain. And where they fall on fields, gardens and forests they draw up the smell of earth. But what exactly is that smell?

Petrichor – the scent of the earth after rain – is a new word, only coined in 1964 by Australian researchers Isabel Bear and Dick Thomas. But it is a word with ancient roots, being a composite of the ancient Greek πέτρα, meaning 'rock', and ἰχώρ, which refers to the watery element in the body of the gods, as well as the liquid element of blood and milk. Prior to Bear and Thomas's paper, this scent was known as 'argillaceous odour' – the smell of sediment-rich rocks.

The word reminds us of the way that places change as they meet weather and time. Smell is never fixed either – a plume of scent is always a symphony full of high and low notes. And our human response to odour is similarly nuanced. Our human nervous systems evolved in synchrony with the world around us, and our senses are tools to literally *make sense* of the complex world around us. Even in our sanitised world our sense of smell continues to shape our experience of the world more profoundly than any other sense.

On stepping into a cool woodland on a hot summer day, we may be consciously aware of the changing light levels as sunlight dapples through the leaves, but it is the smell of the place that hits the nervous system most immediately and deeply. Taste, sight, hearing and touch are all processed through tertiary systems in the brain before reaching the more fundamental areas that control mechanisms like circulation and metabolism. Smell alone travels straight to the limbic system, which manages the foundations of our physical experience, as well as our spatial, emotional and cognitive memory. It is no wonder that in *Swann's Way*, Marcel Proust said that at the end of history the smell of things would act as 'the immense edifice of memory'.

But the scent of cool woodlands in the summer heat appeals to us beyond its romantic and aesthetic qualities. There is an evolutionary benefit, as the human sense of smell has been finely tuned to notice and remember the whereabouts of plant life and the nutrients necessary for survival.

In 1965, the year after petrichor gained its name, the scientists Nancy Gerber and Hubert Lechevalier identified it as belonging to the single compound that they called 'geosmin', a scent which has been present on Earth for more than two billion years. The major source of geosmin is a bacteria which grows like a fungal mould but is in fact a metabolic by-product of certain microbial, fungal and algal species. Geosmin is produced throughout these species' life cycles, but it pours into the soil upon their death. It is released again by the disturbance of the ground caused by rain, perfuming the air with a scent that is distinctively earthy and musty. Human sensory systems are extremely sensitive to geosmin, allowing us the ability not only to sense water across distances, but also to identify 'off' food and drink and protect ourselves from disease. Geosmin is the scent that troubles us if we sip a glass of wine or water that is stale.

In 2020, the researchers Jake Robinson and Martin Breed suggested that this unique sensitivity to geosmin – the smell we call petrichor – is part of what they term the 'lovebug' effect, an interaction between microbes within the human body and microbes in the environment around us. In other words, the pleasure that we derive from inhaling the scent of cool, damp woodlands may be something that is at once deeply human and also external to us, a conversation between our mobile ecosystems and the rooted ecosystem of the woodland. Robinson and Breed call this the 'biophilic drive', the desire to spend time in nature sparked by microbial processes outside of our consciousness.

In this microseason – the hottest point of the year – we pay heed when, in the words of James Joyce in *A Portrait of the Artist as a Young Man*, 'the rain sodden earth gave forth its moral odour'. We encourage you to take to the rain-damp woods and inhale.

ROWAN JAINES

Hot Pokers of Glowing Rosebay Willowherb

Rosebay willowherb, *Chamerion angustifolium*, has painted the modern world, filling its damaged and neglected places with flamboyant colour and a zest for life. It has a way of turning dereliction to delight. In the Second World War, the bomb sites of war-torn cities offered it an enticing mix of bare, uncontested ground containing high levels of carbon and nitrogen, seasoned with lime from pulverised mortar, and the irresistible presence of potash, the residue of burning. As it softened the harsh outlines of shattered brick and concrete, it became known as 'bomb weed'. Today, as it springs up cheerfully in places broken by the destructive forces of heavy industry and commercial forestry, it makes a virtue of disaster. Wherever man has ploughed and cleared, stripped, felled and burned, rosebay willowherb grasps the opportunity to move in and returns colour to scoured landscapes. It is not by chance that many people, who may have minimal botanical knowledge, nevertheless recognise the deep pinky-purple blaze of this plant by its familiar name of 'fireweed'. Indeed, fireweed is so closely associated with our increasingly urban lives that it was voted London's 'County Flower' in a recent poll conducted by the charity Plantlife.

It was not always this way. Historical sources are divided on its presence within the landscape. In 1657, William Coles, the 'herbarist', claimed that it 'grow[s] not naturally in England', while William Camden, in his sixteenth-century survey of Britain, said that it was to be found 'in the meadows near Sheffield, and in divers other places'. More often it was cultivated as a garden plant, valued for its many medicinal and domestic uses.

John Gerard, in his *Herball* of 1597, thought rosebay willowherb a 'most goodly and stately plante', adding that it bore 'brave floures of great beauty . . . of an orient purple colour'. Gerard had identified his rosebay willowherb correctly, illustrating its distinctive four petals and downy seeds, yet for many years it hovered uncertainly somewhere within the loosestrife tribe, sometimes confused with purple loosestrife (*Lythrum salicaria*) and sometimes with its own big brother, the great hairy willowherb (*Epilobium hirsutum*). In fact, modern taxonomy has given it its own genus, *Chamerion*, settling once and for all its relationship with the loosestrifes to that of merely 'cousin'.

Have you noticed how its hot pokers of joyous pink flowers are rarely seen in ones or twos? That's because of its extraordinary ability to produce copious quantities of seed – around 80,000 on each plant – and every one equipped with a mass of fine filaments that enable it to float away on the slightest breeze. These seeds were once used to stuff mattresses and make twine, but it is thought that the plant's sudden spread was dramatically facilitated by the construction of the railway network in the nineteenth century. Opening up long scars of bare ground across the countryside, the new railway tracks formed ideal conditions for a pioneer plant whose tiny seeds were happy to ride the wakes of passing steam engines. The expansion of industrial activity augmented this dispersal system: mining and quarrying, site clearance and building construction all offered tempting, if temporary, homes for rosebay willowherb. Not surprisingly, it acquired a range of local names arising from its location; around the Derbyshire collieries it was called 'pit daisy', while in Scotland it was briefly called Singerweed, after its spectacular colonisation of the bombed-out Singer sewing machine factory on the Clyde during the Second World War. Today it is ubiquitous on construction sites and cleared woodland, where it is considered a spectacle by some and a 'weed' by others.

And, just as it transforms damaged landscapes, so it is valued for its medicinal qualities. Rosebay willowherb has been widely used as a tisane to soothe an upset stomach and as a general anti-inflammatory. In Russia the leaves have traditionally been fermented to make a much-sought-after black tea with the beneficial properties of healing wounds, treating migraine, improving the circulation and promoting male sexual performance. With a reputation like that, it is hardly surprising that by the early twentieth century this 'Koporye tea' or 'Ivan tea' had become so popular that it constituted Russia's second-largest export after wheat. And for those happy people not in need of its medicinal properties, its young leaves and stems can be stewed or steamed and are said to taste somewhat like asparagus.

So the hot pokers of glowing rosebay willowherb have a complex story to tell but they typify this microseason, flamboyant in their appearance, generous in their growth, and a fitting partner to the other signs that characterise the dog days of summer in sultry July.

REBECCA WARREN

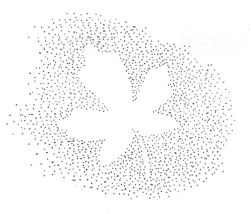

AUGUST

Noticing Exercise

The leaves are still abundant, but they are starting to fall. Now is the perfect time to make a sun print, otherwise known as a photogram.

Go foraging in your local area for newly fallen leaves and try to find out the names of the trees that they belong to. Tape the leaves you've collected to a piece of construction paper (sometimes called sugar paper) and secure the paper to a window, or pin it down outside in the sun. The dyes used in construction paper are unstable in ultraviolet light, and when you take the leaves away the paper below will be marked by the intricate shapes of your foraged treasure. The process might take anything from a few hours to a few days, depending on the strength of the sunlight on the paper.

28 JULY–2 AUGUST

Worts and Weeds for Bees

These few days in midsummer are full of yellow: the stark sun burning long in the sky, the stripe of a bee dancing above a bloom, dandelions smattering lawns, and the star-like flowers of St John's wort. Among the golden weeds, worts and bees chosen to mark this microseason we find stories of undeserved bad reputations and healing, of neighbourliness and stink.

The suffix 'wort' shows that a plant has a long, pre-Linnaean history. It comes from the Common Germanic word *wurtiz*, meaning root, and the Old English *wyrt*, meaning plant. The name is often given to plants and herbs that were used for medicinal purposes. Of the 192 different worts many are named for the ailments they were thought to cure or body parts they resembled. These evocative, vivid names include blushwort, sea milkwort, lustwort, quillwort, lungwort and bruisewort.

There is one wort that has had a bad rap. It is denounced as highly toxic to animals and humans, and even has its own parliamentary legislation designed to control it. Ragwort, *Jacobaea vulgaris*, is part of the *Asteraceae* family. It is thought to have originated on Mount Etna and been introduced to Britain in the seventeenth century. Today it is found in fields, gardens and on waste grounds. Popular opinion has tarnished this wort as one of our 'injurious weeds', with calls for it to be removed in case it poisons cattle and horses. Under the Weeds Act of 1959 and Ragwort Control Act of 2003 a landowner can be ordered to limit the plant's spread, although there is no compulsory duty to remove it. But that didn't stop Lord Tebbit from suggesting in 2014 that young people and offenders should be put to work uprooting it as a form of national service.

So is this 'ragwort hysteria' justified? Ragwort contains alkaloids that make it mildly toxic, but animals will usually avoid it due to the pungent smell that has earned it the name stinking willie. Most cases of poisoning occur in animals who have nothing else to eat or who have eaten hay containing the plant, as dried ragwort loses its off-putting smell, which means cattle and horses can't detect it. There is minimal risk to humans – we would have to eat a huge amount to fall ill.

The plant is currently in decline, which many people may be glad of. But is this really a cause for celebration? Enter the cinnabar moth . . .

Many of us will have seen the distinctive black and yellow caterpillars of the cinnabar moth, *Tyria jacobaeae*, clinging to ragwort stems and leaves. This macro-moth relies on the plant for food and lays its eggs on the underside of the leaves. The emerging caterpillars live on and eat the ragwort, storing up the toxins in their bodies to deter predators. At this time of year the caterpillars are making their way on to the ground to spin cocoons. They will overwinter in the soil and then unfold as red and black moths next summer.

Amazingly, ragwort supports 177 insect species that either depend on it entirely or use it as a significant food source. It also supports fourteen species of fungi and provides a major source of nectar for thirty types of solitary bee. Some people say the honey produced by bees who have visited ragwort has a bitter taste, but that this mellows after a few weeks. There is no evidence to suggest there is any danger in eating this honey, although you might want to let it sit for a while before spreading it on your toast.

How is a wort different from a weed? The latter will often have 'weed' as a suffix, like knotweed or chickweed. But the line between useful medicinal plants and these so-called weeds is blurry – many weeds have health benefits or are edible. And it's not only human uses we need to consider. Weeds provide vital habitats and food for a huge range of insect and animal species.

Common weeds that are beneficial to bees and other pollinators include dandelions, daisies, buttercups, clover and ground ivy. They are part of our cultural land-scape too, inspiring songs, literature and children's games, and carry with them their own traditions. We make daisy chains, hunt for four-leaf clovers to bring us good luck, turn a dandelion's seedy fluff into a clock, and hold glossy butter-cup petals under a chin to see if the person likes butter.

Like the bees and hoverflies, people have foraged for these plants for centuries, enjoying their abundance and nutri-ents. Dandelion root tea is used medicinally to support the digestive system and as a diuretic. Ground ivy has been har-vested since Saxon times, when it was used to clarify beer and gained the name 'alehoof'. It can also be added to salads and is used in herbal medicine as an expectorant. Chickweed is in flower at this time of year and the vitamin C-rich leaves can be eaten like spinach, or used in creams to soothe skin irritations. There are countless tasty, health-boosting plants in our hedges, gardens and verges.

As Richard Mabey argues in his book *Weeds*, we just need to see these plants differently. They are not only integral to biodiversity but resilient and hardy, surviving extremes of weather and our attempts at 'tidying' up our gardens and countryside.

Rather than 'telling it to the bees', perhaps we should *listen* instead, and learn from the way they work, in co-operation with each other and with their habitat. This microseason encourages us to think about how we can work with the natural world we are part of and be more neighbourly to the fauna and flora around us. We can help our bees by ensuring there is a wide range of nectar sources available within a close distance. We can recognise the dandelions, buttercups and worts that dot our gardens and local landscapes as beneficial, vital parts of our community.

LULAH ELLENDER

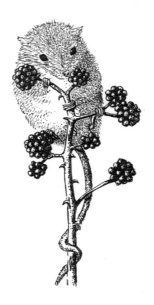

Blackberries Appear

Scrub. The word has a flat, dead ring to it, a sense of messy stuntedness.

Spatially, scrub is the tall vegetation and young trees that appear in between other kinds of habitat. It forms a disorganised edgeland between industrial agriculture and planned settlements, a furred deposit along the arteries of railways and other infrastructures.

Temporally, scrub is what ecologists call a 'successional habitat'. This means that it is a phase through which other landscapes transition, a staging point on the road from open habitat, like grassland and heathland, towards woodland.

Its in-between status makes it easy to dismiss scrub as ruin. It is what happens when we fail to meet the demand to make every inch of agricultural land as productive as possible, when we don't tend gardens or graze hay meadows, when storms topple tall trees, or fire licks through woodland. It is what grows when we are 'neglectful' of our duty to control nature and subordinate every landscape to our human goals.

But ecologists and conservationists have started to realise that scrub is far from a wasteland. Its complex microhabitats contain a humming, buzzing plenitude of life, and its witchy tangles act as a sanctuary for increasingly threatened birds like the turtle dove, tree sparrow and nightingale.

One of the most recognisable forms of scrub contains bramble, *Rubus fruticosus*, a complex of species that are so closely related that they are often treated as one. This pioneer plant is capable of colonising open land with incredible rapidity, a capacity given magical assistance in Perrault's fairy tale *Sleeping Beauty*. After disaster strikes when the princess is pricked by the spindle, the good fairy takes just a quarter of an hour to weave dense thickets of briars around her resting place, where time itself slumbers. But while the castle's inhabitants lay protected by these thickets of thorns in deathly stasis, the surrounding brambles would have hummed with life, surrounded by an audible halo of insects. Sadly, the ecological value of brambles for supporting invertebrates is not always fully recognised in real life: in biodiversity net-gain metrics for the planning system scrub has a 'medium' value, in part because it is seen as an indicator of degraded grassland.

While it might look like a chaotic snarl of organic razor wire, the structure of a clump of bramble has a carefully choreographed regularity. The roots of the plant are perennial, but the shoots are biennial. The canes appear the first year and grow vigorously, at a steady rate. They form arches, rooting where the tip touches the ground. This allows the plant to colonise space, increasing the physical area that it occupies, and also explains why brambles are so likely to snaggle the feet of an inattentive walker. In the second year the canes send out lateral shoots, which are shorter and full of flowers and fruit. In fact, bramble turns time into a spatial structure in such a consistent way that it acts as a kind of 'vegetable calendar'. It is consequently used by some forensic biologists to calculate how long a dead body has been lying in an outdoor environment.

Genetically, the bramble is extremely variable. There are over 300 microspecies in the UK, some of which are very locally specific. The Trelleck bramble, for example, is found in just one place: Beacon Hill in Monmouthshire, Wales. Other microspecies have marked preferences when it comes to soil and habitat: some prefer open ground in sun, others shade; some are specialists of low-lying ground near the coasts, while others prefer reclaimed moorland and heaths. Some flourish on chalk, others on acid soils.

There are so many aggregate species because brambles reproduce both sexually and asexually. They have several sets of chromosomes, which are readily exchanged via sexual reproduction to create new hybrids. But plants can also reproduce themselves asexually, producing seeds by self-pollination (a process called 'apomixis') that create genetically identical offspring. Consequently, brambles are constantly both mixing and conserving their genes, generating and preserving diversity. You've probably noticed this in the fact that some brambles have white flowers, others pink. The fruit can also differ greatly in taste and texture, so if you find a particularly luscious stand, you have stumbled upon treasure!

Blackberry-picking is a traditional rite of late summer and early autumn. Our folklore dictates the traditional timing of this gathering: you shouldn't leave it too late to get your blackberries, because on Michaelmas the devil spits and urinates on all of them, giving them a sour taste. Some legends say that Satan was cast out of hell on that day and that his fall was broken by a blackberry bush, which caused him to curse the plant and to make its berries bitter for the rest of the season. In Ireland, however, you might have longer: here it is the púca (shape-shifting ghosts who often take the form of a horse) that spoil them on Halloween. These days, however, blackberries seem to be ripening ever earlier in response to our changing seasons, making summer picking an increasingly regular occurrence.

There is an intoxicating, absorbing quality to the rhythms of blackberry-gathering, perhaps because the prickliness of the pastime requires a degree of physical focus. In her poem 'August', Mary Oliver describes spending a day blackberrying in a state of hypnotised contentment. Flesh torn by thorns, she gives way to appetite, cramming fruit from surrounding bushes into her mouth. But is this gently animal state equally available to everyone when they pick wild fruit?

In her poem 'Blackberrying Black Woman', the Guyanan-born British writer Grace Nichols draws attention to the ways in which Black participation in British rural customs can become the focus of unwanted attention. Like Oliver's fruit collector, Nichols's Black blackberryer gathers the fruit with 'avid compulsion', her sense of self 'lost in the berriness' of picking. But despite her immediate and instinctive connection to the brambles and the wider landscape, she is nonetheless subject to an othering gaze, as 'passing glances' question her presence and perhaps her level of knowledge of the blackberry lore that dictates the 'correct' time to pick. Ultimately, though, Nichols's poem is hopeful: the gatherer's immersion in her task both protects her from these micro-aggressions and simultaneously refutes the idea that this very British ritual is the exclusive preserve of whiteness. Black blackberrying defiantly belongs in the British countryside.

KIERA CHAPMAN

8–12 AUGUST

Goldfinches Chatter on Thistles

Pass by a drift of prickly thistles or smooth-leaved knap-weeds this time of year, and you may see a telltale shaking of the stems. A charm of feeding goldfinches flitting amongst the stems can seem to disperse as many of the spidery seeds as they consume, as if celebrating their easy abundance with the avian equivalent of a pillow fight. Known as the 'þistel-twige' or 'thistle-tweaker' in Anglo-Saxon, and as *Carduelis carduelis* in Latin (from *carduus*, meaning 'thistle'), the gold-finch is a sociable and distinctive-looking bird. They flock to eat so they don't need to remain as vigilant: in a group, they can handle seeds more quickly and swallow more per minute than solitary birds.

The nomenclature of the goldfinch, which yokes it so tightly to a favourite food plant, feels apt. There is something fluid about the edges of this bird, as if it could become one with its environment to a greater extent than other species. Ted Hughes noticed it in his poem 'Autumn Nature Notes', which commences with a flock of goldfinches trembling and thrilling through an otherwise still laburnum tree that is just turning towards autumn. The arrival of the birds is an animating force, and something vital and green happens in their interaction with the tree that cannot be explained by the mere addition of one organism to another.

The goldfinch's diet extends well beyond the thistles: they will eat seeds from dozens of other plants (along with a small proportion of invertebrates) in varying proportions according to the time of year. Thistledown is replaced by alder, pine and teasel seeds in winter. However, in 1871 Charles Darwin recorded the testimony of 'an old and trustworthy bird-catcher' who said that it was only the male goldfinches who fed on teasel. In the 1960s, the ornithologist Ian Newton confirmed this: netting birds on stands of the plant between December and February, he found that fifty-four of the fifty-six birds that he had captured were male.

The reason behind this is simple. Goldfinches are sexually dimorphic, meaning that male and female birds look slightly different. The beak of male birds is around one millimetre longer than that of females, and is also slightly more curved. A millimetre might seem like an insignificant amount, but it's actually a 9 per cent increase in comparative size. That extra length comes in useful because teasel seeds are hidden away at the bottom of a long, tubular structure among rows of defensive spikes. Observing birds in captivity, Newton noted that female goldfinches had to turn down the spikes of the seedhead before they could reach the food, which slowed them down. In the time that a male bird could eat four seeds, the female could only eat one.

*

This is not the only difference between male and female goldfinches. The red facemask that is so characteristic of these birds extends back further in the male, past the eye. It is also a subtly different colour, though this is difficult to detect with the naked eye: males reflect red more strongly, while females have a more orange face.

In females, the colour may signal the parasite load of the bird. Scientists found that those with higher levels of a blood parasite called *Haemoproteus* tended to have masks that were a yellower shade of orange. Meanwhile, the masks of females with *Isospora* infections in the lining of their intestines didn't reflect UV well. Those poor birds who had both kinds of infection reflected violets more intensely, which may be because they had lower levels of red and yellow pigments compared to healthy birds. So goldfinch masks contain a wealth of information about the immunity and fitness of a female bird.

The red mask has also been key to the symbolism of the goldfinch within European culture. The bird's ease at feeding amid thistly prickles is surely connected to the legend that a goldfinch plucked a thorn from Jesus on his way to the cross, and that Christ's blood caused the red facial stain. In Renaissance art it became common practice to introduce a goldfinch into Madonna and Child compositions, as a symbol of Christ's later suffering on the cross and resurrection. In his 1947 study *The Symbolic Goldfinch* Herbert Friedmann found almost 500 examples of artworks that used goldfinches this way, dating back to sculptures of the thirteenth century. He speculated that the substitution might have had wordplay at its heart: earlier paintings showed Christ with a paper scroll, called a *cartellino* in Italian. Eventually this was replaced by the goldfinch, or *cardellino*, a word which shares the same root, *carduus*, as the bird's later Latin name. The imagery of this bird, as well as its name, returns us to thistles and thorns.

The tradition of treating the goldfinch as a symbol, rather than as a subject in its own right, is arguably broken by the most famous picture of the bird: Fabritius's mysterious painting of a caged goldfinch, created in 1654. As the goldfinch stares quizzically into our eyes, we relate to it almost as we would to a human sitter: this is unmistakably the portrait of a subject with its own character, and perhaps even its own unfathomable inner life. Yet this engagement across the species barrier is possible only because the bird is imprisoned: a delicate metal chain loops from its foot to an iron ring. Behind it is not the greenery of foliage, but a dead, blank, whitewashed wall. To 'see' the goldfinch, Fabritius seems to be saying, we have to hold it artificially still, yet this act of visual and literal incarceration tears it away from its shared, collective life in a green world. In captivity, this bird can no longer bounce and shake its way through shivering seedheads, to the constant sound of irresistible tinkling chirruping.

KIERA CHAPMAN

13–17 AUGUST

Vibrant Rowan Berries

In mid-August the rowan tree blushes red. This hardy little tree also goes by the name 'mountain ash', because of its predilection for upland habitats and the ash-like shape of its leaves. In fact, the rowan (*Sorbus aucuparia*) is not related to true ashes; rather it is a member of the rose family (*Rosaceae*), and the scarlet berries that it produces at this moment in the seasonal year are morphologically similar to its other family member, the apple. Their seeds are also held inside a core, marked by a calyx on their base in the shape of a pentagram. Though less well known than its relations, the apple and the rose, the rowan has a presence in folklore and mythology as vibrant and complex as both.

The rowan tree and its berries feature prominently in Celtic folklore. In this tradition the mountain ash was thought to inhabit three worlds: the earth from which it grows, the air into which it ascends, and the mythical 'Otherworld' to which it is bound. In this way, it touches all levels of existence and bridges every world, and thus offers powerful protection against malevolent magic.

In other cultural traditions, the rowan is also associated with the boundary between the profane and divine realms and forms a point of contact between the Earth, the occult and the sky. In the creation story that underlies ancient Finnish mythology, the rowan is the mother of all plants. It was said that when the goddess Rauni, consort of the sky god Ukko, came upon a barren Earth, she felt distressed to find no flora and so transformed herself into a rowan tree. Ukko was incensed and struck the tree with lightning, which caused it to transmute and multiply, seeding all the plants and trees upon the Earth.

Greek mythology offers another origin story for the rowan. It was said that Hebe, the cup-bearer of eternal youth, had her magical chalice stolen by demons. The gods on Mount Olympus sent an eagle to fight the demons and recover the chalice. The eagle was successful in its quest but was wounded, and when a feather and a drop of its blood touched the earth and mingled with it a rowan tree sprung up. As in Celtic folklore, here we see the rowan as the progeny of three worlds: the earth from which it grew, the eagle's feather from which the leaves took shape, and the drops of blood that became its red berries.

The themes in these myths sometimes found practical application in folk remedies. As in the story of Hebe's chalice of eternal youth, the berries were said to contain the regenerating force of the gods and so provide healing from wounds and illness. They were also thought to act as a conduit for disease: it was believed that if a sick person touched a bunch of rowan berries they would be cured, but that the illness would be passed on to the next unlucky person who brushed against the berries. It was also commonly planted in sacred sites and gardens to offer protection from evil, and in church-yards to prevent the dead from misbehaving.

In pre-modern medicine the berries of the rowan tree were used to treat a variety of maladies. They are reported to have been eaten to treat scurvy in seventeenth-century Wales and used to remedy toothache in eighteenth-century Scotland. They were also recommended as treatments for gout, haem-orrhoids, hypertension and rheumatism, as well as being used as a cough cure, a blood cleanser and a de-wormer in various places across the British Isles.

Many of these healing properties have been confirmed by modern science. Since the 1960s, research carried out on the wider *Sorbus* family (to which the rowan belongs, alongside the service tree and the whitebeam) has discovered more than 250 medicinal compounds. The micronutrients in *Sorbus* berries that influence their colour and flavour have antioxidative capacities that are understood to inhibit oxi-dative stress, which can cause cellular damage and lead to the development of illness. In short, it seems that the rowan really does offer protection against malignant forces.

In keeping with modern medical research, philologists have hypothesised links between the undefined word 'aroint' in Early Modern English and the rowan tree. 'Aroint' appears in Shakespeare's *King Lear* and *Macbeth* in scenes where wretchedness, mental disintegration and the blurring of boundaries are afoot.

In the third scene of *Macbeth*'s first act a clap of thun-der sounds and the wasteland near the royal castle is lit by a bolt of lightning. In this space, three witches appear to Macbeth and tell a gruesome tale of a terrible curse placed upon a sailor, foreshadowing the malignant fate in store for Macbeth himself. The third witch reports an encounter with a sailor's wife, who wards her off, saying, 'Aroint thee, witch!' – a phrase which is usually glossed as 'be gone!' The expression is said to hark back to a corrupt reading of 'I've a rowan tree, witch!', which is to say, 'you cannot come near me, as there is a rowan tree to protect me'.

In this moment of the seasonal year, as the height of summer passes and the nights begin to draw in, winter beckons. Look to these little red berries for inspiration and ask yourself, what will you protect in the coming cold months?

ROWAN JAINES

18–22 AUGUST

Swallows Prepare to Leave

I love watching swallows coursing in late summer, as they fatten up before their long flight to Africa. The deftness of their movements, their flickering aerial attunement to the slightest breeze, their sensitivity to the tiniest deviation of their insect prey is mesmerising. Neither fully gliding nor flapping to a regular rhythm with steady beats, they are live wires, with an electrifying ability to change speed or direction with a whisk of their wings. I can barely follow the movements with my eye, and my body seems embarrassingly earthbound and sluggish by comparison.

How do swallows manage this flexible flight? One part of the answer is that their wings have a very large area in comparison to their body mass. This means that they can generate the power and the asymmetric forces needed to change speed and turn on a dime, switching direction to catch each fresh insect without ungainly flapping.

Then there are those glorious streamer tails. Both swallows

and martins are insect eaters, but martins have squat, square tails and tend to eat smaller, weaker insects (like midges and mayflies) which they catch with a gliding flight. Swallows have those elegant forks and can hunt stronger-flying insects, like horseflies. The distinction lies at the root of their name: the Old English word for a swallow is *swealwe*, a creature that moves to and fro. But the term may also draw on an earlier Proto-Germanic word, *swalwo*, meaning a cleft stick.

For some time, scientists assumed that swallow streamers were a purely sexual characteristic. Female swallows seem to prefer males with longer tails, and research supports the idea that length may be a signal of fitness, since males with longer tails have lower parasite loads and better immune responses to disease. When scientists artificially shortened and lengthened the tails of a group of swallows they found that shorter-tailed males took four times as long to find a mate as longer-tailed males and were less likely to have a second clutch in the same year. Female swallows, by contrast, have shorter tails. Similar experiments to elongate them found a correlation between longer female tails and reduced reproductive success.

Aerodynamically, however, scientists disagree about whether the tails are a hindrance or a help. Many argue that the answer is a bit of both. Growing longer feathers generates significant energy costs, and can make certain aspects of flight more difficult. This means that elongated tails are a characteristic that is at least partly sexually selected via the preferences of female swallows, a kind of 'manageable handicap' that male birds put up with for the sake of attracting a mate. At the same time, other elements of the streamer tails may help the swallows to fly, conferring an advantage that is naturally selected. For instance, the outermost feathers of a swallow can twist in the socket, so that when a bird spreads its tail the streamer feathers bend upwards, making a wide 'U' shape. This creates a vortex at the front edge of the tail, generating lift and possibly allowing the bird to turn more tightly without stalling.

Another element of the swallow's deftness stems from the layer of air in which it chooses to fly. As we learned from our microseason on mosses (10–14 January), air has different layers. It tends to move more slowly close to the ground and faster higher up in the atmosphere. This means that the energy birds need to expend is reduced when they fly low, which coursing swallows frequently do.

What is more, when birds fly, their wings generate little vortices in the air (we will return to this idea for our later essay on migrating swans). When created close to the ground or a water surface, this turbulent air interacts with the swallow's wings, changing the airflow around the bird to reduce drag and increase lift. This is called the 'ground effect': you may have seen cormorants use it when flying close to the water. Swallows exploit the ground effect for around 20 per cent of the time they are in the air on foraging flights.

Different groups of swallows overwinter in different places: we now know that our UK birds will head off to South Africa and Namibia. However, for centuries the disappearance of swallows was a biological mystery. Charlotte Smith's poem 'The Swallow', written in 1797, discusses some of the theories that prevailed in the eighteenth century. She first wonders if the birds

> . . . hide, tho none know when or how,
> In the cliff's excavated brow,
> And linger torpid here

This explanation is ancient: it goes back to Aristotle, who thought that swallows hibernated in caves over winter.

Smith's poem also invokes an alternative, peculiar theory which had been proposed by Olaus Magnus, Archbishop of Uppsala, in the mid-sixteenth century. He thought that the birds huddled underwater during the colder months. Smith imagines them gathering on the 'pliant bough' of willow and sinking in the 'dimpling flood', but wonders how they could possibly know when to emerge again once underwater.

It is clear that Smith herself thought that migration was the most probable solution to the puzzle:

> In Afric, does the sultry gale
> Thro' spicy bower, and palmy grove,
> Bear the repeated Cuckoo's tale?
> Dwells *there* a time the wandering Rail
> Or the itinerant Dove?

In her prose notes that accompany the poem, she mentions the swallow's preparations for departure as evidence for her opinion: 'in September and October they are seen to assemble, as if preparing for their flight, and afterward to have been met in great numbers on the southern coast'.

However, it was only much later, when the practice of ringing birds began, that this question was finally settled. In 1912 a bird that had been ringed in Staffordshire turned up in Natal, South Africa, proving definitively that swallows migrated. Now, with modern satellite tracking data, we know much more not only about their destination, but about the route they take to get there: a 6,000-mile trip down western France, then across the Pyrenees, down eastern Spain into Morocco, followed by a formidable journey across the Sahara to South Africa. With climate change, however, the dates of their arrival and departure are shifting. Unpredictable weather patterns mean that their arrivals don't always marry with periods of insect availability.

In fact, some swallows aren't even making the trip. Instead, they are attempting to overwinter in warmer areas of Britain, often choosing to stay in proximity to sewage works because of their warmth and plentiful supply of insect food. Their chances of making it through the winter are not high, but with climate change it is possible that future Augusts will see fewer birds fattening up and preparing to take to the skies.

KIERA CHAPMAN

23–27 AUGUST

A Shower of Hazelnut Husks from Fattening Squirrels

There are many delightfully evocative collective nouns for animals and birds, but the 'scurry' of squirrels is one of the most apt. Usually seen darting up trees to escape enthusiastic dogs, or scampering across gardens and parks in search of food, squirrels are one of our most visible wild animals. The embodiment of activity, they are rarely still. In late August their busyness is all about preparing for the coming winter. They need to eat 32 per cent more food than is usually required in order to increase their body weight by 25 per cent and get through the cold, hungry months.

Squirrels use these fat reserves to cope with winter, but they can also lower their body temperature by between 1 and 4°C as they shelter in their twig nests, or 'dreys', lined with grass, fir, moss and leaves for warmth. Although squirrels are often thought of as hibernating mammals, they actually survive plummeting temperatures by self-induced torpor, known as facultative heterothermy. This involves a much smaller reduction in body temperature and metabolism than hibernation.

As well as eating seeds, fruits, fungi and bird eggs, squirrels love nuts. To make use of the bountiful nut harvest at this time of year squirrels create caches of nuts, building up their own winter stores. But how do they remember where they have stashed them? Firstly, they store similar nuts in the same places, regardless of where they found them. This 'spatial chunking' is thought to help them locate their caches. Secondly, squirrels spread their hoards about to avoid the risk of a raid or rot wiping out their entire stash, which means they need to revisit several different sites during the cold months. Recalling a series of locations in one area, squirrels create a 'cognitive map' which some researchers have attributed to a higher proliferation of cells in the brain's hippocampus, the area involved in memory and navigation. This argument, that squirrels are able to increase their memory and so their caching capacity, is rooted in the fact that the hippocampus can be developed with activity (as we see with London's taxi drivers, whose hippocampi are larger than other people's due to their constant wayfinding). But other studies have not found a direct connection between larger brain size and caching. While the exact mechanism for remembering caches may be disputed, there is no doubt that squirrels have stellar spatial memory capabilities. And, as well as using their memory to revisit food caches, it is thought that they also use smell to find the exact location.

Squirrelling away nuts and seeds like this means they have a readily available pantry when food is scarce or when they have kittens (baby squirrels) in the breeding season of January to March. But squirrels do not store all the nuts and seeds they gather – they eat some straight away. So how do they decide what to cache and what to eat? The answer may lie in the biochemical make-up of the food itself. Some have suggested that squirrels select food like acorns for storage because they are higher in tannins, which makes them unpalatable. We consume tannins, or polyphenols, in wine, cider and tea, but for many mammals these chemicals can damage their digestive system and reduce water absorption. To get round this some species bury tannin-rich food sources in order to allow the tannins to dissipate. It has been proposed that squirrels cache nuts and acorns for this reason. Yet an Ohio State University study in 1986 revealed that, unlike other mammals, grey squirrels do not experience the toxic effects of high tannin levels in some nuts, meaning there is no need to wait before consuming them. Instead, the tannin content could be a clue to the food's perishability, leading squirrels to take advantage of its preservative effects.

Another possible explanation for how squirrels choose which food to cache is the time it takes to carry and eat different things. A big nut is harder to handle and takes longer to eat, so the squirrel maximises foraging time by burying these for later and eating smaller foods immediately. The urge to cache is probably innate, as there is no evidence of squirrel parents teaching their kittens to bury food. Squirrels are canny in their caching: aware of potential raiders watching them bury food, they will turn their backs to hide their activity and even create fake caches to trick onlookers. When potential competitors are nearby, they often bury food closer to their feeding site, ensuring they can fetch supplies quickly. Researchers have also found that squirrels take particular care to disguise their activities or stop caching when they are storing hazelnuts, one of their preferred foods. Along with walnuts, hazelnuts tend to be cached rather than eaten straight away. And, being more calorific than conkers or acorns, they make an excellent store cupboard staple for the squirrel's winter larder. Interestingly, according to Celtic mythology hazelnuts impart wisdom and inspiration to those who eat them. The Celtic word for nut is *cno* and for wisdom *cnoach*.

*

Most of the studies on caching behaviour centre on the eastern grey squirrel, *Sciurus carolinensis*, which is now dominant in Britain. Originally from North America, the grey squirrel was introduced in the late nineteenth century and has largely displaced our native Eurasian red squirrel, *Sciurus vulgaris*. The success of the larger greys is in part because they are better at neutralising the tannins in acorns and are able to dominate access to hazelnuts, cutting off the reds' preferred food source. The greys also carry the squirrel pox virus, which can be deadly for red squirrels. These endangered reds have now mostly retreated from lowland Britain. Around 75 per cent of them are found in Scotland, where they thrive in coniferous or mixed forests (unlike the greys, which prefer broadleaf habitats).

Attempts are being made to control the grey squirrel population through the encouragement of natural predators like pine martens, and fertility control programmes using species-specific weighted doors that allow only grey squirrels to take bait laced with oral contraceptives. Scientists are also trying to find an effective vaccine against the squirrel pox and exploring ways of reintroducing the reds into the landscape they have forsaken, so in future we might see both species scampering around our trees.

Perhaps because of their ubiquity and busyness, squirrels feature frequently in art, literature and folklore. In illustrations from the Middle Ages we find pictures of pet squirrels, kept on leashes with silver collars and human clothes. And, of course, there is Beatrix Potter's Squirrel Nutkin, characterised by his impertinence but much loved all the same. In Norse mythology, the squirrel Ratatoskr was a messenger running up and down a tree, gossiping and stirring up trouble, gnawing at the 'world tree'. This association with malevolent tittle-tattle may be rooted in their distinctive alarm call, which sounds like two stones being struck together.

The trickster connection continues in Vladimir Nabokov's *Pnin* (1957) – scholars point out the repeated motif of a squirrel that is possibly an embodiment of the protagonist's dead first love, Mira, and a means by which she is able to influence his life from beyond the grave. Franz Kafka describes the creatures as constantly in motion: 'a wild female nutcracker, a jumper, a climber . . . always travelling, always searching'. Again, the scurrying and darting antics characterise so much about our perception of these animals. Prophet, trickster, stockpiler, acrobat – the squirrel lives as much in our imaginations as it does up high in the canopy.

LULAH ELLENDER

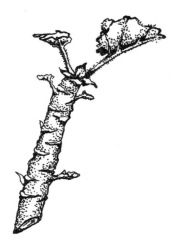

SEPTEMBER

Noticing Exercise

Did you know that you can grow a new plant from just a single leaf? A whole host of shrubs, herbs and perennials can be propagated this way, but pelargoniums make an excellent and unfussy choice. First you'll need to cut a ten-centimetre section of healthy leaf and stem from a mature pelargonium. Early morning is an ideal time to harvest cuttings because plants usually contain the most moisture at this time. Try to make as clean a cut as possible to give your stem the best chance of developing new roots, and remove everything but the top few leaves.

Stand your cutting in a jar or glass of water so that it covers the stem but not the leaves and place it on a sunny windowsill. Change the water every day, and after around four weeks you should start to see the formation of new roots. You can then transplant the cutting into a soil-filled pot. Take care, as roots formed in water are very fragile. With luck, your new plant will thrive all winter on a warm, bright windowsill.

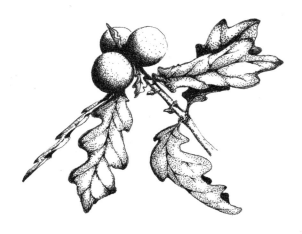

Brown Oak Galls

Question: what connects the Magna Carta, Johann Sebastian Bach and the wasp *Andricus kollari*?

Answer: oak galls!

But before we explore this link, what is a gall? It is a growth produced by the tissues of one organism under the influence of another organism, called the galler. Gallers are often fungi or invertebrates, but sometimes viruses or bacteria. They produce over 2,000 different kinds of structures in Britain which decorate a huge range of plants, fungi, lichens and algae.

The galler warps the normal form of the host, hijacking its young cells and causing them to enlarge, proliferate or differentiate in unexpected ways. The resultant growths range in shape from the large, chaotic tangle of twigs that is a witches' broom (most commonly caused by a fungus that grows on birch) to the compact pink fluffiness of the robin's pincushion on the wild rose (which houses wasp larvae). The objective behind these very different structures, however, is the same: the galler wants to get shelter and nutrients from the host, a relationship that is usually parasitic.

Some of the most interesting galls are those found on oak trees. In Britain, the pedunculate oak (*Quercus robur*), the sessile oak (*Quercus petraea*) and the Turkey oak (*Quercus cerris*) host over fifty different kinds of galls across all parts of the tree. They vary wildly in shape and texture, from tightly furled artichoke-like growths to loose white cotton-wool galls. Many are caused by gall wasps, which look nothing like our familiar garden wasps: most are just a few millimetres long and black or brown rather than warning-striped, with an extremely defined 'wasp waist'.

Some gall wasps have complex life cycles. In many species, a sexual generation emerges, breeds and dies. Their eggs hatch an asexual generation, in which all of the insects are female. However, these females divide into two sub-groups: androphores, which produce eggs that give rise to males in the sexual generation, and gynephores, which produce females.

Sometimes the sexual and non-sexual generations of a gall wasp produce different galls. For example, the sexual generation of the gall wasp *Neuroterus quercusbaccarum* emerges early in the year. The males and females mate and lay eggs on oak buds. A tidy, spherical, berry-like gall, aptly named the currant gall, is the result. Each contains one galler larva, which belongs to an all-female, asexual generation that emerges in June. Their eggs in turn produce flat spangle galls, which look like tiny brown flying saucers, each containing a single wasp larva of the sexual generation. Before the oak leaves fall the fattening galls detach, ensuring that they will be covered by leaf litter over winter, keeping them damp and protecting them from frost. It was the visibility of these spangle galls that inspired the name of this microseason.

Yet quite how gallers manipulate oak trees remains a mystery. It might involve hormonal signalling, gene transfer, or intervention by a third organism, perhaps a virus or bacterium. Very recent research on an American aphid that causes galls on witch hazel suggests that these insects secrete special proteins from their saliva on to their host, which may cause the genes of the witch hazel to be expressed differently.

The high tannin content of oak galls long gave them an economic significance. If you're reading a paper copy of this book, the ink in which these words are printed is probably made from a pigment, quite possibly carbon black suspended in a liquid. But if I were writing out this sentence before the nineteenth century by hand (perhaps adjusting my wig as I wielded my flourishing quill!) I would probably have been using an ink made from oak galls.

Iron gall ink is made from two kinds of gall. Firstly, there are pudgy oak apple galls, produced in response to the wasp *Biorhiza pallida*. Then there are spherical oak marble galls, which form on pedunculate and sessile oaks to house the asexual generation of the wasp *Andricus kollari*. Interestingly, the all-female generation that emerges will lay its eggs on an entirely different species: the Turkey oak. The result is much smaller, pointier galls, nurturing young which will hatch into the next sexual generation.

This *Andricus kollari* wasp was deliberately introduced to the UK in the early nineteenth century because of the commercial potential of its galls as a source of black ink and dyes (Turkey oaks had previously been introduced in 1735). To produce ink, you first ferment the smashed galls in water for a few days. You then react the tannic liquid that results with iron sulphate (also known as 'copperas' or 'green vitriol' in medieval recipes) to blacken it, adding gum arabic to make the fluid stick to the paper. The resulting solution is quite acidic, biting into the writing surface to leave an indelible mark that doesn't fade over time and cannot be removed (unlike some carbon-based inks). Iron gall ink is therefore useful for record-keeping: it was used to write the Magna Carta and, traditionally, for marriage certificates too. (There is a special indelible ink for them, even today.)

Yet there is a weakness. Iron gall ink can sometimes be quite chemically unstable. The reaction that creates the ink can make sulphuric acid, which degrades the woody cellulose in paper, an effect accelerated by excess iron ions and impure ingredients. This means that, over time, iron gall ink can 'halo' on the paper, spreading out in a brown cloud from the written area. It can also 'strike through', so that marks on one side of a page are visible on the reverse. Worse still, 'lacing' can occur, where the inked areas of the paper start to crumble away entirely, leaving an intricate pattern of holes that resembles a laser-cut doily. Some of the manuscripts of Johann Sebastian Bach are particularly badly affected by lacing.

In a computer age in which written characters have become keystrokes, it is tempting to think of writing as something immaterial, the translation of thought into digital code, bypassing anything as mundane as physical matter. Iron gall ink is a reminder that writing is a material process – and perhaps also a warning against the hubris of our aspirations to permanence and indelibility.

KIERA CHAPMAN

2–7 SEPTEMBER

Puhpowee, the Force that Makes Mushrooms Pop up Overnight

In our human world, September is a time for slotting back into the productive rhythms of clock time. The improvisatory freedom of summer holidays is over, and the steady beat of the school and working day resumes. Yet beneath our feet there are signs of a very different cycle, as shortening days and increasing rains call forth a crescendo of our most colourful and fascinating organisms: mushrooms.

Mushrooms are not complete organisms in their own right. Like apples growing on an unseen subterranean tree, they are the visible fruiting bodies of a larger fungal organism called a mycelium. Mycelia can vary in size, from tiny micro-fungi to colossal structures that thread their way across several acres and live for hundreds, perhaps even thousands, of years. They are formed from fine fungal strands, called hyphae, which extend underground like tentacles, producing a filamentous web with no centre and no hierarchy. The space that they occupy is constantly changing, as they reach out for water and nutrients and relay signals about their surroundings back through the fungal network.

Collectively, fungal mycelia weave together an unimaginably complex web of plant and animal life, associating with a vast range of organisms from the tallest trees to the tiniest bacteria. Some of these relationships are parasitic, but many are symbiotic or mutualistic: mycelia often take carbohydrates from plants in exchange for crucial nutrients that those plants require to grow.

Not all mycelia make mushrooms. Those that do form them from the same hyphae involved in making the connective underground web. But to construct the fruit, the long cylindrical cells of the mycelium must co-operate in a new way. First the hyphae knot together in a tiny ball, called the 'fruitbody initial'. This grows, becoming denser, and forms the 'primordium'. The mycelial network will produce many of these, but will select only a few to develop further. For those that are chosen, a complex multicellular structure will develop, and the classic mushroom shape – of a stipe (stem), a pileus (cap) and lamellae (gills) – will begin to emerge.

In many species, the initial phases of mushroom development are completed quietly over several weeks. The final stage of erecting the fruiting body can then happen quickly. The mushroom absorbs air and moisture and 'inflates', a bit like a balloon, which is how it can pop up so quickly, especially after rain. Its purpose thereafter is straightforward: to release reproductive spores.

But is this Puhpowee? The word is Native American, and its popularity is the result of the scientific and literary talents of Robin Wall Kimmerer. In her book *Braiding Sweetgrass*, she describes discovering the term in a book about mushrooms by the Anishinaabeg elder, botanist and conservationist Keewaydinoquay Pakawakuk Peschel. 'Puhpowee' is the Potawatomi word not for the mushroom itself, but for the energy of its unfolding, its 'mushrooming'. What caught Kimmerer's attention is the way that the word pictures nature as a realm of teeming, animated and vital forces that result in the popping up of a mushroom. This is a world of verbs rather than nouns, of relations and processes rather than static objects.

Is this a scientific viewpoint? In some ways not: the power of conventional science, after all, lies in its parsimony. It works by delimiting its object of study, defining hypotheses, controlling variables, breaking down a complex problem and solving it, piece by piece, with every new observation potentially yielding a range of unforeseen applications and uses.

Yet in another sense, the trajectory of modern science from the eighteenth century to the twenty-first could be described as a movement towards an acceptance of interconnectedness, if not of animating forces. For years in the nineteenth century, as we discovered in our microseason on lichens (30 January–3 February), fungi were seen as destructively parasitic in their relationships to other organisms. This made the suggestion that mycelia might engage in more mutualistic relationships simply inconceivable to many scientists. In our microseason on mosses (10–14 January) we met Simon Schwendener, who battled to gain recognition for the dual nature of these organisms as a combination of fungal and algal/bacterial elements. Simultaneously in the mycological world of the 1850s, a scientist called Albert Frank fought to gain acceptance for his idea that fungal mycelia were engaged in what he called 'symbiosis', a mutually beneficial exchange with other organisms.

And yet today modern science affirms that fungi reveal a world of being in which the idea of the 'stand-alone individual' is an increasingly problematic concept. While this is not the same idea as Puhpowee, a 'force' that makes mush-rooms pop up, contemporary science is now developing a much more interconnected and relational view of the world, uncovering the infinitely complex web of exchanges that occur between different kinds of being. These flows of matter and energy through natural systems are a kind of animating force in their own right, after all.

The composer John Cage was fascinated by mushrooms. As a young man he survived on them during the Great Depression. Later, when struggling to establish himself, he supplemented his income selling them to upscale New York restaurants. When he became a recognised composer, he still taught a mushroom identification course and frequently escaped to the countryside around New York to forage for them. They featured in his music and in his mesotics, which are poems like an acrostic, but with the word running ver-tically down the middle rather than at the start of each line. He even appeared on an Italian game show called *Double or Nothing*, on which he won a prize of five million lire (then about $8,000) answering questions about poisonous and edible mushrooms. The final question was 'Name every vari-ety of white-spored mushroom', which he duly did, listing all twenty-four in perfect alphabetical order. He spent his winnings on a new piano.

Most of all, though, Cage saw mushrooms as an occasion for noticing nature in a different way. Part of his fascin-ation was that they defied easy classification: the more you knew about them, he observed, the less easy they became to identify. Something about mushrooms made them hard to pin down. Finding them was difficult too: chance played as much of a role as knowledge.

For Cage, mushrooms offered an opportunity to escape established ways of perceiving the world and to 'de-school' the senses from their tired, everyday ways of looking.

Resolutely opposed to the idea that either life or art was a matter of creating order from chaos, or of reaching towards a sacred nature or a transcendent God, Cage instead used mushrooms as a way of waking up to the present, of seeing and hearing the world around him anew. Wandering in woodland, he thought, was like conducting a silent piece of music. The soundscape was composed in real time, by contemplating the sounds of the natural environment, and being open to chance encounters, like the noises made by startled deer or the wings of birds.

The shift in perspective is similar to that which Cage asks of the listener in his most famous piece, 4′33″. Four minutes and thirty-three seconds without music allows the audience's attention to wander to the kinds of noise that conventional music tries to drown out: the internal sounds of our bodies, the invisible, winged rustlings of the concert hall, even some sounds penetrating from outside, a siren or a car alarm perhaps. In the process we may also have to confront the noise of our own thoughts, whether those are anxious, bored, angry, peaceful or simply bemused. The experience, in other words, is anything but silent, and the kind of listening anything but passive.

Attentiveness to that which we don't usually hear requires a degree of contemplative focus. As does finding something we don't usually see, like mushrooms as they pop up in evidence of vast, hidden subterranean networks of being.

KIERA CHAPMAN

8–12 SEPTEMBER

Arachnids Assemble!

The first reaction of some people to the idea of arachnids assembling will be one of fear, kidney-punching, heart-racing, chest-tightening fear. I understand: I used to be an arachnophobe myself. In fact, when I studied biology I would not only let out an involuntary yelp at the mere sight of a spider, I also had to get my partner to put sticky notes over every picture of them in my textbooks. I'm only really able to write about them today because over the years I've learned a bit more about them and become less terrified as a result. So if you are scared of spiders, please don't skip this micro-season. Stay with me for a while and we can explore them together, and perhaps conquer just a tiny bit of that fear.

There are about 670 species of spider in the UK, but most of them prefer to avoid human houses altogether. Only ten species or so are commonly seen indoors. Those that become very apparent at this time of year, the 'assembling arachnids' that people noticed in our poll, are generally the house spiders, five kinds of spider in the *Eratigena* and *Tegenaria* genera.

House spiders have been the subject of some taxonomic controversy. Part of the problem is that the *Eratigena* spiders are so similar to one another that they can only be distinguished under a microscope. They are all pale brown, with yellow-coloured chevrons on their abdomen, which can look a bit like a brown and yellow skeleton costume. However, they do have a distinctive geography. *Eratigena duellica* is widespread in England but less common in Cornwall, western Wales and most of Scotland. *Eratigena saeva* likes the West Country and Wales, but tends to avoid eastern England. Meanwhile, *Eratigena atrica* is very local, being mainly a Geordie spider living in and around Newcastle (with another cluster in Perth and Dundee).

Then there are the *Tegenaria* spiders. *Tegenaria domestica*, found throughout Britain but more scattered in the west and north, looks like a smaller, paler version of the *Eratigena* species. Confusingly, however, the biggest of the lot, with a leg span of up to twelve centimetres in males, is *Tegenaria parietina*, the cardinal spider, found in the south-east of England. Legend has it that it is so named because it is found predominantly around Hampton Court, where it apparently terrified Cardinal Wolsey in the early sixteenth century. (However, the earliest historical reference I have managed to find to it is much more recent: Edward Jesse's 1832 *Gleanings in Natural History*.)

I say that house spiders 'become apparent' in our homes in the autumn because they've probably always been indoors, merely becoming more noticeable at this time of year. So when we encounter a giant *Eratigena* house spider in our bathtub on autumn mornings it's more likely that this incy-wincy spider was on a night-time ramble and fell in than that he crawled up the drainpipe or clambered in from outside. When you think about it, this is a reassuring thought for arachnophobes: for most of the year these retiring creatures assiduously avoid us.

Many of these autumn house-roving spiders are males, venturing out bravely into the open because they are seeking a mate. Notice them more closely, and it's easy to distinguish them from females. Both male and female house spiders have two appendages (called 'pedipalps') that look like miniature legs at the front of their bodies. In males, these have thickened areas at the end. The last bit acts as a spider penis, transferring sperm into the female during courtship.

These big and beefy house spiders contrast sharply with the spindly cellar spider, *Pholcus phalangioides*, a tangle of delicate legs around a tiny body. You may have seen it finding a home in the corners of your room, where it will reside in an almost invisibly fine web. Leave *Pholcus* in place long enough and its web will get bedecked with the carcasses of small flies, midges and mosquitoes, testament to the efficiency of this spider at removing small insects from your environment. An ecosystem service, free of charge!

The story of *Pholcus* is one of successful colonisation. Originally it was a cave-dwelling species, but 300 years ago it was introduced to central Europe from Asia. It has since spread across the continent so successfully that it may now be present in virtually every single European building. What is more, global commerce has introduced it to Australia and the Americas, where numbers are also increasing.

Yet the cave-dwelling past of *Pholcus* is still evident in its behaviour. If you've ever pulled a thread of this spider's web with a duster, you might have seen it go into a dramatic spasmodic vibration, vigorously shaking the entire structure in a way that shows off its extraordinarily reverberant and elastic nature. This 'whirling' may be a clever strategy to avoid becoming prey to hungry predators, from other spiders to cave-dwelling birds like swallows. The shaking makes it very difficult for a predator to locate the spider visually, allowing it to escape an attack.

Even though the giant house spider looks huge compared to the cellar spider, *Pholcus* actually predates *Eratigena*. If you find dried-up remains of house spiders in your house, legs neatly tucked back towards the body like some strange kind of industrial cog, this may well be the work of *Pholcus*. It finds the house spider, sits next to its funnel-shaped web, and vibrates it in a way that mimics an insect. When the house spider appears, *Pholcus* attacks from a distance, throwing silk at it to encumber its movements. Only when the larger spider is suitably immobilised does it move in closer to paralyse it with venom. So if you have *Pholcus* in your home, you're unlikely to have house spiders for very long. In fact, so effective is their campaign against their larger relatives that it's hard not to feel sorry for our larger house spiders, and to value their presence in our homes that little bit more.

KIERA CHAPMAN

13–17 SEPTEMBER

Dew-drenched Cobwebs

Arachnids are named after the Greek myth of Arachne, a woman of humble origins, who was famed for her preternatural prowess as a weaver. She boasted that she had developed a skill greater than that of Athena at producing cloth, without tuition from the goddess. Angered by her claim, Athena challenged her to a weave-off to compare their work.

In Ovid's version of the story, each woman creates a tapestry that reflects her world view and understanding of power. Athena's shows a unified scene, depicting her victory over Poseidon in their battle to name the city of Athens. In the centre, twelve gods are illustrated in all their dignity and majesty, while the four corners depict stories in which mortals who challenge divine power are firmly punished by being metamorphosed into animals.

Arachne's tapestry, by contrast, does not have a clear, centralised organisation. It shows a succession of scenes in which it is the gods who deliberately metamorphose into animals to deceive and rape a succession of female victims. Instead of representing a hierarchically ordered cosmos and the glory of divine power, her work piles up example after example of divine wrongdoing. The tapestry itself, however, is technically flawless in execution.

Infuriated by her rival's success and the subversiveness of her design, Athena attacks Arachne with the hard shuttle used to thread the weft through the warp. Tortured by the pain, Arachne puts a rope around her neck, driven to the brink of hanging herself. Instead of allowing her to die, however, Athena condemns her to a life of being suspended in mid-air, spinning a web. She is metamorphosed into a spider.

The conventional interpretation is that there is a cruel contrast in Arachne's punishment between the glory of her human weaving and the apparently repetitive, unskilled nature of her labour as a spider. This reading links her artistry in weaving to her narrative ability: as a spider, she can spin but she can no longer tell a story, or challenge the status quo with tales that question the gods.

This detrimental comparison between human and arachnid weaving continues in much later work. For Karl Marx, writing in the 1860s, a spider's work resembles that of a weaver, but with a crucial difference: humans execute a rational mental plan when they labour, whereas the spider works on instinct alone. In this view, humanity is special because we take the materials of nature and mould them to a pre-designed purpose, marshalling our will to realise an idea in the world.

But the comparison between the spider's web and pictorial art ignores a crucial feature of webs. They may not be visually representational – in fact, in most cases they are designed not to be seen – but they are an opening on to the world, an extraordinarily dynamic and mobile way of gathering information about three-dimensional space. The spider at the centre is not suspended in a meaningless vacuum, but is the living heart of a pulsing network. In this way, the web functions not merely as a kind of prosthetic extension of the spider's body but as an extended perceptual system that delivers and processes large amounts of tactile, mobile and spatial data.

Despite having eight eyes, most species of web-building spider have rather poor vision. Instead, they sense the world via vibration. Our recognition of this phenomenon is relatively new: for a long time, scientists dismissed the notion that vibrations carried through the medium of a substance could act as signals. It wasn't until the late 1970s that conclusive evidence emerged demonstrating that scorpions could detect prey via vibrations in sand. Since then a great deal of research has shown that many invertebrates, as well as several species of mammal, bird and amphibian, gather information about the world in this way. The scientific study of the many ways in which animals use the transmission of vibrations through various media is called 'biotremology'.

So how do spiders pick up vibrations? To understand, we need to grasp three features of their anatomy. Their bodies, and especially their legs, have lots of hairs connected to nerves that detect touch directly, in a way that is familiar to us as humans. However, they also have a special type of hair, called a trichobothrium, which is extremely fine and highly sensitive to air movement at a distance. This lets them detect the buzzing of an insect's wings in the surrounding air. Finally, they have holes in their exoskeleton called 'slit sensilla'. The slightest movement of the spider's skin (or cuticle) deforms the shape of the hole, triggering a nerve. This allows the spider to orientate itself in space, but also enables it to detect tactile vibrations along strands of silk. Slit sensilla are especially numerous in the legs of species that spin webs.

But spiders also use vibration to communicate proactively with their surroundings. For example, web-spinning spiders can pluck the threads of their webs, sending a pulse of compressed energy down the silk. The vibrations they detect in response tell them about the web's condition and the position of any ensnared prey. Many can also make vibrations by moving the threads sideways in space, bouncing up and down on the silk like a trampoline, or shaking their abdomens to vibrate a strand. In some species these tremulations act to deter predators; in others they may play an important role in courtship, allowing males to signal to females that they are a potential suitor, not potential prey.

This sensitivity to movement, and its extension in space enabled by a web, is the subject of the artist Tomás Saraceno's *Arachnid Orchestra* installations. Saraceno places a number of web-dwelling spiders in cases, lighting them to show off the unearthly architectural beauty of their creations. He then uses a host of microphones, transducers, piezoelectric pickups and vibrometers to capture their subtle, spidery vibrations within these webs, translating them into sounds that we can hear. The result is an avant-garde series of breathy whomps, roars and machinic grunts.

At some gallery events, Saraceno has invited human musicians to improvise alongside the spiders, creating more-than-human songs across the species barrier. His latest work takes the idea even further, suspending humans in vast, dimly lit webs where we are encouraged to experience the world as spiders do. Attuned to the vibrations around us, we encounter other human visitors as a series of constantly changing haptic signals.

So when dew magically reveals the otherwise invisible cobwebs around us, consider that you're looking at a vital part of a sophisticated sensory system. And perhaps take a moment to close your eyes and imagine being at the heart of its quivering silk network.

KIERA CHAPMAN

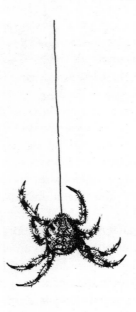

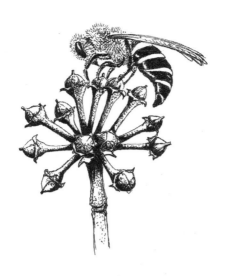

18–22 SEPTEMBER

Bees Cling to Ivy

Picture an abandoned building or a ruined castle. It might have brambles looping around its perimeter or moss carpeting its floors. Chances are you've conjured up some ivy creeping across the walls and windows, concealing the stone and stories beneath. Ivy cloaks things in mystery with its evergreen tendrils winding their way over, up and around structures or plants. It evokes a sense of the unknown, the hidden, the disappeared. We imagine what lies under its vines. Yet in September its surface is teeming with life, a shroud that is also a source of support and sustenance.

Ivy has aerial roots covered in fine hairs that enable it to grow up to twenty-five to thirty metres high and grip surfaces. This ability to climb over and cover up has given the plant something of a bad reputation for pulling down buildings or depriving trees of moisture and food. These fears are largely misguided. Ivy is not parasitic. In fact, it draws its nutrients from roots in the soil rather than the host plant and does not harm trees in areas where it is native. It will usually only worsen already weakened masonry or old mortar rather than create new problems. English ivy, *Hedera helix*, is more aggressive and potentially damaging if the surface is already compromised; but there is also evidence that ivy can sometimes act as a thermal blanket for walls, protecting them from frost damage.

As well as being known for its resilience and prolific spreading, ivy is traditionally associated with Christmas as one of the few evergreen plants suitable as a festive decoration in winter. But it was also used by pre-Christian pagans in their winter celebrations and is linked to the Greek god Dionysus (or the Roman Bacchus), the god of fertility, agriculture and wine who wore an ivy wreath around his head to prevent intoxication or a hangover. This connection with wine continued in the Middle Ages, when ivy was hung outside taverns, perhaps because its flowers and berries resembled grapes, but possibly due to the classical bacchanalian connection.

The word 'connection' is fundamental to our perceptions of ivy. From the vines binding the graves of Tristan and Isolde to bridal bouquets and druidic fertility rituals, ivy symbolises peace, fidelity and protection. It lives for many years and is strong, adaptable and persistent. And it plays a vital role within the environment, especially during the more barren months.

Ivy is an incredibly important source of nectar, pollen and shelter once the weather turns cold and other plants retreat. While it might hide the surface below, at this time of year the flowering ivy is visibly alive, abuzz with bees and thrumming with energy. Only mature ivy will have flowers and it can be identified by its oval leaves, whereas juvenile plants have three- or five-lobed leaves. It is closely entwined with the life cycle of one type of bee in particular: the ivy mining bee, or *Colletes hederae*. These bees are relatively new to Britain, with the first recorded in Dorset in 2001. They are predominantly found in southern England but are slowly spreading.

Unlike its long-lived host, the ivy mining bee lives for just six weeks. In September the females are busy gathering pollen and nectar to take back to their nests. Unlike the colonial bumblebees we met back in our March microseason, these are solitary bees, but they will create aggregated nests in sandy, exposed soil and cliffs. The females excavate burrows in the soil or sand, laying their eggs in individual nests lined with pollen for the larvae once they have hatched. When the female has collected enough food for her future offspring, she seals up the entrance – another concealment, this time a less conspicuous one. Soon she will die, her work completed.

The following August the now mature adult male bees emerge. They dance around the nests waiting for the females, which leave the nests around one month later. As the females surface they release pheromones that are irresistible to the males, causing them to dive upon their chosen mate in extraordinary bundles, tumbling in sex-crazed scrums until one male is left. Once they have mated the female begins nesting, making her home close to some ivy, her main supply of nectar.

The plant is not only essential for the ivy mining bee; it is also a key food source for hoverflies (including the rare golden hoverfly), solitary wasps and butterflies like the holly blue and red admiral. Around 80 per cent of the nectar collected by honey bees in September comes from ivy. Brimstone butterflies hibernate in its tendrils, and it also provides shelter for small mammals, bats and birds over winter when many trees are bare. The sweet-scented green-yellow umbels turn into glossy black berries that provide winter food for birds like thrushes, wood pigeons and blackbirds. There is a striking contrast between the human urge to destroy ivy, for fear it will damage our homes, and the hospitality the plant offers to so many creatures.

The life cycles of the ivy and the bees are knitted together. And this entanglement reveals the importance of tenacity and mutual support – of connection.

LULAH ELLENDER

23–27 SEPTEMBER

Cacophonies of Conkers

In late September the air is perfumed with the idiosyncratic scent of the fruits of the horse chestnut. The pretty pink and white flowers that adorned the branches of this tree in May have been pollinated by insects, and have spent the summer developing into glossy auburn seeds encased in a spiky green husks. At this moment in the seasonal year, the fruits ripen, hang heavy and fall, releasing an earthy, fungal, sweet fragrance; the smell of autumn.

Today the horse chestnut is one of most commonly sighted trees in Europe. They line streets, parks and gardens all over the British Isles. The seeds are known as conkers and have been used in childhood games since at least the eighteenth century. This connection to childhood makes this tree seem as though it is one of Britain's native species; however, this is not so. The journey of the horse chestnut from a 'new discovery' to a ubiquitous sight in the most ordinary of public places is one that took place over centuries.

The horse chestnut (*Aesculus hippocastanum*) is native to the Balkan peninsula, but for nearly three hundred years

247

most botanists believed that it had arrived in Europe from Asia.

The first known report of the horse chestnut appears in a letter dated 26 July 1557 from Willem Quackelbeen to Sultan Süleyman (the Magnificent) written in Istanbul. Quackelbeen describes a species of chestnut common to Istanbul, which has horse as its second name because, he says in his letter, when fed to horses three or four at a time the seeds were thought to give relief to equine chest complaints such as coughs and worm disease. This letter was published shortly after its receipt and was followed in 1563 by the first known botanical illustration of the horse chestnut, in the form of a woodcut in Mattioli's *New Kreüterbuch* (herbal book), in the chapter 'on the chestnut tree' under the subheading *Roszkastanien* (chestnut), *Castanea equina*.

The documentation of this new tree led to imports of the horse chestnut into European gardens. One of the first of these arboreal transplants took place in 1576 when the Artois botanist Charles de l'Écluse brought horse chestnut seeds from Constantinople to Vienna, where he planted them in the imperial gardens.

The next significant record of the horse chestnut's journey towards naturalisation in Europe comes from 1615, when the French botanist François Bachelier brought two saplings from Constantinople to be planted in Paris. The first was set in the courtyard of the Hôtel de Soubise, in the up-and-coming Marais neighbourhood – and there it grew until 1840. The second sapling was planted in the Jardins du Roy (known today as Jardin des Plantes), where it lived until 1767. During this time the horse chestnut received the common name *marronier d'Inde* (the chestnut of Turkey) and was a popular sight in the city. The beauty of this tree inspired Louis XIV to order the gardeners in the Jardin des Tuileries and Versailles to plant lines of horse chestnuts, which captured the imagination of landscape gardeners all over Europe and transformed the horse chestnut into one of the most commonly planted ornamental trees of the eighteenth century.

When the time arrived for the taxonomic botanist Linnaeus to write his definition of the horse chestnut in 1753, it was already enshrined in scientific folklore that the tree originated from the northern areas of Asia. Linnaeus encoded this into scientific 'knowledge' proper in his *Species Plantarum*. The Asian origins of the horse chestnut remained a 'fact' until the late nineteenth century, even flying in the face of discoveries to the contrary.

In the late eighteenth century, the gentleman traveller John Hawkins discovered a horse chestnut growing wild in the Pindus Mountains of Greece. He published his hypothesis that the tree was actually a Balkan native, only to have his report met with widespread disbelief from the botanical community. It took until 1879, over eighty years after Hawkins's discovery, for the scientific world to acknowledge their error and confirm that the mountains of Bulgaria, Albania and the north of Greece are the native habitat of the horse chestnut.

In this Balkan region the horse chestnut grows wild in mixed woods alongside the common alder, the ash, the Norway maple and the common walnut. Here the Greek common name for this tree is the 'wild chestnut', and researchers discovered that, as in the Turkish regions where Europeans first 'discovered' this tree, the fruits were used in folk medicine to cure coughs in horses.

*

In modern medicine the properties that gave this tree its equine name have been researched more fully. Coughs and chest complaints in horses are often caused by fluid building up in the lungs during the early stages of heart failure. This manifests itself in difficulty breathing and coughing. Research has shown that chemical compounds in the horse chestnut seed, or conker, control inflammation and swelling and reduce the accumulation of fluid. In clinical trials these compounds have been found to strengthen the circulatory system, in particular the venous system. In short, contemporary research has confirmed the efficacy of at least one of the traditional uses of this tree, which endured through all the years of taxonomic confusion in Europe.

This microseason, let the falling of horse chestnuts bring to mind the huge journeys and long processes that brought the most familiar of British plants to the seasonal landscape. There is an argosy of histories inside each glossy seed, nestled within the horse chestnut's spiky shell, and above all there is the wonder of cracking it open and inhaling the scent of autumn.

ROWAN JAINES

OCTOBER

Noticing Exercise

This month sees some of the most brilliant colour changes in woodlands. But the moment feels so fleeting and transient: wouldn't it be wonderful if we could preserve some of this autumn colour, to carry forward into winter?

Well, it is possible to preserve leaves, and at least some of their vivid colour. All you need is a solution of one part glycerin (available from pharmacies or in the baking section of the supermarket) to two parts water. Put your leaves in a flat container – a shallow pasta bowl or a polystyrene plate is ideal – and pour in enough solution to cover them. Put another bowl or plate on top and add a weight to keep the leaves submerged. Leave the whole thing for two to six days and then remove the leaves, drying them off. They should emerge in a pliant, pliable and preserved state.

28 SEPTEMBER–2 OCTOBER

Beech Nuts Fall

A flock of bramblings, with russet and black wings, yellow beaks and white go-faster stripes on their wings, are pecking busily at the ground in a field at the edge of a wood. Suddenly, in unison, they lift in a trembling wave and fly up over the trees. They are here for the beech nuts, their favourite food.

Bramblings are just one of a huge range of species that find food and shelter in a beech wood; some are native and others, like these small finches, are seasonal visitors. The main areas of beech woods in Britain are in the south of England and Wales. They have been here for at least 1,000 years, though their exact origin is disputed: some claim they must have been brought here after the Romans because Julius Caesar states there were no beeches in Britain in his *De Bello Gallico* of 58–49 BCE. Yet excavations in Wales unearthed traces of beech pollen in charcoal dating back to the Iron Age.

Whenever and however these trees came to Britain, the European beech is now one of our best-loved species. Its woodland habitat is reflected in its name, *Fagus sylvatica* (from the Latin *sylva*, meaning wood). With their grey bark and toothed, bright green leaves the trees are fairly easy to identify by their foliage alone, but at this time of year there are other clues: carpets of triangular beech nuts wearing spiny casings that resemble four-pointed fairy hats. Like the hazel we looked at previously, beech trees are monoecious, meaning they have both male and female flowers. The female flowers turn into these spiky 'fruits' which break open in autumn to reveal the distinctive beech nut, or mast. In some years, known as 'mast years', the trees produce bumper crops of nuts. There is no hard and fast rule about the gaps between mast years, but it is roughly every two to three years.

It is thought that this spacing, an example of predator satiation, helps ensure the trees' survival. One year they produce a large quantity of beech nuts that no amount of squirrels, mice or birds can completely deplete, and then the following year or two they do not produce many. This reduces and regulates the numbers of animals in their habitat as they either die of starvation or fail to breed. Interestingly, all beech trees in the same area will follow the same nut-producing pattern. We do not fully understand how they communicate this, but there are plausible theories: airborne chemical signals, and messages sent via mycorrhizal networks. Some believe mast years are a response to the weather and environment. In warm temperatures beeches produce more nuts, which seems to bear out this idea. This has implications in terms of climate change as increasing temperatures may mean too much mast, which will encourage spikes in rodent populations.

You might find empty husks with no nuts inside. They are not fakes, but nuts that were never pollinated. These hollow cases are made from carbon, which does not use as much energy to produce as the nuts, which are made using nitrogen. But if you do find a nut, don't rush to eat it. Beech nuts *are* edible, and the ancient Greeks believed they were the first food eaten by early humans. They are high in protein and fat, making them an excellent food source for birds and mammals, but the taste is pretty unpleasant. They can also be toxic in large quantities, so should best be left to the bramblings.

Another creature whose history is intimately connected with the beech tree and its nuts is the pig. In areas like the Sussex Weald, Hampshire's New Forest and Surrey beech forests there is a long history of 'pannage' – the right to graze pigs on beech nuts and acorns in certain forests.

Pannage helped shape the landscapes of the past in post-Roman Britain, and it is still practised in the New Forest. Over this area's 219 square miles, around 700 'commoners' have the right of pannage; they also cut wood for fuel and pasture. This grazing right is connected to their property, and some have a family heritage of 'commoning' stretching back generations.

Throughout the year they will turn out livestock on to the heathland, bogs and wetlands, and in mid-September they let loose up to 600 pigs and piglets in the forest. For around two months visitors can watch the pigs snuffling around, foraging for beech nuts and acorns with rings through their noses to prevent them doing too much damage to the tree roots and soil. This might sound like an awful lot of pigs, but in the nineteenth century up to ten times more enjoyed this beechy bounty. The purpose is not just to give the animals a feast; they are actually mopping up acorns that can be harmful to other grazing herbivores like cattle and horses.

Prohibitive house prices in the area preclude new (especially young) people from having the opportunity of buying a property with commoning rights. And there are some who argue that commoning is causing overgrazing. Yet this small-scale farming system increases biodiversity, supports local communities and promotes co-operation and mutuality as the commoners help each other at different times of the year. It is an example of living collaboratively and sustainably, with a fairer distribution of resources.

There is a body of research pointing to a severe decline in beech forest habitats as the trees suffer in increasingly hot droughts. This will impact not only the commoners of the New Forest, but all the thousands of creatures and ecosystems that depend on these majestic trees. The sight of an undulating murmuration of bramblings descending on a blanket of beech nuts feels all the more precious and wondrous.

LULAH ELLENDER

The Sound of Migrating Geese and Swans

Silent is my garment when I tread the earth
or dwell in the towns or stir the waters.
Sometimes my trappings lift me up over
the habitations of heroes and this high air,
and the might of the welkin bears me afar
above mankind. Then my adornments
resound in song and sing aloud
with clear melody – when I do not rest
on land or water, a moving spirit.

Exeter Book, riddle 21

One thousand years ago, a series of Anglo-Saxon riddles were collected in the *Exeter Book*. This one asks us to guess the identity of a being whose clothes are silent when on the ground or on water, but that sing in the air. Further, this raiment has magical properties, lifting the being far above the human world, to become one with the might of the sky.

The answer to the puzzle is the mute swan, *Cygnus olor*. Despite its name it is not silent, but makes a number of different vocal sounds, including a positively inelegant grunt not unlike that of the hungry pigs we met in the last essay. However, the *Exeter Book* riddle centres on the sound made by the swan's wingbeats. On take-off, these are surprisingly percussive, almost glockenspiel-like, but quickly acquire an eerie, almost extraterrestrial quality, a sawing, breathy oscillation that is audible at a distance. According to one interview with the composer's widow, the pulsating sound may have inspired Wagner's *Ride of the Valkyries*.

With its distinctive orange beak and bulbous black nose knob, the mute swan is resident in the UK year round. So, when we think about 'the sound of *migrating* geese and swans' in this microseason, we are talking about other species. They include Bewick's and whooper swans, which are smaller, neater birds than mute swans, with yellow bills and smooth noses, and a number of different species of geese (brent, barnacle, greylag, pink-footed).

Each has its own distinctive set of calls in the air, which are rather different from their sound on the ground. Dark-bellied brent geese travel all the way from the Russian Arctic tundra in long, wavering lines that are held together by their stuttering, reedy alto calls. Pink-footed geese fly in V-shaped wedges from Iceland and Greenland, with a higher, faster, almost seagull-like call that can seem to echo around the autumn sky. Thriving resident populations of greylag geese are boosted in winter by rasping, honking incomers from Iceland.

Flying in formation may help the birds to save energy. When a large bird, like a swan or a goose, flaps its wings to generate lift, a small vortex is created at their tips. This generates an upwash of air. A following bird can capture its energy, to make its own flight easier. But co-ordinating the formation also takes work, and this may be where their

vocalisations come in: they provide constant feedback, allowing the birds to maintain their relative position in the flock.

One of my favourite sounds of autumn is the migratory call
of the whooper swan. Though lighter than mute swans, they
are longer-winged, which helps around 11,000 of them reach
the UK from Iceland each year. In good conditions they can
cover the 900-mile distance in as little as thirteen hours,
though many birds take considerably longer.

Whooper wings make a quiet swishing sound, but it is
their flight call that is extraordinary, at once reedy and resonant, a natural bugle. In fact, sound reverberates through
the whooper's Latin name: *Cygnus cygnus*. The word comes
from the Greek *kuknos*, meaning 'honker', though northern
European terms are rather more romantic: in Norwegian
the whooper is the *sangsvane*, in German the *Singschwan*
and in French the *cygne chanteur*. The English 'swan' comes
from the root 'swen' – to resound – which also gives us 'sonos',
sound itself.

How does the whooper produce this extraordinary noise?
Whereas mammals make sounds using vocal chords in their
larynx, birds sing with a syrinx deeper in their chest. The
walls of the syrinx form a vibrating membrane which is con-
trolled by surrounding muscles. The same principle is used
in wind instruments like the bassoon, where sound is produced via two pieces of reed that vibrate against each other.
In birds, a delicate bar of cartilage called the pessulus modu-
lates the sound. However, other parts of the anatomy also
contribute: the whooper swan has a particularly long wind-
pipe, or trachea, which runs down its elongated neck and
coils around its breastbone. This gives its voice extra depth
and power.

To me, the sound is filled with joy, vigour and life.
Nowhere is it captured more affirmatively than in the finale
to Sibelius's Fifth Symphony. The first three movements are

anxious and wandering: molten themes seem to emerge and develop organically through repetition rather than the workings of conventional musical form.

But in the final sections these fragments resolve into an emphatically resonant, swaying 'swan theme', carried high on the sonorous voice of the horns. Above it floats a glorious long line of major-key melody in the strings. The moment is one of musical and spiritual epiphany, and it was directly inspired by the sight, and above all the sound, of flying swans. In his diary Sibelius reverently wrote:

Today at ten to eleven I saw 16 swans. One of the greatest experiences of my life! Lord God, how beautiful! They circled for a long time well above me. Then disappeared into the haze of the sun as a silver ribbon, which flashed now and then. The sounds are of the same woodwind type as the cranes, but without tremolo. The swans are closer to the trumpet, though with a clear sarrusophone timbre. A low ambient refrain, reminiscent of the crying of a small child. Nature mysticism and the pain of life! The fifth symphony's final theme [Sibelius here breaks off to sketch out the notes of the musical idea] legato in the trumpets!! Dear God! The mystery of nature and romance and God knows what! – That this should happen to me, who has been an outsider for so long. So I've been in the sanctuary today, 21st April 1915.

All too easily seen as a season of mists and mellow fruitfulness, autumn is often written off as a final burst of colourful activity before the year fades into the monochrome and silence of winter. But the noise of migrating swans and geese filling our skies reminds us that it can also be a time of sonorous arrivals and bustling new beginnings.

KIERA CHAPMAN

8–12 OCTOBER

Owls Duet

I can tell you the exact moment I became obsessed with owls. I was seven, and was lying in the grass of an orchard, under an apple tree that was wracked with the cracks and crevices of age. As I stared up into its branches I suddenly became aware that a pair of polished onyx eyes were peering back at me. I was looking straight up at a young tawny owl.

We stared at one another, one of those odd moments of inter-species exchange in which our human reckoning of time stops. The owl seemed as curious about me as I was about it. Then the spell was broken; it blinked, turned its head through an impossible number of degrees, and went back to sleep.

Thereafter I produced endless very bad owl drawings, read every book I could order about them from the local library, and collected hundreds of ornaments from charity shops (many of them truly hideous) to transform my bed-room into an Owl Shrine.

The owl duets that characterise our nocturnal soundscape at this time of year are from male and female tawny owls, *Strix aluco*. If you want to hear one, then a warmish, clear, still, moonlit night in a non-urban area with broadleaved wood-land offers ideal conditions. You're most likely to hear them directly after sunset, as they tend to become quieter later in the evening.

Autumn is not the primary courtship period for tawnies. That happens in early spring, when males call and feed females to demonstrate their worthiness to mate. Females respond with soliciting vocalisations, reminding males of their duties. Once eggs hatch, males tend to quieten down, though the female starts to make soft nasal 'feeding calls' to her mate, and also gives brief hoots in response to deliveries of food. Any potential threat near the nest is also greeted with raucous calls of alarm, to distract the predator and cry for help. The autumn calling period starts in September, well after the young have left the nest, and is all about both males and females establishing and advertising territory. The owls then quieten down over winter, becoming more vocal again as the spring breeding season approaches.

If you hear the classic 'Twit-Twoo-o-oooo' of owls, beloved of television sound engineers who wish to suggest a slightly spooky nocturnal atmosphere, you're probably listening to two birds duetting. Conventional wisdom is that the 'Twit', perhaps better rendered as 'Ku-Wick', is the female's solicit-ing call and the 'Twit-Twoo-o-oooo' is the male's hooting response. However, according to The Sound Approach, a collective of ornithologist sound engineers who have made a special study of owl calls, males can also produce a solicit-ing call, at a lower pitch than females, and both sexes can produce the compound hoot. It's often still possible to tell males and females apart, however: female hoots tend to be higher-pitched with two separate notes in the middle, whereas males tend to have just a single middle note.

The tawny owl's hoot is often associated with melancholy and foreboding, but it becomes something deeper in Edward Thomas's 1915 poem 'The Owl', written when the poet was hesitating about whether to enlist to fight in the First World War. Finding refuge at an inn, the poem's narrator tries to bar out the night, but cannot avoid hearing the cry of an owl, which becomes both a vocalisation of his unspoken individual feelings of guilt and a mouthpiece for a collective and precarious humanity that otherwise lacks a voice:

> Shaken out long and clear upon the hill,
> No merry note, nor cause of merriment,
> But one telling me plain what I escaped
> And others could not, that night, as in I went.
>
> And salted was my food, and my repose,
> Salted and sobered, too, by the bird's voice
> Speaking for all who lay under the stars,
> Soldiers and poor, unable to rejoice.

Thomas enlisted shortly after writing the poem and was killed in action in 1917.

While we hear a sense of guilt or melancholy in the sound, owls themselves hear a great deal of information about the caller. In fact, if you unburden yourself of your cultural associations and listen afresh, even your human ears may well be able to distinguish between individual birds. The call tells owls the size, weight, health (parasite load) and level of aggression of the caller. That information conveys, by proxy, something about the bird's ability to keep hold of its territory in the face of rivals and its fitness as a mate. Males with the highest level of testosterone call more often and for longer, and are often experienced parents with high-quality territories.

Owls probably duet to help each other establish and defend the breeding territory in the autumn. The two voices together signal to other birds that the area is defended by a pair who are co-operating well.

Calling can also be an aggressive response to intruders, particularly in the breeding season. In such cases, you might expect that the intruder would be seen off most vigorously by the owl of the same sex in the established pair. Males, in this theory, would be more threatened by a male intruder, who might displace them, than by a female intruder, who might be a fitter mate. Research conducted during the breeding season suggests that this is broadly true of tawnies. However, there is evidence that male birds who have already bred successfully with their partner in previous seasons also chase off strange females. The success or failure of a tawny owl nest is strongly related to the experience and body weight of the female, so it may be that these males are protecting an investment they have made in courtship feeding early in the year.

However, as we discovered in our microseason at the start of the year, 'Birdsong Builds', bird vocalisations are not just the product of an individual 'caller'. They are three-dimensional spatial events. In dense forest cover, higher, shorter notes are absorbed and reflected by intervening foliage and branches, while lower notes travel much more effectively. Owls respond to this vocally: in open habitats they have higher hoots, and in woodland cover they tend to call at a lower pitch.

When we hear this cry, then, we are hearing not just the owl but a whole place, with innumerable intervening twigs, leaves, roofs and rocks. The pulse of sound is like a sonic search-light, and in its beam we hear the nocturne of the forest.

KIERA CHAPMAN

13–17 OCTOBER

Chestnuts Glisten

Sweet chestnuts are one of autumn's treasures. As falling temperatures and shortening days trigger leaf drop, chestnut trees cover the ground with a thick carpet of large, orange leaves that rustle and crackle underfoot. And scattered among these leaves are chestnuts, some lying exposed, their skins bright and alluring, asking to be touched. Others remain huddled in their spiny cases, jostling with their siblings for a chance to burst out into the light.

Can anyone resist picking up newly fallen chestnuts? The skins shine like highly polished veneer, a glowing mix of auburn, henna, mahogany, amber, tawny . . . no single word catches the depth and range of browns that make up the colour of a ripe chestnut. The sight of them spread out at our feet, beautiful and tempting, awakens some primitive instinct within us, the desire to gather in food, to put by nourishment for the coming cold weather. And their appearance, as the days darken and the skies fill with cloud, brings with it welcome hints of warmth and celebration – cosy winter fires and popping chestnut skins, perhaps the smoky smell of chestnut roasters in city streets, or turkey stuffing and bowls of Brussels sprouts . . . Indeed, for many of us the arrival of chestnuts in the shops is a foretaste of Christmas.

The association between chestnuts and Christmas may be ancient, but it was undoubtedly fostered by the writing of Charles Dickens, who had a perceptive eye for detail. He deliberately used the seasonality of chestnuts to help to create his image of a 'traditional Christmas':

> There is probably a smell of roasted chestnuts and other good comfortable things all the time, for we are telling Winter Stories [. . .] round the Christmas fire; and we have never stirred, except to draw a little nearer to it.

In his much-loved novella *A Christmas Carol* he brought chestnuts to the forefront of what counted as 'festive fare' in his depiction of 'Christmas Present', where his anti-hero, Ebeneezer Scrooge, was shown an idealised view of seasonal feasting and jollity:

> The poulterers' shops were still half-open, and the fruiterers' were radiant in their glory. There were great, round, pot-bellied baskets of chestnuts, shaped like the waistcoats of jolly old gentlemen, lolling at the doors, and tumbling out into the street in their apoplectic opulence.

Later on, in the joyful celebrations of Bob Cratchit and his family, a 'shovel-full of chestnuts' is put on the fire and they sputter and crackle noisily as Bob declares: 'A Merry Christmas to us all, my dears. God bless us!' This is one of the most memorable Christmas scenes in literature, but underneath the jollity it is also an acute observation of a society in which chestnuts are not just a symbol of festive warmth and good cheer but an unmistakable marker of social class. In Dickens's time chestnuts were primarily a food of the poor, and their appearance in the Cratchits' home would have immediately signalled their domestic penury to more affluent readers.

In fact, the chestnut has had a complicated place in the British diet. Over the centuries, it has consistently failed to be elevated to a desirable, or even staple, ingredient and has remained resolutely a food of last resort. Several bad harvests in the 1590s led the Elizabethan writer and inventor Hugh Platt to commend their consumption to the poor as a response to famine, and they appeared occasionally in recipes for meat-stuffing or in pie fillings and hashes in the years following. In 1612, the intriguingly named royal surveyor Rooke Church noted that:

> There is also a fifth kind of timber tree, of which few grow in England, and which is little inferior to any [of] the rest, and that is the chestnut tree, which beareth good fruit, that poor people in time of dearth may with a small quantity of oats or barley make bread of.

He was, rightly, rather more enthusiastic about the trees as a source of useful wood. A few years later, in 1631, the geographer and writer Daniel Widdowes made a similarly ambivalent case for the chestnut, stating that they are 'hard to digest, and beget lice: but good if roasted and eaten with salt, pepper, and sugar'. He added that 'the powder of dry chestnuts voydeth urine'. It was hardly a compelling recommendation.

There have, however, been a few attempts to elevate its place on the table. In 1670 in *The Queen-like Closet*, the cookery writer Hannah Woolley was using them with oysters, butter and claret to stuff chicken or to make a sauce for roast mutton. And, in Dickens's own time, the chestnut was sometimes raised to the height of Victorian splendour in the form of Nesselrode Pudding, with its mix of chestnuts, cream, rum and dried fruit, or as a 'chestnut cream' or as a glacéed fruit or *marrons glacés*. Such desserts were descendants of an eighteenth-century French fashion for chestnuts, nurtured by the pharmacist and agronomist Antoine-Augustin Parmentier. Parmentier successfully promoted the use of potatoes as a human rather than animal food, and this led him to investigate the production of flour and sugar from chestnuts. His efforts, however, failed to impress the Emperor Napoleon, who offered his support instead to the development and use of sugar beet.

Napoleon was undoubtedly right. In a world hungry for sugar, the chestnut was neither the best nor the most reliable source for its manufacture. Chestnuts like warm climes and are slow to fruit. As a Corsican, Napoleon would have been familiar with them on his native island, where the Mediterranean climate suits their pernickety requirements. Disliking damp or limey soils, they grow best in the mountainous regions of France, Italy and the Iberian peninsula, offering a useful source of nutrition in regions where other staples including rice, corn and wheat will not thrive. So while the chestnut has enabled communities to survive in places that would otherwise have been impossible, this has solidified its reputation as peasant food. And the difficulty of using chestnut flour, which lacks both gluten and protein, has meant that its popularity has remained very limited, even to the present day.

And yet, if the chestnut does not play a starring role in the culinary culture of Britain, it nevertheless retains its seasonal symbolism. So, as the days darken and the skies fill with clouds, the sight of chestnuts lying among fallen leaves is something to savour, a foretaste of the midwinter pleasures of warmth and celebration.

REBECCA WARREN

18–22 OCTOBER

Acorn-caching, Forest-planting Jays

I don't remember ever seeing as many acorns as I did in the autumn of 2020. Once every five to ten years, in response to cues that we don't yet understand, oak trees synchronise to produce a bumper crop of nuts, the 'mast year' mentioned in our microseason on beech (28 September–2 October). So plentiful were they that the ancient oak woodland near my home had a thick, crunchy russet carpet for several weeks. These were fat days for the local wildlife; not even the greediest grey squirrel could gobble them all up.

However, the following autumn, when our poll took place, the oaks had a far leaner year, producing only a few acorns. With this sudden dip in their food the jays in my area seemed to change character. Usually shy woodland birds, they began to venture into domestic gardens, fighting the resident magpies and crows for a replacement food: peanuts. Perhaps this atypical visibility was one of the reasons they were nominated in our poll.

Jays are ecosystem engineers. From September onwards they collect thousands of food items for the winter, with acorns a particular favourite. They prefer larger nuts, and can carry five of them at a time: four in an adapted gullet in their throats and one in their beaks. This precious cargo is then cached, often by burying it in the ground in open areas with loose soil where the food will be safe from mice.

These birds have great spatial memory: they probably use landmarks like bushes and rocks to remember where their caches are located, and will return year-round to grab a snack. Nevertheless some of the acorns go uneaten, meaning that the jays have effectively planted them. Assisted by the fact that there is a dip in the adult jay's consumption of acorns from April to August, these neglected acorns will produce a crop of fresh oak seedlings to regenerate the forest the next spring.

But, like the squirrels we met in August, jays also have a sneaky side. They can use both sound and vision to observe and remember the location of caches made by other birds, which they then steal. The more dominant the bird in the social hierarchy, the more aggressive its thieving. To try to avoid this, subordinate birds cache in more secretive locations, using crevices in walls rather than exposed ground to avoid being observed. Socially dominant birds, by contrast, store more food in the ground but move their cache more frequently, perhaps in an effort to confuse any watching subordinates.

Some experiments suggest that jays understand when they are being watched. In one piece of research, they cached food in out-of-sight places when they knew another bird was looking, but were far less discreet when they thought that they were unobserved. What is more, they appear to understand that noise can give them away. Researchers found that birds avoided caching nuts in a loud, crunchy-sounding gravelly substrate when they knew another jay could hear but not see them.

More contentiously still, some scientists think that jays may have a degree of insight into the mental state of their fellow birds. A team of researchers at the groundbreaking lab of psychologist Nicola Clayton at the University of Cambridge tested this by focusing on a specific behaviour: the fact that male jays feed females during courtship.

The team began by separating bonded male and female pairs. Some females were fed exclusively on wax moth larvae; others were given only mealworms; while a third group was fed a mixed diet. The idea was to induce a state of boredom with one kind of food in the females of the first two groups. While this happened, the male jays watched what their partners ate.

Males with satiated partners were then offered a choice: they could feed their partner either wax moth larvae or mealworms. Males who had watched their partner being fed just one kind of thing tended to select the opposite food. However, when the experiment was repeated without the males being able to see what the females had eaten, they chose food randomly.

According to the researchers, this shows that jays can attribute a 'desire state' to their partner. The males appear to have reasoned from observation that their partners were bored of eating the same food. However, this idea remains controversial: others argue that male jays might just be picking up on behavioural cues that are invisible to human observers.

If you're walking in woodland, you may well hear the raucous wheeze of a jay before you see it. However, you may also hear a jay making more unusual sounds. These birds are notoriously good mimics of other species, able to do a startlingly accurate impression of a whole range of noises.

In his essay on animal intelligence, Plutarch tells the story of a barber in Rome who trained a jay to reproduce not only animal cries but human speech. When a wealthy man was buried in the neighbourhood, to the fanfare of many trumpets, the jay fell completely silent, and stopped asking her keeper for food or water. Passers-by wondered if she had been deafened by the music, or even poisoned by a jealous rival bird trainer.

However, the jay was actually refitting her voice to imitate trumpets, and soon burst forth into a perfect imitation of the instrument, to the wonder of onlooking crowds. For Plutarch, the story offers an example of a non-human creature using self-discipline in a way that implies a rational and self-directed will to learn. Though this interpretation is dubious, the jay's modern Latin name nonetheless reflects both its vocal abilities and its favourite food: *Garrulus glandarius*, the chatterbox lover of acorns.

KIERA CHAPMAN

Wind Swirls Through Fallen Leaves

The leaves are turning – from green to red or orange. Noticing the fire and beauty of this spectacular autumnal colour show is one of the first ways in which we sense the changing seasons as children, suddenly aware of the palette of our world, as well as new shapes and textures at our feet. As soups and slippers replace salads and sandals, the surest sign that winter is near are the drifts of fallen leaves carpeting parks, streets, fields and gardens. Stomping through these piles of leaves on a cold, sunny autumn morning is one of life's great joys, and a compensation for the loss of colour to come.

The garden writer and poet Vita Sackville-West's family loved leaf-stomping so much that they developed the phrase 'through leaves' to describe similar everyday sensuous pleasures. In a 1950 BBC broadcast she explained what the phrase meant:

> the small but intense pleasure of walking through dry leaves and kicking them up as you go. They rustle; they brustle; they crackle – and if you can crush some beech nuts underfoot at the same time then so much the better. But beech nuts aren't essential. The essential is that you should tramp through very dry, very crisp brown leaves.

She illustrates this with a list of similar satisfying sensory delights, like cracking the thin layer of ice on a puddle, running a stick along iron railings, drawing curtains that glide smoothly on their rods and pulling a cork with a corkscrew. As autumn deepens, perhaps we could all take some time outside to find our own version of this 'top-note through leavery'.

Vita Sackville-West stipulated brown leaves for her 'through leavery', presumably because they are the driest and crunchiest. But have you ever wondered why leaves change colour? There is some debate over exactly why, with suggestions that it is to do with preventing light or insect damage, and that it helps the tree conserve energy over winter. The answer most likely lies in both hormonal and seasonal changes. Leaves contain four colours that come from three groups of pigments: green (chlorophylls), red (anthocyanins and carotenoids), yellow (flavonoids and carotenoids, including a sub-group called xanthophylls) and orange (carotenoids). During spring and summer the dominant chlorophyll turns water and carbon dioxide from the air into starch and sugars that feed the tree. This amazing process of making food from sunlight is known as photosynthesis. The green leaves send essential nutrients along the branches to be used and stored by the tree.

As the days shorten and temperatures drop, chlorophyll production slows and eventually stops entirely. The carotenoid and xanthophyll pigments become more visible and the leaves begin to make anthocyanins, giving them their beautiful autumn hues. As autumn approaches their exact colour depends on the weather – warm, sunny days with cool nights boost anthocyanin concentration, which gives the leaves a redder tone, while those leaves containing more carotenoids will tend to be more orangey. Early frosts can inhibit anthocyanin production and result in less vibrant reds, but daylight has the greatest impact on changing leaf colours.

There are some days when you notice the leaves beneath your feet, and others when you are caught up in their dance with the wind as they fall. What makes them fall? Evergreen trees don't lose their leaves in one go – which gives the impression that they don't lose them at all. In fact, they replace old leaves continuously and retain them throughout winter thanks to inbuilt antifreeze fluid and a special wax coating that protects their foliage from frosts. But deciduous trees shed their leaves each year in the blazingly beautiful process of abscission, or leaf fall, that begins with the colour changes we start to notice in early autumn. The change in colour signals the imminent end of the leaf's life on the tree. By the close of autumn most branches will be bare and the leaves will have floated to the ground. Some leaf-shedding is the result of strong winds, but the majority of fallen leaves haven't exactly *fallen*. They have been dropped.

So how does leaf drop work? It appears to be a genetically programmed process, but weather patterns and temperatures also play a part in a leaf's final days. As the season turns, levels of the hormone auxin decrease. Auxin is what helps fruit and leaves stay attached to their stems, and when levels begin to fall it triggers the start of abscission. The veins carrying fluids inside the leaf slowly close, causing a build-up of anthocyanins. A specialised layer of cells called the abscission zone develops where the leaf stem meets the branch. To safeguard against infection or branch damage a layer of cork cells forms, sealing off the leaf from the tree, and cells on the leaf side of this are degraded, which eventually pushes the leaf away from the stem. The tree is essentially creating a deliberate fracture line which eventually causes the leaf to fall off.

The leaf falls to the ground, often assisted by the wind. The tree is now dormant but very much alive, just biding its time for the coming spring. Over winter it sends some of its energy down to its roots, which keep growing alongside the mycorrhizal fungi, and the bare branches still provide shelter for many beings. Next spring, as the sap rises and takes nutrients up to the branches, the leaf buds we noticed in February will begin to emerge and the cycle continues.

In times of drought trees may start to drop leaves in an attempt to save essential energy and survive. They may also respond to pathogens or parasites by abscising. But abscission is not confined to trees. It occurs in animals that shed body parts in response to a threat, and in fungi releasing spores too.

Leaf fall is a cleverly evolved survival mechanism. The severance and shedding provides protection. Perhaps we can learn from this example of getting rid of what we no longer need in order to free up essential energy, bringing a deeper meaning to our 'through leavery' this jewel-toned autumnal microseason.

LULAH ELLENDER

NOVEMBER

Noticing Exercise

Using our memories can alert us to how much we fail to notice in the world around us. This month try closing your eyes and thinking of a tree, one that you see every day. Imagine how you would draw it. What is its size, its colour, its shape and its texture?

Then go outside and really look at this tree, noting the ways it surprises you and the things you missed. Imagine how you would draw it now.

28 OCTOBER–1 NOVEMBER

Reddening Dogwood

Sometimes noticing is about the things we *don't* notice. Like those plants in supermarket car parks, motorway service station slip roads or corporate landscaping schemes. These plants make up the horticultural equivalent of elevator music. Yet they all bring something to the world, whether it's a bounty of nectar for pollinators, shelter for small creatures or a blaze of colour in the midst of winter, like the dogwood.

Although it has pretty white flowers in spring and berries beloved of birds in autumn, the dogwood often becomes part of the background, part of the unremarkable planting we overlook simply because it's always there. Until winter, when it really comes to life and seems to catch fire. Some of the cultivated varieties are green and yellow but the best-known are the red dogwoods, whose stems glow ruby-bright among all the greys and browns of this season, creating a sweep of molten colour right through until spring returns. For this microseason we are celebrating the seasonal firecracker that for much of the year goes overlooked but commands attention right now.

Dogwood is part of the *Cornaceae* family, which contains thirty to sixty species. Common dogwood, *Cornus sanguinea*, displays its vivid crimson branches from late October to March. It likes damp hedgerows and woodlands, and its name comes from a traditional use for the stems, which were employed by butchers as skewers for meat. These skewers were known as 'dags' or 'dogs'. The second part of its Latin name, *sanguinea*, means 'bloody' and reflects its red colour.

As well as being a butcher's implement, dogwood has been used around the world for thousands of years, thanks to its hardness and durability. Native Americans made arrow shafts from their species of dogwood and also used the stems as fire drills and for basket-making. Remember the ice man found with sloes in his possessions from our Blackthorn Spring microseason (15–19 April)? He had dogwood arrows in a quiver, which shows that this plant has been a useful tool for humans at least as far back as 5,300 years ago.

Dogwood is also thought to have been used in the creation of crucifixes, and there is a story that links it with the cross on which Jesus Christ was crucified. In response to his Son's death God was said to have cursed the tree so it could never grow large enough to be used for such torture again. He is also said to have created reminders of Jesus's death within the fabric of the tree, from the four-petalled flowers set out like a cross and with nail-like indentations to the bloody hue of the wood. There is a proliferation of supposed relics of the 'true cross', but none appear to be dogwood. And, in fact, it is more likely that Roman crucifixes at that time would have been made from local oaks.

In addition to making use of the dogwood branches' strength, people have also made medicines from parts of the plant. The bark has similar properties to quinine and was used to treat malaria, fever and babesiois, a rare tick-borne disease also known as redwater fever. The leaves were made into poultices to heal wounds, and people chewed the stems to clean their teeth. Despite having high concentrations of vitamin C the berries have an unappealing taste.

What do you think of when you think about the colour red? Blood, lipstick, fire, love, danger, anger, cherries, passion, roses maybe. Probably not trees. We normally expect trees to have green leaves and brown or grey bark. So why does dogwood have red bark? The answer lies in those anthocyanins we talked about when looking at why leaves change colour in the previous microseason.

A similar process occurs in dogwood stems during the winter. But to understand this we need to dive a little deeper into the structures of bark. Made up of layers of tissue and straw-like pipes, bark's function is to insulate and protect the tree from cold, wind, sunlight, pathogens and pests. Bark is often described as having four layers: a cork outer layer (or phellen); the cork cambium (or phellogen), where cork cells are produced; the phelloderm; and the phloem, where fluids containing sugars are transported from the leaves. Then there are layers that are not bark but a part of the cross section of a tree: the vascular cambium below the bark that makes xylem and phloem; and the secondary xylem, or sapwood. Both xylem and phloem are found in the rings by which we can measure the tree's age, and contribute to the tree's growth in girth.

Now to the colours that make this tree such a fiery feature in these colder months. The cells in the inner layers contain green chlorophyll and can actually photosynthesise, just like leaves, thanks to food-producing organelles called chloroplasts. Despite what we might expect, tiny bits of light penetrate bark through minute pores and fissures. These holes possibly aerate the wood and are essential for the gas exchange needed for photosynthesis, but we do not know for sure why bark can also photosynthesise (as well as the branches and stems). One explanation is that it gives a tree another energy source after leaf fall. The chloroplasts are vulnerable to too much light and can't photosynthesise well, which is where those anthocyanins step in. They create a kind of sunscreen to ensure photosynthesis can happen efficiently. Anthocyanins are red pigments which reflect red and blue wavelengths, giving the tree its distinctive ruby tones.

Bark with a high tannin content tends to be red-brown, but the dogwood can also have orange, yellow or lime-green stems; this will be governed by the levels of chlorophyll and anthocyanins inside the bark. So, although less compelling perhaps than the idea that it is an accursed plant reminding us of Jesus's death, the explanation for the dogwood's ruby tones is down to chemistry. And it is a brilliant example of the complexities and miracles going on all around us, if we only take the time to stop and look.

LULAH ELLENDER

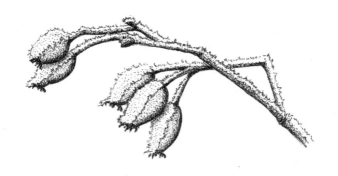

2–6 NOVEMBER

First Frosts

Crunching across stiff grass. Fingers tracing fractals on window panes. The light dancing off whitened ground. Boots tapping on icy puddles. Clouds of freezing breath exhaled into early-morning air. It is easy to be bedazzled by frost. The sunlight is more luminous, the world seems to sparkle. Yet frost can be damaging and dangerous, resulting in iron-hard earth, stone-like water and wilting plants. Frost bites.

No wonder, then, that frost has captured our collective imagination in those parts of the world that experience seasonal chills. The character of Jack Frost personifies the dynamism and trickiness of a phenomenon that seems to come from nowhere, blanketing the world in a dusting of ice and then retreating once more. Jack Frost has appeared in literature and film in various forms around the world: a mischievous spirit who takes people by the nose, a gnome, a powerful general, the malevolent nose-nipper in Nat King Cole's 'The Christmas Song'. In Slavic countries their equivalent, Moroz, or Grandfather Frost, is a more benevolent, Santa Claus-like persona who also brought gifts to children, accompanied by his granddaughter, Snow Maiden. Moroz was a pagan construct, a divine character linking the earthly and eternal worlds, associated with death, resurrection and the cooling of passions. He was caught up in the tension between Christian Orthodoxy and traditional paganism but his image persists today.

Since their publication in the 1950s, C. S. Lewis's *Chronicles of Narnia*, tales of a frozen land ruled over by a white witch, have enchanted and terrified children. And then there is the mega-blockbuster film *Frozen*, which retells Hans Christian Anderson's story *The Snow Queen*. The film is about unpredictable power, and the ways in which love can help us control and live productively with that power – in this case, to freeze. Its success was not purely due to great animation and belting songs. It tapped into something elemental about cold and ice, something capricious, potentially destructive yet simultaneously alluring.

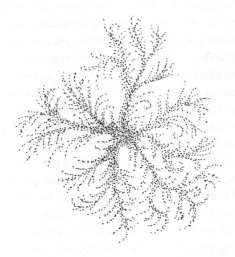

We experience frost when temperatures drop below 0°C, and it is also characterised by a thin layer of ice on the ground. These two features can be harmful for tender plants and animals not equipped to survive plummeting temperatures.

Many creatures go into hibernation in order to get through winter, and hardy plants have adaptations like antifreeze fluids or, as with the seemingly delicate crocus, a waxy cuticle that protects their leaves and flowers to ensure they can endure even heavy snow.

This is one of the microseasons that perhaps best illustrates our regional differences, with northern Britain experiencing colder temperatures earlier than the south. While we see variations according to where we are in the country, the first autumn frosts in general are starting later year on year as a result of climate change. We explored the impact of late-spring frosts on plants in our chapter on leaf buds, and now we can see that there are changes happening on both sides of winter. The growing season is effectively stretching, with later first frosts and shorter winters. Data collected by the Central England Temperature record project shows that between 1861 and 1890 the growing season averaged 244 days; between 2006 and 2015 it averaged 280 days. We have had six of the ten longest recorded growing seasons in the last thirty years. These shorter winters dupe plants into putting on their spring growth too early, making them vulnerable to snap frosts once their shoots and leaves are emerging.

These changes can also enable invasive species to take hold as they are not killed off by cold weather. And they have a huge impact on the interdependent relationship between pollinators and plants. As phenology (the seasonal timing of cyclical biological events) is disrupted by climate change we will see declines in pollinators whose life cycles do not fit with the plants they need for food, breeding or shelter. This will have ripples across ecosystems. Late-autumn frosts can be a matter of life or death.

So what are prime frost conditions? We mostly see frosts when there is a period of high pressure that creates clear skies and light winds. With no clouds to trap the thermal radiation emitted from the soil, heat escapes and the soil cools further, causing water droplets on the surface to freeze. Soil that is rain-damp is more prone to frost, and as the nights get longer we see greater radiational cooling (the rapid drop in temperatures resulting from clear skies and calm weather). Different topography and terrain affect frosts too. Cold water within rocks freezes and causes cracks. The cells carrying nutrients inside many plants freeze and expand, cutting off the supply of energy and killing the plant. Leaves may become scorched. Animals without sufficient body fat, shelter, food or hibernatory habits may die. Birds and insects can't find water.

But frost is not all bad. It makes certain types of berries, like rose hips and sloes, more palatable. Some plants actually require frosts and cold temperatures in order to awaken their seeds from dormancy. This is known as cold stratification and involves regular exposure to below-zero temperatures to break down the outer layer of the seed's shell before it can germinate. So we see the duality of frost – it can be deadly, and also essential. It preserves and provokes into life. Sometimes it can provide a source of entertainment, as with the famous Frost Fairs in London, which took place on the frozen River Thames from 1608 to 1814. During this period the Thames completely froze over twenty-four times and stayed frozen for several weeks. This was due to the river being shallower and wider, and thus more likely to freeze in the harsh winters of the 'Little Ice Age'. After 1814 the old London Bridge, which used to contribute to the freezes by slowing down the water, was widened and the river was dredged. There is probably never going to be a time when it freezes again, so we have to imagine the scenes of the Frost Fairs: stalls selling hot food, shouts from gambling booths, the awful noise of bear-baiting, people playing nine-pin bowls, royalty promenading and children laughing at puppet shows.

All against the glorious white of a frozen ribbon of water and a city blanketed in snow.

Frost Fairs may be consigned to history, but we can still have some easy fun with frost. On a clear, still winter's evening, fill a jam jar lid or saucer with water then add any interesting berries, leaves or feathers you can find nearby. Place a piece of string so one end is in the water, then leave it outside overnight. In the morning, carefully prise it out of the container and you should have a beautiful ice sculpture which you can hang outdoors until the thaw comes.

LULAH ELLENDER

Fog, Drizzle and Mist

Fog and drizzle sit upon a spectrum; between them lies mist. All three forms of murky dampness are the effect of condensed water droplets hanging in the air, and all reduce our ability to see the world around us with clarity. On November days the sky frequently falls upon us and we find ourselves oozing through clouds, our clothes and hair damp and dewy to the touch. In this particularly autumnal spectre the world is made gloriously sibylline, and we can let our imaginations go into overdrive as we attempt to auger the blurry shapes coming towards us in the near distance.

The atmospheric conditions of this time of year are deeply entwined with our images of modern English cities, most notably London, thanks largely to the way they've been depicted in Victorian novels. From Oscar Wilde and Charles Dickens to Robert Louis Stevenson and Arthur Conan Doyle, nineteenth-century writers were instrumental in transforming a weather event into an affective atmosphere. These writers used the visual imperceptibility and material mois-ture of drizzle, mist and fog as a symbol of society's ability to obscure truth in the face of evidence.

This is realised perhaps most elegantly in Oscar Wilde's 1891 novel *The Picture of Dorian Gray*, in which two aspects of one human are monstrously separated through the dis-connection between their social image and their true self. (A similar theme is explored in Stevenson's similarly foggy *The Strange Case of Dr Jekyll and Mr Hyde*.) In the opening to Wilde's novel, the handsome young anti-hero Dorian Gray has his portrait painted by the sensitive and deeply moral artist Basil Hallward, which brings him into the orbit of aris-tocratic society. Enthralled by the hedonism and vanity of this world, Gray wishes that his portrait would age and fade while his body remains young and beautiful. He has his wish granted, but the fulfilment of this desire for eternal youth has abhorrent repercussions.

Towards the end of the novel, when Dorian has thrown himself into an increasingly louche and dubious lifestyle, the painter Hallward perceives his former subject through the mist of a November evening and insists on a social call. In the two short pages that follow there are four mentions of fog, through which lamplight struggles and threatens to obscure Gray to the last person who saw him as whole. Gray bids Hallward: 'Come in, or the fog will get into the house. And mind you don't talk about anything serious. Nothing is serious nowadays. At least nothing should be.' Things do not end well for either Hallward or Gray as the desire to remain under the cloak of fog intensifies violently.

While fog was used by novelists as an atmospheric and allegorical tool to stage drama, it was also a daily reality in the period. The Industrial Revolution, which had led to a consumer revolution – in which more and more of the same could be produced, and the old and worn-out could be replaced by the new and pristine – also produced thick smog.

This filthy smoke belched out from factory chimneys and the homes of the workers who staffed the production lines, and drifted across the newly crowded cities.

In the opening passages of Charles Dickens's 1853 novel *Bleak House* he describes the 'implacable November weather', in which smoke lowers 'down from chimney pots, making a soft black drizzle with flakes of soot as big as full-grown snowflakes – gone into mourning, one might imagine, for the death of the sun'. A combination of air pollution and damp weather conditions held the particles released from chimneys in suspension, creating a pea soup of smothering smog.

Even before the Industrial Revolution and its sprawl of modern cities, fog had associations with evil and obscuration. Fog and mist and drizzle played a role in Elizabethan theatre, where they added texture and nuance to the binary of light and darkness and were associated with deception and confusion. Characters in the plays of Shakespeare, for example, are often blindsided by these atmospheric conditions, both metaphorically and literally. This occurs perhaps most famously in the last lines of scene one in *Macbeth*:

> Fair is foul, and foul is fair,
> Hover through the fog and filthy air.

These words are uttered by the three witches, who speak throughout in ambiguous language; their words indicate a moral confusion at the centre of the play's world and imply that nothing is quite what it seems.

The use of fog to indicate duplicity and uncertainty in the human realm is perhaps no surprise, as it blurs our understanding of the very order of the world. Speaking meteorologically, fog is a very low layer of cloud that often falls so that it touches the ground; the heavens that usually crown us come to lie at our feet.

*

But what causes these low-slung, creeping clouds? They are made up of tiny water droplets, light enough to hang suspended in the air. These droplets form when the temperature of the air dips below the 'dewpoint' – the temperature at which the moisture capacity of the air is reduced and airborne water condenses into liquid, saturating the air with water vapour.

During November the conditions are perfect for this process of condensation: the nights are lengthening, the temperatures are falling and the air is moist. The ground still retains some of the warmth of the summer sun, and the heat that it radiates is rapidly cooled by the frigid air; liquid water begins to condense on the surface of things, such as blades of grass and particles of dust in the atmosphere. Light reflects off the airborne droplets in all directions, forming the whitish haze that we associate with fog, drizzle and mist. On days when the sun is strong it heats up the air after dawn, increasing its capacity to hold moisture, and the air clears. As autumn gives way to winter, the sun's rays grow weaker and the moisture in the air is no longer 'burned off' with the coming of day.

While fog, drizzle and mist obscure our normal view, they also make the invisible content of the world around us suddenly manifest. Particles of dust, that material expression of lived history, are enveloped in water and literally cloud our vision. As the ocular sense upon which we so rely to navigate the world is compromised by these weather conditions, the familiar is made strange. We focus more carefully on the things close by, looking for clues as to what is ahead or beyond. As we walk on earthbound clouds this microseason, what smells and sounds might we notice that usually fly below our perceptual radar?

ROWAN JAINES

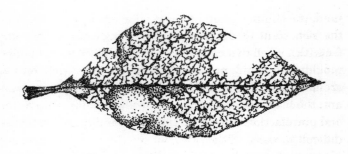

12–16 NOVEMBER

The Smell of Decaying Leaves

By mid-November, many deciduous trees have shed their leaves. Some have floated lazily down on calm, still days of weak sunshine to coat the ground in a light quilt of colour. Others have been torn from their branches by high winds, sudden gusts shaking down a rain of bronze, amber and gold on to the shoulders of passers-by. And now the fallen leaves lie in deep, rustling drifts. The season is changing and winter is eager to claim its own.

Within days these bright, brittle leaves will have begun that long, necessary journey back into the cycle of life, claimed once more by the soil that gave them birth. Rain and humidity will have stripped them of their individuality, and they will have become instead a soggy mass of nondescript organic matter. They will be returning to the earth; not leaving, but changing. Decay is, after all, a process of rebirth, a moving from one form to another; a renaissance.

Being in woodland is a balm for the soul, a therapy for the weary mind; even in early winter, there is joy to be had in the company of trees. In November, a walk through the forest is still a treat for the senses: the liquid sound of squelching mud, the shining green of ivy, vivid against grey bark, and the rich scent of decaying leaves turned over by passing feet. It's a smell that catches in the back of the nose, neither mouldy and foetid, nor acrid and harsh, just a rich, earthy aroma, damp and dark. Decomposition *can* smell unpleasant: the black silt of neglected, leaf-filled ponds reeks of rot and putrefaction, a product of decay without oxygen that is difficult to wash off the skin. But the smell of decomposing leaves on the woodland floor is different, a warm mix of soil, leaf and rain, a memory of life, not a message of death. But what is going on down there? What is happening to these once-bright leaves to turn them from windblown receivers of light to soil-bound givers of nutrients?

Leaf decay is a complex process of deconstruction carried out by an equally complex array of microorganisms, fungi, animals and physical processes. Perhaps the most important of the 'detritivores' are the fungi, which rapidly spread their minute hyphae over and into the fallen leaf matter, extracting the nutrients they need for growth and beginning the breakdown of organic material. Rain and frost accelerate the attack, rupturing connecting tissues and leaching their chemical compounds back into the soil. Bacteria, insects, molluscs and worms contribute further to the process, recycling the constituent parts of each leaf until it no longer exists as a distinct entity. Some leaves, of course, take longer to decompose than others, especially those with high levels of lignin, a polymer that is one of the building blocks of cell walls in plants. Lignin helps to reinforce the veins of leaves and is responsible for the delicate, ephemeral leaf skeletons we sometimes find lying on the ground like tiny stained-glass windows, retaining their tracery even though the coloured glass between has long gone. But even lignin breaks down, and eventually all leaves will succumb to the natural processes of rot. And as they do, they produce the characteristic smell of woodland in autumn.

Yet how does this process give off its distinctive scent? Leaves contain a complex association of sugars, starches and proteins. As they die at the end of the summer they release a cocktail of volatile organic compounds including terpene and isoprenoids. Some of these compounds are detectable by the human nose and produce that distinctive leafy smell. Once the leaves are on the ground and undergoing the actual processes of decay, more volatile compounds are released, filling the air with a light but distinct autumnal scent. It is the kind of smell that triggers memories, taking one back to a particular time or place. Perhaps it reminds you of playing in the garden? Building a bonfire for Guy Fawkes night? Walking in the woods with the dog, as it nosed and scuffled through the leaves? We all have our special moments, places in the memory to which we are instantly returned by a particular aroma.

The peculiarly vivid association between memory and smell is a well-known phenomenon, as we discussed in our chapter on the smell of cool woodlands in summer heat (17–22 July). It results from the unique relationship between the olfactory 'bulbs' in the brain that receive the compounds that create 'smell' and the hippocampus, where memory is effectively created and stored. Stimuli from other senses, such as taste or sound, travel first to a region in the brain called the thalamus for processing, before being passed on to the amygdala, where emotion is generated, and then on to the hippocampus. Odour, however, is sent directly to the amygdala and hippocampus, a virtually instantaneous action. The immediacy of this process and the close proximity of these two regions of the brain explain why the memories triggered by particular scents are especially vivid and evocative.

But, of course, for most people the smell of decaying leaves is not a doorway into a specific memory; it simply contributes to the sensory background of a place or an experience. It is the aromatic wallpaper to a walk in the forest, to foraging for conkers, or to raking up fallen leaves in the garden. The positive connection between mental wellbeing and exposure to nature is now well established, so perhaps, when we are out in the countryside or walking through the park, we should pay more attention to these background scents. Perhaps we could learn to navigate through our environments using our sense of smell as well as our eyes and ears? Perhaps we might be able to 'read' the landscape differently, knowing that the scent of decaying leaves might be as much a marker of time and place as a signpost, a landmark or a distinctive sound. We could even try to relish the complexity and richness of decay in the same way that we savour fresh coffee or a fine wine. After all, it's good for you, widely available and entirely free.

REBECCA WARREN

17–21 NOVEMBER

Chattering Starlings

A starling seems like a bird with two souls. One is singular, the other collective.

A starling murmuration has to be one of the grandest natural spectacles in the UK. A liquid swirl of birds in a twilight sky, like billowing smoke become animate, rippling and pulsing in an aerial ballet of contoured Henry Moore figures, sometimes shimmering and transcendent, sometimes ominously threatening. The unearthly sound of their wings overhead, like the sound of the distant sea.

But then, suddenly, without warning, the spell is broken. The starlings tornado down into the roosting reeds, a squabbling cacophony of earthy individuals, screeching obscenities at one another as they settle down to sleep. These are the chattering starlings familiar from our gardens, yet their noisy assertiveness seems a world away from the birds of the fluidly co-operative flight.

How can we reconcile the two sides of this bird?

The cause of murmurations is mysterious, though data suggests that both their size and duration increase when predators are nearby and engaged with the flock. If this is correct (and some do dispute it), it suggests that starlings build a swirling bird assemblage to confuse raptors, making it difficult for these predators to lock on to any individual bird. Safety in conspicuous, free-flowing numbers.

This explains those mesmerising variations in a murmuration's form. Recent research has studied the various shapes of these lines of collective flight, and related them to the predatory behaviour of peregrine falcons. When starlings are relaxed in a murmuration they are generally 'diluted', spatially spread out, which gives the flock a light-grey appearance. When a falcon is flying in the vicinity, or actively pursuing the flock – putting the birds on a level of medium alert – the most frequent responses are 'blackening', where starlings group together, darkening the appearance of the murmuration, and a 'wave event', when a darkened band pulses through the murmuration as a result of birds moving closer together in sequence. The latter is more likely to happen after medium-speed attacks.

When a peregrine attack comes at speed and from above, raising the level of alert to emergency, the flock can undergo 'flash expansion', when birds scatter radially away from a centre. Occasionally a murmuration will split to avoid the predator, and in some cases the two sections remain connected by a thin ribbon of birds, called a 'cordon'. In rare instances the flock develops a 'vacuole' or a hole in the middle.

How is all this co-ordinated? Starlings do not use a centralised system in which birds follow key individuals who have been picked out as 'leaders'. There's a good reason for that: the ability of the whole group to respond rapidly to a highly mobile threat, like a falcon, is limited if information has to be centralised before it is acted upon. A hierarchy in which certain birds are regarded as too unimportant to notice means that fast-moving predators can be missed.

But if the murmuration is decentralised, what is the relationship between individual birds and the collective flock? In the 1980s, the computer scientist Craig Reynolds was trying to build a model to simulate flocking behaviour. He called his project 'Boids', and started out from the assumption that collective movements like murmurations were the result of decisions made by individual birds following the same basic rules. Firstly, each bird would seek to avoid colliding with others. Secondly, every individual would try to match its speed and alignment to those of other birds. Thirdly, each starling would endeavour to move towards a central position compared to its nearby flockmates (this affects birds on the edge of the flock more than birds already in the middle of it).

The result of Reynolds's work was a computer simulation in which little triangles flew in a surprisingly lifelike formation. In fact, it was so realistic that it was used as the basis of early CGI animations of group behaviour, including a bat swarm and an army of marching penguins in Tim Burton's *Batman Returns* (1992). More deeply, the work suggested that a murmuration could be explained as a self-organising form that came down to surprisingly simple laws of individual behaviour.

More recent research has built on this idea, with scientists arguing that starlings orientate themselves in space by correlating their flight with other birds. In other words, each starling positions itself in relation to a number of immediate neighbours, possibly the nearest six or seven birds. Researchers have shown that this works even at different densities of birds, so the flock stays cohesive even when it is undergoing blackening, a wave event, or a flash expansion.

But there is still a problem: how does this interactive co-ordination in small parts of the flock propagate outwards to affect the entire murmuration, which can include hundreds of thousands of birds? Normally we would expect a correlation like this to decay with distance, so that an adjustment made by one bird is copied by its immediate neighbours but is gradually watered down as we look at birds further away. But what is visually striking about a murmuration is the fact that a change of direction by one little bird ripples out across the *entire* flock.

So how can one starling change the course of hundreds of thousands of others? Some scientists think the answer is that starling murmurations are exhibiting something called 'criticality'. To understand this difficult concept, it helps to think of an everyday example. We all know that the properties of water change with temperature and pressure: ice melts from solid to liquid, and when we put that liquid in a kettle and boil it we see water vapour, a gas. However, at very high temperatures and pressures, water starts to behave in very strange ways. It takes on the physical characteristics of both solids and liquids at the same time, and it loses some of its normal properties. This is water's 'critical point'.

Systems in this critical state are poised between order and disorder, with an unusual degree of connectivity between their parts. This means that they exist at a tipping point, when transitions from one state to another can happen very abruptly because changes get copied through the whole with great rapidity. Scientists who have studied murmurations from the perspective of statistical mechanics think that they are exhibiting the mathematical characteristics of a critical state. So, rather than a single starling's change of direction decaying as we move out from the individual bird's location, the murmuration exists in a state where the whole thing can suddenly switch.

If this is right, then it means that the trick of each starling correlating its movements with its nearest neighbours only works to co-ordinate the entire murmuration because the flock is *already* tuned to the biological equivalent of the critical point, ready to change direction in the blink of an eye. Effectively, the criticality of a starling murmuration means that information from any bird can be transmitted across the whole with incredible speed, and without loss.

The apparent split in starlings between their individual squabbling, chattering selves and their smooth collective murmuration may be altogether stranger than we realise. A single bird can lift the casual billow of the flock not through an act of leadership or will, but because the dance of the murmuration itself is primed to respond to such individual lines of flight.

KIERA CHAPMAN

22–26 NOVEMBER

Even the Light Grows Cold

Head colds, chest colds; cold toes; the cold shoulder, being left out in the cold, being cold-blooded, cold-hearted, as cold as ice; cold wars, cold sores, cold sweats, a trail gone cold; cold calls; cold readings, going cold turkey, getting cold feet, putting the thing on ice; cold frames, cold comfort, cold lunches. A person might freeze in frigid air, find themselves suddenly numb or bitter in the sharp climate of this gelid microseason, in the cold light of a winter's day.

In the late nineteenth century there emerged in northern Europe a new school of artists who became known as the Impressionists. One of their aims was to get closer to a true representation of landscapes in this cold winter light. Prior to this, artists had attempted to portray the chromatic landscape using what we might call 'local colour', which captures the hue of an object in neutral, bright, flat light, with no adjustment for shadow. 'Local colour' means green trees, blue skies, white snow. The Impressionists became interested in the way that light in the northern hemisphere shifts throughout the seasons and creates divergences between local colour and real colour as it is perceived under specific atmospheric and temporal conditions. Though not the first to notice this phenomenon, the Impressionists used novel techniques in their attempts to take the variable perception of light seriously as a way of capturing life through the medium of painting.

The Impressionists painted hibernal scenes in blue or violet hues that viscerally captured the icy light of short winter days by using unconventional colours, like purples, to capture light. Think of Claude Monet's *The Magpie*, where the lonely black magpie sits upon a gate amid a snowy landscape that glows with coloured shadows; or Camille Pissarro's *White Frost*, in which a solitary figure is weighed down not only by a load on his back but by the visceral substance of the winter landscape which he traverses. By using knifework to form the impression of frost on ridges, Pissarro produces the oppressive sensation of a closed landscape where the blue-tinged ground has a perceptible crystalline crunch.

These paintings convey something of the seasonal chromatic shifts in the way we see the world around us. Our experience of colour occurs as a result of different wavelengths of light within our visual perception. In the retina of the human eye there are three types of cones: blue, which is sensitive to short wavelengths of light; green, which is medium-wavelength sensitive; and red, which is long-wavelength sensitive. The interaction of light with these optic cones produces signals which travel along the optic nerve to the visual cortex in the back of the brain. From here these signals dialogue with 'higher-level' brain systems such as memory, attention and experience to integrate this visual information into objects and scenes; in short, to make meaning. And perhaps that's why, when we see a scene in one of these Impressionist paintings, we understand, almost viscerally, what a particular shade of light means. We too have stood in a landscape which feels exactly that blue hue of bone-chilling cold.

We are used to thinking of colour as one thing, but the way that colour interacts when it is mixed as a pigment is different from the ways it acts in our eyes. That is because making colour for paints or dyes involves the stacking-up of particles of pigment in order to imitate the way that light hits the eye. Take green, for example, which in art theory is not a 'primary colour' because green mediums have to be made by mixing blue and yellow. However, green means something quite different when we think about colour as part of a spectrum of light that is visible to the human eye. In the visible spectrum, green is a 'pure' or 'unique' colour that sits between yellow and blue rather than a composite. The effect that we call 'green' is produced in our eyes when we encounter light within a specific range of wavelengths. The best way to picture this is by thinking of a rainbow, in which visible light is dispersed through atmospheric water so that we can see the spectrum of colours laid out as a smooth gradation of unique colours.

As well as green, the human eye can generally also identify three other 'unique' hues that don't appear to contain mixtures of other colours – blue, yellow and red. But the way in which each of us sees a particular colour – in other words, the point on the rainbow that a person might identify as red, blue or green – is influenced by culture as well as individual perception. Of these four unique colours, only yellow retains a stable identity and hue across cultures, though evidence suggests that it might shift between seasons. Why might this be?

One possibility is that unique yellow acts as a colour balance calibrator; in other words, it appears in some circumstances to mediate our perception of light between summer and winter. In this way, this colour is a compass for the seasons.

The Earth's annual traverse around the sun results in light coming at us from different angles as the year unfolds. The summer sun shines directly down upon northern Europe around the summer solstice, resulting in long, warm days. In these seasonal conditions, plant life thrives and from the smallest weed to the tallest tree the light that reaches our eyes is infused with the green of vegetation reaching towards its life-giving rays.

Some scientists suggest that our colour vision may adapt in tune with these seasonal shifts. In one small study researchers found that in summer, people who were asked to identify unique yellow in a darkened room identified the colour at shorter wavelengths than in winter. This may be because our visual system compensates for the bombardment of green that we experience in summer months. As November unfurls the light lowers, casting long shadows. This is the moment in the year when the bronze and golden leaf fall comes to its end, and in these conditions our eyes recalibrate, much like shifting the colour balance on a television. This recalibration of our vision moves our perception of yellow towards longer 'reddish' tones, and the winter landscape is cast in that cold mauve aspect identified by the Impressionists.

The winter scenes painted by the Impressionists help us understand that the changing colour palette through the year isn't just determined by the emergence of flowers in different colours, of trees in different phases of leaf; it is also profoundly influenced by the light. The blue and mauve shadows that Monet and Pissarro mixed pigments to replicate and daubed into their winter scenes are an effect of the light and the way in which our eyes adjust to different light conditions, as is the golden glow that we associate with a summer's eve.

The root from which the word colour emerges in Indo-European languages comes from the Latin verb *celare*, indicating a cover or a skein rather than an inherent quality of a thing. Our colour vision shifts in late November, when the axis of the Earth has shifted so that the sun's rays reach us at oblique angles and the colours of deciduous foliage have first transmuted and then disappeared altogether.

In trying to capture the exact shade of the winter landscape before them, the Impressionists were engaged in an act of recalibration akin to the shifting of unique yellow in our visual perception that occurs at this point in the year. Their paintings show that paying close attention to what is in front of us can make what is apparently fixed suddenly strange, curious and exciting. If we think of our experience of winter as a shift in perception, a movement away from the yellow warmth of the sun, the cooling of the winter light is revealed as more than an optical phenomenon. It is rather an indication of how fluid our senses are, and how our perception is always mediated as much by our environment as it is by any desire to make meaning.

ROWAN JAINES

DECEMBER

Noticing Exercise

It can be easy to think of December as a time when little happens in nature, but going twigging can be a way of attuning yourself to the changes that are quietly happening in the cold months of the year. When you look closely, twigs are fascinatingly different shapes and colours: the matt black buds and flattened wood of ash are completely different from the elongated, spear-like buds of beech.

You can go twigging in 'advanced mode', collecting samples from plants near you, taking them home and identifying them without any contextual clues. But if you're relatively new to tree identification, it can be much more satisfying to get to know the other winter aspects of trees too. If you number your twigs as you gather them and photograph the tree they belong to, you will gain some valuable extra clues to help you identify them.

A small number of questions can really help to narrow down the species. Ask yourself how the buds are arranged: do they alternate left and right up the stem, or are they in pairs? How many leaf scales does each bud have? What colour and shape are the wood and the bud? Many tree guides have sections on twigs, and the Field Studies Council publishes a special booklet on the winter identification of trees.

27 NOVEMBER–1 DECEMBER

Teasel Brush Silhouettes

As we discover more about the plants and ecosystems around us, the clearer it becomes that death is just part of a continuous cycle. Leaves turn into compost, flowers transform into seedheads that are eaten by birds and deposited elsewhere in droppings, vegetables set seed ready for next year's crop. One plant that embodies this idea of continuity is the teasel, perhaps because its tall, spiny stems and bristly seedheads are so prominent at this time of year. Wild teasels, *Dipsacus fullonum*, are predominantly biennial, appearing every other year in field margins, waste ground and damp grasslands. They are not actually thistles, despite the visual similarities. Thistles have soft down that helps disperse seeds, as well as more bracts than teasels, and less spiny flowers. They are mostly from the *Asteraceae* family, and the teasel from the *Dipsacaceae*. Teasels can grow up to three metres tall and have purple, egg-shaped flowerheads that provide precious nectar for pollinators in summer. In the autumn these become dry cones edged with a cup of spiky bracts, like a faded gemstone coming free from its clasps.

Teasels invite comparisons: hedgehog, microphone, brush, grenade. If you see one, run your fingers gently up and down the prickly seedhead and listen to the sound it makes. The writer Melissa Mouchemore brilliantly describes them as a 'two tone zither with a third tone twang'. You might remember teasels from the *Little Grey Rabbit* series of children's books by Alison Uttley, in which the squirrels used teasels as tail brushes. Folk names like 'barber's brushes', 'donkey's thistle' and 'brushes and combs' reflect the plant's appearance and bristliness. Another name, 'Venus's basin', comes from the way in which water collects in the cup of leaves at the top of the stem.

It is the spiky seedheads, beloved by goldfinches (as we saw in our earlier microseason) and other birds in winter, that give the teasel its common name. These seedheads also provided early clothworkers with a valuable tool, and the plant with its common name. The fuller's teasel, *D. sativus*, a sturdier cultivated species, was used to 'tease out' damp cloth and raise the nap, making it soft – a job for which the Romans used hedgehogs. Teasels were an important part of the textile-making process in England at least as far back as the thirteenth century, when teasel-farming developed as a profitable industry, particularly in Somerset. In fact, these farms sent so many teasels to Europe that it caused a shortage in England and led to exports being banned.

In Tudor times the plant was used as a symbol for the Clothworkers' Company, a group formed from two textile workers' guilds in the reign of King Henry VIII. The spiny teasels provided the perfect balance of suppleness and abrasion. Originally, the seedheads were fitted into a wooden frame called a 'teasel hand' or 'handle' and brushed against the cloth by hand, but in the eighteenth century the process began to be mechanised. Teasel gigs or gig-mills combined the natural attributes of the plant with technological developments, fastening around 3,000 teasels into a metal drum. This machine was more efficient at spinning the teasels over the cloth to raise the nap, and a 'teasel man' would travel around keeping the machines in good order. Teasels are still used today on snooker or billiard table baize.

The plant also has a long history of use in herbal medicine. The root was thought to have antibacterial and antiviral properties, and was used in the Middle Ages as a diuretic and to treat warts and wounds. People also believed the water that collected in the leaves would cure eye problems or purify the skin, and it was applied to treat acne.

A fascinating line of research might make us think differently about these apparently commonplace plants. Experiments carried out in the 1870s by Francis Darwin, Charles Darwin's son, led him to posit that teasels are carnivorous. He believed that the cupped bracts were there not only to collect water and prevent insects from damaging the flowerhead, but also to catch prey. If you look closely at a teasel seedhead you might see lots of decomposing insects inside the cup. Could they be there by design? After adding raw meat to the cupped area of the teasel, Darwin recorded what he thought was movement in the protoplasmic filaments emerging from the plant's glands. He argued that this action was intended to help the plant absorb meat from these insects.

Francis Darwin's theory had his father's support. Charles believed he was on to something exciting, writing that he should 'Take care and do not overwork and kill the goose that lays the golden eggs.' Francis wrote a paper on the subject that was eventually published by the Royal Society in 1877, but he met with rebuttals and eventually stopped researching teasels.

Recent studies, however, took up where Darwin left off. In 2011 research appeared to show differences in seed production rates between teasels supplemented with animal substances and ones that weren't. For many, this provided proof confirming Francis Darwin's argument that teasels were carnivorous. But in 2019 another study appeared to refute this, claiming that the differences were due to poor soil conditions rather than the absorption of meat.

The debate continues. And although there is no definitive answer, it is exciting to think that these strange statuesque plants dotting our wild landscape might in fact be meat eaters, and so play a different role in the cycle of life than we might previously have imagined.

LULAH ELLENDER

2–6 DECEMBER

Robins Defend Winter Territories

Orange trees first arrived in Europe from Asia in the late fifteenth century. With them came the Sanskrit word *naranga*, the origin of the word 'orange'. Before this, the English language didn't have this colour concept: things that we would now term orange were described as either yellow or red. This is the reason that the robin, which has a conspicuously orange front, was originally called the 'ruddock' or 'redbreast'. It came to be known as 'robin' for the simple reason that people added this diminutive, alliterative nickname for 'Robert' – and it stuck.

Robins are unusual among British birds because they have both autumn/winter and summer territories. Winter territories are fiercely protected by single birds and are smaller; summer breeding territories cover a wider area and are held in pairs. Researchers using dummy robins showed that those with red breasts stimulated a more aggressive territorial response from other robins than those with duller, brown breasts.

The sound of a rival's song also stimulates territorial behaviour. Robins sing in the winter as well as the summer, but their tone changes with the seasons. The scratchy attack of the summer song is replaced by a softer, more thoughtful-sounding note in winter, when testosterone levels are lower. The third stanza of Keats's famous 'Ode to Autumn' begins:

> Where are the songs of spring? Ay, where are they?
> Think not of them, thou hast thy music too –

but then notes that birdsong has not fallen completely silent: 'The red-breast whistles from a garden-croft'.

Robins are a favourite bird of the winter season for many. As Richard Mabey says, there's something particularly beguiling about the way they cock their heads and look beadily at us. Their shining black eyes are slightly larger than those of similarly sized birds, adapted so that they can find food in the low-light conditions of a forest floor. UK robins are more confiding than their European counterparts, hopping around gardeners to steal worms and millipedes from disturbed soil.

Our winter population of robins is boosted by birds that migrate from Europe to escape harsh winters (a small number of British birds travel in the opposite direction too). Many of them fly at night, which begs the question: how on earth does this bird find its way in the dark? The answer may reveal a whole new dimension to those glittering eyes.

Avian navigation is complex, and mechanisms vary between species of birds, but there is increasing evidence that at least part of the robin's navigational ability comes down to an internal biological compass that responds to the magnetic field of the Earth. Exactly how this works remains something of a mystery. The problem, stated simply, is that the Earth's natural geomagnetic field is far too weak to be able to break the chemical bonds that normally hold molecules together, which is the most obvious way in which a directional signal could be produced. In fact, it's so subtle that the robin's detection mechanism would need to be extraordinarily sensitive to be able to pick it up.

How might such a signalling system work? The answer might lie in an emerging field that studies the role of very tiny particles in living organisms: quantum biology. The mathematics of quantum physics is notoriously complex, and we can only deal in a simplified way with the basic principles here. The central actor in our theory is a particle called a *radical* in the eye of our robin. As you may recall from school, atoms have three main bits: positively charged protons, neutral neutrons, and negatively charged electrons. A radical has at least one unpaired electron, which makes it unstable and liable to react with other atoms and molecules.

When two radicals are created together their electrons can start to interact, forming a short-lived 'radical pair'. Fleetingly, the two electrons correlate with one another: they become 'entangled'. This entanglement involves one of their most important properties: their 'spin'. We think of spin in our lives as rotation (like a spinning top), but electrons are so tiny that they cannot really be described in this way. So physicists think of spin as a kind of angular momentum that is inherent to matter itself: it is a property intrinsic to the electron, not a rotational movement.

Paired electrons do not spin willy-nilly but oscillate between two states many million times a second. They can spin in parallel (↑↑) or antiparallel (↑↓) directions. The difference in energy between the two states is tiny (much smaller than the amount of energy needed to break a chemical bond), which means that small inputs will get them to switch from ↑↑ to ↑↓. Importantly for our robin trying to find its way in the dark, all particles with spin are magnetic. The theory is that even a force as weak as the Earth's geomagnetic field could potentially influence whether a radical pair spins in parallel or antiparallel directions. This gives us the basis for a highly sensitive compass.

The final piece of the puzzle is that this is a chemical reaction, and each spin state produces a different chemical product. This product could potentially form the start of a signal, to tell the robin about its orientation in relation to the Earth's magnetic field.

This might seem like wild speculation, but there is some experimental evidence for the theory. Radical pairs are 'tuned' to magnetic fields at a particular frequency. Caged robins who are subjected to an oscillating radiofrequency field that disrupts their ability to sense the Earth's geomagnetic field are not able to orient themselves in space. This loss of directional sense occurs even when the field used in the experiment is 3,000 times weaker than the Earth's magnetic field.

It may be those beady, curious eyes that hold the secret of this quantum mechanism. In a robin's retina, there is a molecule called cryptochrome. Experiments have shown that when a photon of blue light hits it, a radical pair is created. Further, laboratory experiments on this molecule in vitro suggest that it is magnetically sensitive. The theory is controversial, however, and there remain many mysteries still to be solved. Perhaps the greatest of them is the question of how the minuscule lengths of time over which quantum reactions take place could be lengthened sufficiently to become the basis for a geomagnetic detection system.

The next few years should be an exciting time, as leading researchers unravel the secrets of the robin's polished onyx eyes. In the meantime, we can enjoy their cock-headed, cheeky company and twiddling cold-weather whistling as we potter around our winter gardens.

KIERA CHAPMAN

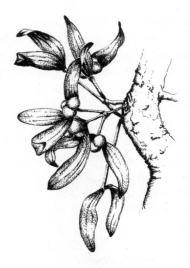

7–11 DECEMBER

Mistletoe Boughs Drip from Branches

A fleeting kiss under mistletoe hung from a doorway or ceiling is as much part of the festive season as mince pies and exchanging gifts. But this spontaneous moment of connection belies the complex, slow processes that brought the plant into its current state.

Mistletoe, *Viscum album*, is present all year round but it is most visible in winter, growing in drooping boughs on bare trees. You can see its pendulous swags adorning the upper branches of oaks, apples, limes, poplars, hawthorns and plums, among others. In December it puts out berries, dotting its bundles with white globules that look like mint imperials or fat pearls. It may be associated with Christmas simply because this is when its decorative berries appear, but our connections with the plant are more complex and tangled than mere availability.

Like many Yuletide customs, the link to Christmas may have its roots in pre-Christian pagan culture. We know from the Roman historian Pliny the Elder that the Celts saw mistletoe as an augury of good luck. In his *Natural History* Pliny describes a druidic ritual that occurred on the closest new moon to the winter solstice, when a white-clad druid would climb a sacred oak tree to harvest some mistletoe with a golden sickle. The elixir produced was used to treat infertility and as an antidote to snake poison, showing that mistletoe has played an important part in midwinter rituals for thousands of years. Another example is the Norse legend of Baldur, which describes how he was killed with an arrow made of mistletoe wood because his mother and wife forgot to mention the plant when asking all living things to leave him to live in peace. Mistletoe was hung to show it was never again overlooked.

Since the nineteenth century, Christmas has been a time of ghost stories, and mistletoe gives us one particularly spooky tale, later developed into a carol. In this story a bride is said to have hidden from wedding guests by climbing into a wooden chest. She was trapped inside and died, her family only discovering her body years later, the wedding dress now a shroud for her skeleton. The first appearance of the story in print, in an 1822 poem by Samuel Rogers, has no connection to mistletoe, but later Victorian versions by T. H. Bayly reset the story at Christmas, with a chorus repeating 'Oh the mistletoe bough'. Later, Sir Henry Bishop set the poem to music and it became a popular carol, particularly in Sheffield and north Derbyshire, where it is still sung today by locals to mark the beginning of the festive period.

Mistletoe is hemiparasitic, meaning that although it does photosynthesise through its leaves, it obtains most of its nutrients and carbohydrates from a host plant. The host, therefore, plays a key role in keeping its guest alive and mistletoe has evolved to make the best use of tree branches through a fascinating growing process that only culminates in flowers after five years.

After a seed has germinated, for the whole first year of its life it grows inside the host. The embryonic mistletoe uses a gravity-based signal to move towards the branch; then, as it finds its way inside the bark to the xylem, it produces viscin, a gooey substance made up of cellulose and muco-polysaccharides that helps it stick to the branch. It breaks down the bark, probably through enzymes, and begins to build the haustorium (a root-like structure that enables it to extract nutrients from the host). The next year, one shoot develops and a node is added annually until year four, when it branches for the first time. In its fifth year, flowers and berries develop. As the tree puts on its yearly rings of growth, so the mistletoe's haustorium expands. Mistletoe has roots that grip on to the branches, enabling it to grow high up and maximise sunlight for photosynthesis.

But once the mistletoe is suspended aloft, how does it reproduce and colonise other trees? This is where things get even more interesting. The berries are full of sticky viscin, which acts like a kind of super-glue gloop. As birds feed off the berries they pass the seeds out in their faeces. The viscin makes their faeces sticky, so that rather than falling to the ground it adheres to their feet or feathers, or to the branch the bird is sitting on. They also get viscin on their beaks as they eat the berries. To clean it off they wipe themselves on branches, depositing the seed on to a new host. The viscin then glues the seed to the branch. This is where the plant gets its common name, from the Anglo-Saxon 'mistel tan', meaning 'dung on a stick'. Viscin also led the Celts to associate mistletoe with the semen of Taranis, the god of sun and thunder, and inspired the ancient Greek name for it: oak sperm.

Each berry can produce up to two metres of viscin and it has been found to stick to a wide range of both natural and man-made surfaces, as well as to skin and cartilage. As a result, researchers are investigating possible biomedical and biomechanical uses for the substance, such as a biodegradable sealant or as a treatment to heal wounds.

Humans have found myriad other uses for this fascinating plant for thousands of years, and across the globe. In Nigeria African mistletoe was traditionally used to treat diabetes; Native Cherokee people used American mistletoe to induce abortions; and in China and Northeast Asia the plant is indicated to treat uterine bleeding in pregnancy. Studies have shown its efficacy in regulating blood pressure and relieving anxiety, and some HIV-positive patients take it to boost their immune system and inhibit disease progression. Mistletoe is also being studied as a potential treatment to relieve the pain of endometriosis. But a note of caution: the berries are poisonous and should only be used with medical supervision or advice.

As we have seen in relation to other plants with medicinal uses, the Doctrine of Signatures has influenced how mistletoe was prescribed – in this case the semen-like substance was used to treat conditions in the reproductive system. The association with fertility may also be because mistletoe flowers when little else does. In Europe the flowers appear in autumn, when much around us is dying, and in Africa mistletoe flowers in the middle of the dry season. There is something about its abundance in a time of sparsity, of shiny berries against skeletal branches, that exudes fecundity, resilience and hope.

Hung from ceilings and doorways this season, mistletoe does not just invite us to embrace for a seasonal kiss. It also challenges us to think about our perceptions around individualism, agency and autonomy in the natural world. Should we view parasitic plants as ecological freeloaders, sapping strength from an unwitting host? Or, by looking aslant at the notion of parasites, should we remember that interdependence is actually the essence of all living things?

LULAH ELLENDER

12–16 DECEMBER

The Black Month Deepens

Our contemporary calendar is divided into twelve distinct months, but it hasn't always been this way. The period of the year that runs from the end of the harvest season, marked by Samhain (1 November), to the end of winter and the beginning of the lambing season, which is marked by Imbolc (around 31 January), was known in the Celtic languages as 'the black month'. These three months were sometimes referred to separately as 'the black month' (November), 'the black month before Christmas' (December) and 'the black month after Christmas' (January), but they were generally considered as one period of deepening darkness rather than separate calendrical entities.

In the Celtic tradition, the 'black month' is the polar opposite of early spring. In Welsh, Celtic and Breton folklore and poetry the month of May is personified in the image of a noble knight who defeats winter and conquers the land, dressing all living things in his green livery. By contrast, the 'black month' is an absence or a pause, not one singular unit of time but rather the night between the dusk of autumn and the twinkling of spring. It is often personified by the female figure of the 'midwinter woman', who marks the intrusion of darkness into the seasonal calendar. This female figure is not the ripe feminine body of creation but is rather the figure of the crone, an old, wrinkled hag who embodies the absence of fertile forces. Wrapped in a shawl, she appears to wreak violent havoc on those who do not pay heed to cultural taboos against productive activities in the midwinter period, particularly those associated with female labour such as spinning.

This ominous figure would have featured often in the stories told around the fire – for the black month was the season for the telling of tales, a period after the work of the harvest had been completed when the cold, dark days encouraged families and neighbours to gather in the warmth in the women's realm that was, during the rest of the year, dedicated to spinning and sewing. These spaces were re-formed as sites for conversation and storytelling, and perhaps it is no surprise that the act of sharing anecdotes is still today known as 'spinning a yarn'.

In the Gaelic folklore common to Scotland and Ireland there is a particular tradition of tales of hags or Cailleacha woven into this dark winter period. These mythical female figures are builders of stone monuments, wells and hills, and they are deeply connected to ideas of old age and winter. The Scottish Cailleach is said to have worn a great grey hood, which she washed each year at Samhain in the Gulf of Corryvreckan, the dangerous narrow strait between the islands of Jura and Scarba. It was said that the tidal floods which roil and ferment there were caused by the Cailleach laundering her great shawl. When she had finished her washing the Cailleach's hood was pure white, and she laid it over the landscape in a deathly blanket of snow.

These early conceptions of the black months as a period covered over by a deadening spell crops up many centuries later in the writings of an eighteenth-century botanist called Richard Bradley. In his 1718 tract, *The Gentleman and Gardeners Kalendar, Directing What Is to Be Done Every Month*, Bradley briefly summarises the usual climate for each month, using data he collected over several decades. When it comes to December he states that it is 'commonly called the Black Month' because 'it is subject to every sort of weather that is fatal to plants of a tender nature. All vegetables of our climate seem now to sleep; the days are short, and every little warmth from the sun makes every curious lover of gardens wish for the spring.'

Bradley was fascinated by seasonal variations and what they mean for those who take care of plants. By 1721, he was experimenting with collecting even more precise data on weather. For 2–7 June 1721 he recorded data collected at three-hour intervals (excepting midnight until 9 a.m.) from a barometer, a hygrometer and a thermometer, along with indications of weather. This meant that when an exceptionally severe winter hit England at the end of 1728 and beginning of 1729, Bradley was primed to write an in-depth examination, not only of the winter itself but also of the earlier signs that augured its ferocity.

In his book, titled *A philosophical enquiry into the late severe winter, the scarcity and dearness of provisions, and the occasion of the distemper raging in several remote parts of England*, Bradley reported to have been forewarned of the 'black months' of that biting winter by an unusual source: a mole catcher who found moles living a foot deeper in the ground than was usual.

Bradley hypothesised that this uncharacteristic burrowing behaviour was driven not by hibernation but as a hunting strategy: the moles followed their main food source, earthworms, which he claimed were sensitive to impending weather conditions because of their 'structure and tender disposition'.

This theory was at least half right. Contemporary ecologists have found that as the weather grows colder, earthworms push deeper into the ground, taking organic matter with them. In the depths of the earth they build burrows and curl up tightly, insulating themselves from dehydration using protective slime.

While some contemporary scientists have been looking to the micro-movements of earthworms, others have been taking their cold-weather cues from the larger patterns. Meteorologists have discovered that it is possible to predict cold weather in Europe through monitoring autumn snowfall in Siberia. When this vast region of Russia and northern Kazakhstan experiences high snowfall, the resultant cold air animates atmospheric disturbances which spread into the upper layer of the atmosphere and warm the polar vortex. This action pushes the jet stream south, and leads to colder winters in the United States and Europe and warmer weather in the Arctic. And in this macro-model, there is a connection back to the micro-world of the mole and the worm. Since earthworms are sensitive to barometric pressure, it does make sense that Bradley's mole catcher caught the scent of a particularly cold winter. There's a connection back to Celtic lore too. Researchers have found that tidal movemements in the Outer Hebrides, where the Cailleach's washtub is situated, are stimulated by low-pressure systems brought by the jet stream following snowfall in autumnal Siberia.

But even if we now know about the atmospheric conditions that bring about this unpredictable churning of the seas, in this dark period in the year it is still possible to imagine the Cailleach's hood growing thicker and heavier, as the black month deepens and we huddle closer together around the fire.

ROWAN JAINES

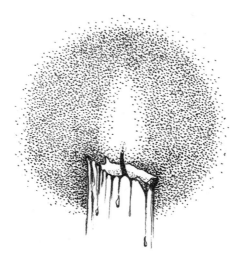

17–21 DECEMBER

Darkness and Light Hold Hands

Some of the changes we have been noticing over this year are experienced at slightly different times depending on geographical location, topography and weather patterns. And some occur at exactly the same time but in completely opposite ways, like this microseason's winter solstice, which sees the shortest day of the year in the northern hemisphere and the longest in the southern hemisphere. In the northern hemisphere we are sensing the slight, subtle shortening of the days that peaks on 21 December, at the end of this microseason. The gentle shift in day length as we approach and then move away from the solstice can be felt by most people in this part of the world. We share the pause as, in Annie Dillard's words, the 'planet tilts just so to its star, lists and holds arching in a fixed tension between veering and longing, spins helpless, exalted, in and out of that fleet blazing touch'.

The solstice is a moment of suspension before the start of a new cycle of time that emerges from darkness. As we saw in our 5–9 January microseason, solar and clock times are different, which means the solstice is the shortest day in the northern hemisphere but doesn't have the latest sunrise or the earliest sunset. Somewhat counter-intuitively, although 21 December has the most darkness, the evenings have actually been getting lighter for the last ten days!

This strange time of stasis has been marked by different cultures and peoples for thousands of years. The fifteenth-century citadel of Machu Picchu, built by the Inca, and England's Stonehenge show how important the solstices were to our ancestors. These monuments were built to capture the exact alignment of the sun at specific points in the year. At the spectacular Maeshowe chambered cairn on Orkney you can watch a livestream of the sun illuminating a spot just near the tomb at sunset on the solstice, as it has done for millennia – an amazing feat of engineering and a reflection of the significance of the sun's movement for Neolithic people. The need to notice, mark and capture the shifts in light and time has a constancy across time and culture, from the Roman Saturnalia festival (held on 17 December in honour of the sun god) to China's Dong Zhi solstice celebrations. Part of this impulse to celebrate must surely be an expression of relief and gratitude that the light is returning and the world is reawakening. And part of it could be sheer awe and wonder that, in an ever-changing world, these moments recur year after year at the same time, in the same place. There is a deep and abiding comfort in that.

But for now we are still in the darkening phase, approaching the tipping point but not quite there yet. For the five days of this microseason darkness still holds sway. The sun is at its lowest and is casting the longest shadows of the year. So what are we to make of these shadows, these patterns of light that have been witnessed by every sighted human that has ever lived? They represent repression, disappearance, erasure and danger; but also protection and reprieve. They leave space for the imagination to wander, and they intensify the contrasting light. They define objects and spaces, giving things a realness and drawing our attention. As the architect Louis Kahn said, 'The sun never knew how wonderful it was until it fell on the wall of a building.'

As we learn more about how and why ancient peoples moved huge slabs of stone to create temples and monuments, we see how our long-held fascination with light and shade has spurred acts of creation. Since Pliny's description in his *Natural History* of how a woman named Dibutades sketched her lover's shadow on a wall, we have seen how artists have incorporated shadows in their work, not simply as realistic representations of objects or people but also as psychological or emotional markers. Rembrandt gave his name to a method of lighting that cast one half of the subject's face in shadow but left a triangle of light around the nose and eye, while Vermeer, Da Vinci and Hammershøi spun shadows into beauty.

We can consider the ways in which shadows have featured in photography, an art form that began with the goal of simply 'fixing a shadow'. From the work of Clementina Hawarden to Fan Ho and Henri Cartier-Bresson, the dance of shadow and light has been central to many iconic images. Painters, too, have manipulated the light and used shadow to draw the eye or to create atmosphere. We can remember Jane Eyre's assertion, in the 1996 Franco Zeffirelli film version of the book, that 'the shadows are just as important as the light'.

Or we can simply observe. As these chiaroscuro days bring us to the end of the year, what are the shadows we see around us? What do we want to consign to darkness rather than carry with us into the new year? What are the things we need to bring out into the light? Pause. Watch. Wait.

LULAH ELLENDER

22–26 DECEMBER

Jolly Holly

What could be more seasonal at this time of year than a sprig of glossy holly, with gleaming red berries? In her 'Christmastide Poems', Christina Rossetti compares holly to more superficially attractive and popular plants. In her view, it has a democratic, everyday cheerfulness that fits our winter celebrations better than more exotic flora:

> A rose has thorns as well as honey,
> I'll not have her for love or money;
> An iris grows so straight and fine
> That she shall be no friend of mine;
> Snowdrops like the snow would chill me;
> Nightshade would caress and kill me;
> Crocus like a spear would fright me;
> Dragon's-mouth might bark or bite me;
> Convolvulus but blooms to die;
> A wind-flower suggests a sigh;

Love-lies-bleeding makes me sad;
And poppy-juice would drive me mad: –
But give me holly, bold and jolly,
Honest, prickly, shining holly;
Pluck me holly leaf and berry
For the day when I make merry.

Yet the jolliness of holly seems counter-intuitive when we consider its bristling prickliness. As you may have found to your cost, collecting decorative sprigs definitely comes with its risks! But look closely, and you may notice that holly leaves have very different shapes. On the same plant they can be spiky, with jagged teeth turning away from the plane of the leaf to tear into the surrounding air, or surprisingly smooth, with a shape that resembles a fat bay leaf. This ability to pro-duce differently shaped leaves is called 'heterophylly', and it is shared with another stalwart of the Yuletide season: ivy.

The production of prickles is a response to animals chew-ing on the leaves. Researchers in Spain found that, where trees showed evidence of browsing by herbivores, 76 per cent of twigs had prickly leaves, compared to 19 per cent in trees that had no signs of being eaten. What is more, the damaged – and therefore prickly – areas correlated with the 2.25-metre reach of the largest herbivore in the environment, the red deer.

The spikes, then, are signs of the holly tree fighting back! But how does the holly mount this surprisingly nuanced response to environmental cues? Each of its leaves has the same underlying genetics, after all. The answer is something called 'epigenetics', which describes how behaviour and environmental cues can change the way that genes work.

DNA is made up of molecules called 'bases' that arrange themselves into two chains, coiled around one another in a double helix shape. Two of these bases have a methyl group attached to them, which is a combination of one carbon atom and three hydrogen atoms. Scientists found that these methyl groups were relatively absent in pricklier leaves, compared to smoother ones from the same height and location. Prickliness therefore seems to result from DNA 'demethylation', which changes the way that genes are expressed without changing the underlying DNA sequence.

We don't tend to think of holly as something animals like to eat, so the idea that its prickliness depends on damage caused by hungry deer seems strange. However, before turnips were introduced in the eighteenth century, holly was an important winter feed for cattle and sheep, particularly in areas like the Pennines where winter grazing was poor. The practice of cutting it for feed is very old: in a bawdy medieval satire on the Franciscan monks, written in around 1440, an old horse is put out to pasture on holly: 'Lyarde es ane olde hoa'se . . . He, salle be putt into the parke holyne for to gnawe.'

Its usefulness to farmers meant that, unlike other scrub, holly trees weren't cleared as common land was enclosed in the seventeenth and eighteenth centuries. In the 1770s, Thomas West commented that in Furness 'large tracts of common pasture are so covered with these trees, as to have the appearance of a forest of hollies'. In the Sheffield area, a 'hag of hollin' was a stand of holly trees growing in the commons of the manor.

So when you're stuffed with Christmas dinner, why not go out and see if you can find differently shaped holly leaves on the same bush? Extra bonus points if you discover a leaf that looks like the one in the picture.

This wandering pattern is a leaf mine, and it has been caused by a fly called *Phytomyza ilicis*. The fly lays its eggs on the underside of the holly leaf in June. They hatch and the larvae enter the midrib of the leaf and eat their way down. Sometime in September to November they run out of midrib and bite through into the inner tissue of the holly leaf, where they leave these meandering trails. The adults will emerge next year, in May to June, after gnawing a triangular trapdoor in the leaf to get free, and the cycle will start all over again.

KIERA CHAPMAN

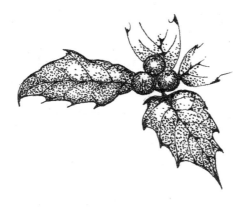

27–31 DECEMBER

Tree Skeletons and Sky

The silhouettes of tree skeletons standing stark against the sky may seem a bleak place to end our microseason calendar. But, as we have seen throughout our observations and noticings, there is more to their story than may at first appear. Shorn of their leaves, the trees' shapes are more clearly visible – from the size and frame of their crowns to the texture and girth of their trunks; and, stripped of their summer floof, their height is altered. The naturalist Anna Botsford Comstock wrote that 'it is during this winter resting time that the tree stands revealed to the uttermost, ready to give its most intimate confidences to those who love it'. So, let's listen to the stories these trees are telling us as they stand lung-like, branches resembling bronchi, waiting out the winter.

The fact that most trees remain standing through gales and storms is testament to some clever engineering. In order to be able to bend without breaking, all materials have what is known as an 'elastic range'. If a tree's elastic range is exceeded due to a force, such as high winds, it has a trick up its sleeve: it uses structural damping to dissipate the force and prevent damage. This is when the branches sway in a different direction from the trunk, which distributes the energy from the gust and converts the force into heat at the roots.

Despite this mechanism for literally 'taking the wind out' of the wind, some trees do still fall. One reason for this is 'windthrow', a lever-like action caused by a gust that particularly affects trees in leaf. The force is sent down to the roots and can topple the tree – root ball and all. A tree's risk of being uprooted is higher in wet soil. Loose, claggy soil doesn't provide good stability, especially if the ground is tarmacked over and water is funnelled in channels towards trees. Sometimes trees fall because of root damage, where roots have either been cut or so restricted by hard landscaping or compacted soil that they can't support the tree any longer. To properly anchor a tree against the particular prevailing winds the roots need to be able to grow in the right place, and where this is not possible their structure is more unstable. And sometimes trees fall because of a structural weakness resulting from disease or damage. Yet trees of all sizes can withstand extraordinary extremes of weather.

To cope with years of buffeting, bleaching and icing, trees have learned to be adaptable. As the ecologist and biologist Robin Wall Kimmerer notes, 'Plasticity is possible because trees have myriad growing points, or meristems, a reservoir of adaptation poised to respond to changed circumstances.' It is not only their dancing branches that move to meet the wind, their very tissues change according to conditions and need. Trees can drop parts of themselves they can't sustain and grow new parts when necessary. Slowly, incrementally, they build themselves and bend themselves and bare themselves, year after year.

In deepest December it can look as if not much is going on in these delicately filamented, brittle-looking trees. But beneath the soil they are engaged in an incredible system of communication.

Thanks to the pioneering research of the ecologist Suzanne Simard we know that trees share nutrients and information through root and mycorrhizal fungi networks (as we saw in our Puhpowee microseason). Like Wall Kimmerer, who points out that to indigenous peoples trees are 'respected as unique, sovereign beings equal to or exceeding the power of humans', Simard argued that trees are social beings with intelligence. They recognise and prioritise nutrients for their own species, especially when they are young saplings. Yet Simard's work showed that trees also compensate for shading out smaller trees of other species. She observed that birch trees which were shading Douglas fir saplings increased the photosynthetic sugars transmitted to these saplings, ensuring the younger trees survived. Trees work collaboratively to support a mutually beneficial society, responding to environmental signals in order to find resources. This may be in a forest, garden or field – they are all striving together for a healthy community. And in turn this ensures a healthy planet for us all – which is why it is so important to protect our forests. As the environmental journalist R. Schiffman notes, forests are 'not collections of isolated organisms but webs of constantly evolving relationships'. When we damage one part of the web we damage the whole.

It is this idea of relationships that is so compelling and essential. As the year turns to a close these tree skeletons are deceptively full of life. Stand in the cool damp of a winter wood. Turn to the trees. If you look closely you will see they are not bare at all. You might spot catkins or bud nodes, or hibernating invertebrates tucked under the bark. And you can imagine the flow of energy, information and life going on in the earth beneath your feet.

The physical and psychological benefits of forest bathing are now well known. This ancient Japanese practice, called *shinrin-yoku*, involves being calm and quiet among the trees and consciously connecting with the natural environment. Even on a leaden winter's day, the simple act of being in the presence of trees can feel both rejuvenating and restorative. But could there be more to this experience of connection than the immediate sense of relaxation? Are there deeper, more fundamental lessons we can learn from woods and forests?

The poet Ross Gay asks, 'How does a healthy forest supply us [with] a model of how to be in practices of care and interaction and interdependence?' We can remember the incredible mycorrhizal telegraphing taking place in the soil and the mutual care different tree species take of each other. And perhaps we can reflect on our human role and responsibility within this shared ecosystem. Carry this question with you into the next season and the next, as you emerge from winter ready to put out fresh shoots, to unfurl ideas, plans, hopes for the coming year. Ask the trees how we should *be*.

LULAH ELLENDER

Notes

5–9 JANUARY: THE LIGHT STEALS BACK

inspired artists: J. Lack, *In Praise of Shadows: Artists Inspired by Darkness*, christies.com, 21 January 2021.

the 'Equation of Time': D. W. Hughes and C. Y. Hohenkerk, 'The Equation of Time', *Monthly Notices of the Royal Astronomical Society*, 238 (1989), pp. 1529–35.

solar time: M. Müller, 'Equation of Time – Problem in astronomy', *Acta Physica Polonica A*, 88 (Supplement) (1995), pp. 49–67.

10–14 JANUARY: MOSSES GLOW GREEN

changing their traits over time: S. McDaniel, 'Bryophytes are not early diverging land plants', *New Phytologist*, 230(4) (2021), pp. 1300–04.

damper, cooler environment: R. Kimmerer, *Gathering Moss*. London: Penguin, 2021.

wind vibration can assist dispersal: V. Johansson et al., 'Release thresholds for moss spores: The importance of turbulence and sporophyte length', *Journal of Ecology*, 102 (2014), pp. 721–9.

when re-wetted: P. Alpert, 'Constraints of tolerance: Why are desiccation-tolerant organisms so small or rare?', *Journal of Experimental Biology*, 209(9) (2006), pp. 1575–84.

uronic acid and phenolic compounds: R. Clymo and P. Hayward, 'The Ecology of *Sphagnum*', in A. Smith (ed.), *Bryophyte Ecology*. London: Chapman and Hall, 1982, pp. 229–89.

difficult for competing plants to grow: H. Rydin and J. Jeglum, *The Biology of Peatlands*. Oxford: Oxford University Press, 2nd edn. 2013.

Sir Edward Ward: J. Porter, '*Sphagnum* moss for use as a surgical dressing: Its collection, preparation and other details', *Canadian Medical Association Journal*, 7(3) (1917), pp. 201–7.

to British military hospitals: T. Griffiths, I. Rotherham and C. Handley, '*Sphagnum*: The healing harvest', in I. Rotherham and C. Handley (eds.), *War & Peat: The Remarkable Impacts of Conflicts on Peatlands and of Peatlands on Conflicts – A Military Heritage of Moors, Heaths, Bogs and Fens*. Sheffield: Wildtrack Publishing, 2013, pp. 201–20.

an antimicrobial effect: H. Mellegård et al., 'Antibacterial activity of sphagnum acid and other phenolic compounds found in *Sphagnum papillosum* against food-borne bacteria', *Letters in Applied Microbiology*, 49(1) (2009), pp. 85–90; T. Stalheim et al., 'Sphagnan – a pectin-like polymer isolated from *Sphagnum* moss can inhibit the growth of some typical food spoilage and food poisoning bacteria by lowering the pH', *Journal of Applied Microbiology*, 106(3) (2009), pp. 967–76.

25 per cent of soil carbon: J. Loisel et al., 'Expert assessment of future vulnerability of the global peatland carbon sink', *Nature Climate Change*, 11 (2021), pp. 70–77.

'wastes': V. di Palma, *Wasteland: A History*. New Haven: Yale University Press, 2014.

'mamba': Roxane Andersen, cited in V. Gewin, 'How peat could protect the planet', *Nature*, 578 (2020), pp. 204–8.

two billion metric tonnes: H. Joosten et al., 'The Role of Peatlands in Climate Regulation', in A. Bonn (ed.), *Peatland Restoration and Ecosystem Services*. Cambridge: Cambridge University Press, 2016, pp. 63–76.

12–40 per cent: J. Leifeld, C. Wüst-Galley and S. Page, 'Intact and managed peatland soils as a source and sink of GHGs from 1850 to 2100', *Nature Climate Change*, 9 (2019), pp. 945–7.

15–19 JANUARY: SNOWDROPS EMERGE

the deathless gods: Homer and S. Butler, *The Odyssey Rendered into English Prose*, Book X. New York: Jonathan Cape, 1925, p. 154.

Plaitakis and Duvoisin: A. Plaitakis and R. C. Duvoisin, 'Homer's moly identified as Galanthus nivalis L.: Physiologic antidote to stramonium poisoning', *Clinical Neuropharmacology*, 6(1) (1983), pp. 1–6.

20–24 JANUARY: SMALL BIRDS FLUFFING

the evolution of feathers: R. O. Prum and A. H. Brush, 'The evolutionary origin and diversification of feathers', *Quarterly Review of Biology*, 77(3) (2002), pp. 261–95.

the cultural history of feathers: T. Hanson, *Feathers: The Evolution of a Natural Miracle*. New York: Basic Books, 2011.

25–29 JANUARY: BRIGHT WINTER ACONITES

Gerard's Herball: L. Knight, *Of Books and Botany in Early Modern England: Sixteenth-Century Plants and Print Culture*. Abingdon: Routledge, 2009.

Carl Linnaeus: P. White, *Sex, Botany and Empire: The Story of Carl Linnaeus and Joseph Banks*. Thriplow: Icon Books, 2004.

The Botanical Magazine: F. J. Chittenden, 'History of Curtis's Botanical Magazine', *Curtis's Botanical Magazine Index*. London: Royal Horticultural Society, 1956, pp. 251–69.

Richard Salisbury: R. K. Brummitt and C. E. Powell, *Authors of Plant Names*. Kew: Royal Botanic Gardens, 1992, p. 555.

Capability Brown: J. Dubow, ' "From a view on the world to a point of view in it": Rethinking sight, space and the colonial subject', *Interventions*, 2(1) (2000), pp. 87–102.

30 JANUARY–3 FEBRUARY: LICHENS ON BARE BRANCHES

Lichens are an association: D. Richardson, 'War in the world of lichens: Parasitism and symbiosis as exemplified by lichens and lichenicolous fungi', *Mycological Research*, 103(6) (1999), pp. 641–50.

human politics and social questions: J. Samyn, 'Intimate ecologies: Symbioses in the nineteenth century', *Victorian Literature and Culture*, 48(1) (2020), pp. 243–65.

Schwendener: S. Schwendener, 'Die Algentypen der Flechtengonidien', *Programm für die Rectorsfeier der Universität Basel*, 4 (1869), pp. 1–42. See also J. Sapp, *Evolution by Association: A History of Symbiosis*. Oxford: Oxford University Press, 1994.

injures and ultimately destroys: M. Cooke, 'The dual lichen hypothesis', *Grevillea*, 7(43) (1879), pp. 102–8 and 44, pp. 117–26, this citation p. 119. James Crombie makes a similar point: 'Other plants, from which parasites draw their nourishment, usually become speedily exhausted and finally perish', 'On the Algo-Lichen

Hypothesis', *The Journal of the Linnean Society: Botany*, 20 (1886), pp. 259–83, this quotation p. 268.

Fungal master: both quotations are from J. Crombie, 'On the lichen-gonidia question', *The Popular Science Review*, 13 (1874), p. 263 and p. 276.

universally accepted: for an account see M. Mitchell, ' "Such a strange theory": Anglophone attitudes to the discovery that lichens are composite organisms', *Huntia*, 11(2) (2002), pp. 193–207.

Fenzl: see https://www.hubert-fenzl.de/

4–8 FEBRUARY: WINDS HOWLING IN THE NIGHT

Augustine in his *Confessions*: P. Plass, 'Augustine and Proust on time and memory', *Soundings: An Interdisciplinary Journal*, 73(2/3) (1990), pp. 343–60, p. 350.

soundscapes: M. Akiyama, 'Transparent listening: Soundscape composition's objects of study', *RACAR: Revue d'art Canadienne/ Canadian Art Review*, 35(1) (2010), pp. 54–62.

World Soundscape Project: B. Truax, 'R. Murray Schafer (1933–2021) and the World Soundscape Project', *Organised Sound*, 26(3) (2021), pp. 419–21.

the jet stream is likely to shift north over time: M. B. Osman et al., 'North Atlantic jet stream projections in the context of the past 1,250 years', *Proceedings of the National Academy of Sciences*, 118(38) (2021):e2104105118.

9–13 FEBRUARY: BIRDSONG BUILDS

birds sing for joy: L. V. Riters, 'Pleasure seeking and birdsong', *Neuroscience and Biobehavioral Reviews*, 35(9) (2011), pp. 1837–45.

birdsong has a positive impact on wellbeing: D. M. Ferraro et al., 'The phantom chorus: Birdsong boosts human well-being in protected areas', *Proceedings of the Royal Society B*, 287(1941) (2020): 20201811.

impact of human noise on birds: A. S. Injaian, C. C. Taff and G. L. Patricelli, 'Experimental anthropogenic noise impacts avian parental behaviour, nestling growth and nestling oxidative stress', *Animal Behaviour*, 136 (2018), pp. 31–9.

a joy so great it becomes unbearable: Reb Nachman quoted in D. Rothenberg, *Why Birds Sing*. London: Allen Lane, 2005.

birdsong in schools, hospitals and airports: D. Winterman, 'The surprising uses for birdsong', *BBC News Magazine*, 8 May 2013.

'What the birds are "saying"': S. Lovatt, *Birdsong in a Time of Silence*. London: Penguin Books, 2021.

14–18 FEBRUARY: SPARROWS SQUABBLE

chances of winning: A. Liker and Z. Barta, 'Male badge size predicts dominance against females in house sparrows', *The Condor*, 103(1) (2001), pp. 151–7.

fifty times bigger: K. Todd, *Sparrow*. London: Reaktion Books, 2012.

blind sparrows: M. Menaker, 'Extraretinal light perception in the sparrow, I. Entrainment of the biological clock', *PNAS*, 59(2) (1968), pp. 414–21; M. Menaker and H. Keatts, 'Extraretinal light perception in the sparrow, II. Photoperiodic stimulation of testis growth', *PNAS*, 60(1) (1968), pp. 146–51; M. Menaker et al., 'Extraretinal light perception in the sparrow, III. The eyes do not participate in photoperiodic photoreception', *PNAS*, 67(1) (1970), pp. 320–25; J. P. McMillan et al., 'Extraretinal light perception in the sparrow, IV. Further evidence that the eyes do not participate in photoperiodic photoreception', *Journal of Comparative Physiology*, 97 (1975), pp. 205–13; H. Underwood and M. Menaker, 'Photoperiodically significant photoreception in sparrows: Is the retina involved?', *Science*, 167(3916) (1970), pp. 298–301.

fight off disease: for an overview see J. Falcón et al., 'Exposure to artificial light at night and the consequences for flora, fauna, and ecosystems', *Frontiers in Neuroscience*, 14 (2020): 602796. For effects on tree sparrows see J. Jiang et al., 'The effects of artificial light at night on Eurasian tree sparrow (*Passer montanus*): Behavioral rhythm disruption, melatonin suppression and intestinal microbiota alterations', *Ecological Indicators*, 108 (2020):105702.

two days longer: M. E. Kernbach et al., 'Light pollution increases West Nile virus competence of a ubiquitous passerine reservoir species', *Proceedings of the Royal Society B*, 286(1907) (2019): 20191051.

19–23 FEBRUARY: DAFFODIL SPEARS

Pliny: W. H. Jones (trans.), *Natural History* (10 vols.), vol. 6. London: Heinemann, 1961, p. 255.

Modern Curiosities of Art: N. Lémery, *Recueil des curiositez rares et nouvelles des plus admirables effets de la nature et de l'art*. Paris: Louis Vendosme, 1685, p. 265.

24–28 FEBRUARY: LEAF BUDS FATTENING

Fibonacci . . . spirals: C. Surridge, 'Leaves by number', *Nature*, 426(237) (2003), p. 237.

early leaf-out: R. B. Primack and A. S. Gallinat, 'Spring budburst in a changing climate', *American Scientist*, 104(2) (2016), p. 102.

implications of earlier leaf-out: C. Pollgar, R. B. Primack and A. S. Gallinat, 'Drivers of leaf-out phenology and their implications for species invasions: Insights from Thoreau's Concord', *New Phytologist*, 202(1) (2014), pp. 106–15.

1–5 MARCH: FROGSPAWN WOBBLES

twenty tonnes of toads killed on roads: Froglife, https://www.froglife.org/what-we-do/toads-on-roads/facts-figures/ (accessed 29 September 2022).

toads as objects of detestation: Thomas Pennant, quoted in D. Hart-Davis, *Fauna Britannica*. London: Weidenfeld & Nicolson, 2002.

frogs as bioindicators: A. Venturino et al., 'Biomarkers of effect in toads and frogs', *Biomarkers*, 8(3–4) (2003), pp. 167–86.

witches' familiars: recorded by W. W., *fl.* 1577–82, at the Essex witch trials, printed in London, 1582; H. Parish ' "Paltrie Vermin, Cats, Mise, Toads, and Weasils": Witches, familiars, and human-animal interactions in the English witch trials', *Religions*, 10(2) (2019), p. 134.

6–10 MARCH: WOODPECKERS DRUMMING

cranial kinesis: S. Van Wassenberg et al., 'Cranial kinesis facilitates quick retraction of stuck woodpecker beaks', *Journal of Experimental Biology*, 225(5) (2022): eb243787.

woodpeckers removing stuck bills: K. Knight, 'Stuck woodpeckers "walk" their beaks free for liberty', *Journal of Experimental Biology*, 225(5) (2022): eb244092.

shock-absorbing tissue: C. Lesté-Lassere, 'Woodpeckers don't have built-in shock absorbers to protect their brain', newscientist.com, 14 July 2022.

11–15 MARCH: CHIFFCHAFFS RETURN

two million pairs: https://app.bto.org/birdfacts/results/bob13110.htm and https://www.rspb.org.uk/birds-and-wildlife/wildlife-guides/bird-a-z/chiffchaff/ (accessed 3 August 2022).

the rigours of migration to southern Europe: http://www.cheshireandwirralbirdatlas.org/species/chiffchaff-wintering.htm (2008) (accessed 3 August 2022).

'functional green space': https://www.ons.gov.uk/economy/environmentalaccounts/bulletins/uknaturalcapital/urbanaccounts (accessed 4 August 2022).

hungry chicks: C. M. Perrins, 'Tits and their caterpillar food supply', *Ibis*, 133(s1) (1991), pp. 49–54.

healthy terrestrial ecosystems: D. Goulson, *Insect Declines and Why They Matter*, South West Wildlife Trust, 2019.

16–20 MARCH: BUTTERFLIES EMERGE

early months of the year: https://butterfly-conservation.org/butterflies/first-butterfly-sightings-2022 (accessed 10 August 2022).

21–25 MARCH: THE THUD OF DOZY BUMBLEBEES

later in the season: for an account of bumblebee life cycles see D. Goulson, *Bumblebees: Behaviour, Ecology, and Conservation.* Oxford: Oxford University Press, 2010; T. Benton, *Bumblebees.* London: Collins, 2006.

shiver rapidly: B. Heinrich and H. Esch, 'Thermoregulation in bees', *American Scientist*, 82(2) (1994), pp. 164–70.

summer heatwaves: D. Kenna, S. Pawar and R. Gill, 'Thermal flight performance reveals impact of warming on bumblebee foraging potential', *Functional Ecology*, 35 (2021), pp. 2508–22.

Bumblebee Economics: B. Heinrich, *Bumblebee Economics.* Cambridge, MA: Harvard University Press, 1979. The preface is to the new 2004 edition.

cautions against them: see B. Heinrich, 'ZZZZzzzzzMMMMMmmmmmmm', *New York Times*, 25 May 1979.

two French entomologists: A. Magnan, *Le Vol des insectes.* Paris: Hermann, 1934.

successful in explaining bumblebee aerodynamics: R. Bomphrey, G. Taylor and A. Thomas, 'Smoke visualization of free-flying bumblebees indicates independent leading-edge vortices on each wing pair', *Experiments in Fluids*, 46(5) (2009), p. 811–21.

Göran Persson: quoted in S. Thakur et al., *Sweden's Welfare State: Can the Bumblebee Keep Flying?.* Washington: IMF, 2003, p. 3.

economists and financial journalists: see, for example, D. Crouch, *Bumblebee Nation: The Hidden Story of the New Swedish Model.*

London: Blink Publishing, 2019; S. Steinmo, 'Sweden: The Evolution of a Bumblebee', in *The Evolution of Modern States: Sweden, Japan, and the United States*. Cambridge: Cambridge University Press, 2010; G. Svendsen and G. Svendsen, *Trust, Social Capital and the Scandinavian Welfare State: Explaining the Flight of the Bumblebee*. Cheltenham: Edward Elgar, 2016.

$160 and $689 billion: see table 4.9 in V. L. Imperatriz-Fonseca et al., *The Assessment Report of the Intergovernmental Science-Policy Platform on Biodiversity and Ecosystem Services on Pollinators, Pollination and Food Production*. Bonn: Secretariat of the Intergovernmental Science-Policy Platform on Biodiversity and Ecosystem Services, 2016.

26–30 MARCH: CHERRY BLOSSOM FESTIVAL

poetess Kunaikyō: *The Thirty-Six Immortal Women Poets*, trans. A. Pekarik, London: Barrie & Jenkins, 1991, p. 171.

'To learn how to die': *The Sound of Water*, trans S. Hamill. Boulder, CO; Shambhala, 1995, p. 104.

In 1896 the writer A. E. Housman captured the spectacle of wild cherry blossom: A. E. Housman, *A Shropshire Lad*. New York: John Lane Company, 1906, p. 76.

31 MARCH–4 APRIL: HALLUCINOGENIC MAGNOLIAS

Aztec poetry: D. Damrosch, 'The aesthetics of conquest: Aztec poetry before and after Cortés', *Representations*, 33 (1991), pp. 101–20.

On pollination ecology: K. Faegri and L. Pijl, *The Principles of Pollination Ecology*. London: Pergamon, 2013.

5–9 APRIL: HAILSTONES AND SUNSHINE

Kate Fox: *Watching the English: The Hidden Rules of English Behaviour*. London: Hodder & Stoughton, 2004.

Bill Bryson quote: B. Bryson, 'The man who'll make you love Britain anew', *Scottish Daily Mail*, 13 August 2016.

Kay Ryan, 'Hailstorm': *The Atlantic*, December 2003, p. 104.

10–14 APRIL: BLACKBIRDS BICKER

blackbird song: D. W. Snow, *A Study of Blackbirds*. London: George Allen and Unwin, 1958.

William Henry Hudson: Hudson, 'The Secret of the Willow Wren', in *Birds and Men*. Redditch: Read Books, 2016.

biosemiotics: A. Anastasi, 'Biology, learning, and evolution of vocality: Biosemiotics of birdsong', *Cognitive Semiotics*, 10(1) (2017), pp. 19–39.

noise pollution and birdsong: J. Sierro et al., 'European blackbirds exposed to aircraft noise advance their chorus, modify their song and spend more time singing', *Frontiers in Ecology and Evolution*, 5 (2017), p. 68.

as far back as the ancient Greeks we find evidence of birdsong as a model for poetic and rhetorical form: https://www.racar-racar.com/uploads/5/7/7/4/57749791/2010_35_1_7_akiyama.pdf (accessed 12 August 2022).

15–19 APRIL: BLACKTHORN SPRING

blackthorn poison injuries: H. Sharma and A. D. Meredith, 'Blackthorn injury: A report of three interesting cases', *Emergency Medicine Journal*, 21(3) (2004), p. 392.

Neolithic sloe berry use: P. Hunt, 'Otzi the Iceman's medicine kit included sloe berries (*Prunus Spinosa*)', *Electrum Magazine*, 5 June 2019, http://www.electrummagazine.com/2019/06/otzi-the-icemans-medicine-kit-included-sloe-berries-prunus-spinosa/ (accessed 6 September 2022).

20–24 APRIL: LLYGAD EBRILL
(APRIL'S EYE – THE CELANDINE)

asexual and sexual reproduction: K. Z. Mattingly et al., 'Genetic and morphological comparisons of lesser celandine (*Ficaria Verna*) invasions suggest regionally widespread clonal and sexual reproduction', preprint accessed 14 August 2022, now available at https://link.springer.com/article/10.1007/s10530-022-02921-4.

protoanemonin and saponins: A. E. Axtell, A. di Tommaso and A. R. Post, 'Lesser celandine (*Ranunculus ficaria*): A threat to woodland habitats in the northern United States and southern Canada', *Invasive Plant Science and Management*, 3(2) (2010), pp. 190–96.

liver damage: B. Yilmaz et al., 'Lesser celandine (pilewort) induced acute toxic liver injury: The first case report worldwide', *World Journal of Hepatology*, 7(2) (2015), pp. 285–8.

greater celandine uses: M. Woodward, *Gerard's Herball*, from the edition of T. H. Johnson, 1636. London: Spring Books, 1964.

25–29 APRIL: BLUEBELLS BLANKETING WOODS

bluebells and fungal friends: J. P. Clapp et al., 'Diversity of fungal symbionts in arbuscular mycorrhizas from a natural community', *New Phytologist*, 130 (1995), pp. 259–65.

Highland species champions: https://www.johnogroat-journal. co.uk/news/highland-councillors-to-champion-iconic-species-172572/

30 APRIL–4 MAY: MAY DAY GORSE CROWNS

Beltane: J. G. Frazer, *The Golden Bough*. London: Macmillan and Co., 1890.

Celtic folklore of Beltane: J. Rhys, *Celtic Folklore: Welsh and Manx*, vol. 1. Oxford: Clarendon Press, 1901.

Taliesin: M. Haycock, *Legendary Poems from the Book of Taliesin*. Aberystwyth: CMCS Publications, 2015.

theory of non-human minds: N. Malcolm, 'Knowledge of other minds 1', *Journal of Philosophy*, 55(23) (1958), pp. 969–78 and H. H. Price, 'Our evidence for the existence of other minds', *Philosophy*, 13 (1938), pp. 425–56.

5–9 MAY: FIRST SWIFTS

denial: K. Whyte, 'Too late for indigenous climate justice: Ecological and relational tipping points', *WIREs Climate Change*, 11(1) (2020): e603. For a thought-provoking version of the need to consider the uneven geographical contribution to carbon emissions see K. Yusef, *A Billion Black Anthropocenes*. Minneapolis: University of Minnesota Press, 2018.

drought and flooding: M. Glantz (ed.), *La Niña and Its Impacts: Facts and Speculation*. Tokyo: United Nations University Press, 2002.

bad for swift survival: C. Foster, *The Screaming Sky*. Beaminster: Little Toller, 2021; G. Boano et al., 'Climate anomalies affect annual survival rates of swifts wintering in sub-Saharan Africa', *Ecology and Evolution*, 10(14) (2020), pp. 7916–28.

more El Niño years: R. Seager, N. Henderson and M. Cane, 'Persistent discrepancies between observed and modelled trends in the tropical Pacific Ocean', *Journal of Climate*, 35(14) (2022), pp. 4571–84; B. Orihuela-Pinto, M. England and A. Taschetto, 'Interbasin and interhemispheric impacts of a collapsed Atlantic Overturning Circulation', *Nature Climate Change*, 12(6) (2022), pp. 558–65.

10–14 MAY: LILAC TIME

unlucky to bring indoors: for anecdotes and recollections of this superstition see https://www.plant-lore.com/lilac/ (accessed 16 May 2023).

varies with the time of day: X. Yang et al., 'Analysis of floral scent emitted from Syringa plants', *Journal of Forestry Research*, 27(2) (2015), pp. 273–81.

Persian in origin: H. W. Lack, 'Lilac and horse-chestnut: Discovery and rediscovery', *Curtis's Botanical Magazine*, 17(2) (2000), pp. 109–41.

in full flower: however, Sibthorp's discovery was posthumously suppressed by his literary executor, James Edward Smith, with the result that credit for making the connection between lilacs and the Balkans is often granted instead to later botanists, including Anton Rochel. For Sibthorp's journal excerpt see MS Sherard 216 in the Bodleian Library, transcribed in E. D. Tappe, 'John Sibthorp in the Danubian lands, 1794', *Revue des Études Sud-est Européennes*, 5(3–4) (1967), pp. 461–73.

Jefferson: all dates are from T. Jefferson, *Thomas Jefferson's Garden Book: 1766–1824, With Relevant Extracts from His Other Writings*. Philadelphia: American Philosophical Society, 1944. For the 'microseason' letter of 11 April 1818 see pp. 578–9.

volcanic eruption: J. Dai, E. Mosley-Thompson and L. Thompson, 'Ice core evidence for an explosive tropical volcanic eruption 6 years preceding Tambora', *Journal of Geophysical Research*, 96(D9) (1991), pp. 17361–66; A. Guevara-Murua et al., 'Observations of a stratospheric aerosol veil from a tropical volcanic eruption in December 1808: Is this the "Unknown" 1809 eruption?', *Climate of the Past Discussions*, 10(2) (2014), pp. 1901–32.

Lowell: Amy Lowell, 'Lilacs', *BROOM*. Rome and New York: The Broom Publishing Company, 1(1) (1921), pp. 41–4. These citations are on pp. 43 and 42 respectively.

15–20 MAY: FERNS UNFURL

commonest single plant species: https://www.woodlandtrust.org.uk/trees-woods-and-wildlife/plants/ferns/bracken/ (accessed 15 August 2022).

21–25 MAY: FROTHY HAWTHORN

I had found the Spring: E. Thomas, *In Pursuit of Spring*. Beaminster: Little Toller, 2016.

whole path throbbing: M. Proust (C. K. Scott Moncrieff trans.), *Swann's Way*. Dover: Chatto & Windus, 1922.

thick, white cream: D. Hockney for *A Bigger Picture* exhibition, Royal Academy, 2012.

26–30 MAY: BUTTERCUP MEADOWS

Culpeper: N. Culpeper, *The English Physician Enlarged*. London: John Streater, 1666, p. 80.

acting as a reflector: S. Vignolini et al., 'Directional scattering from the glossy flower of Ranunculus: How the buttercup lights up your chin', *Journal of The Royal Society Interface*, 9(71) (2012), pp. 1295–301.

shininess: S. Galsterer et al. 'Reflectance measurements of glossy petals of *Ranunculus lingua* (Ranunculaceae) and of non-glossy petals of *Heliopsis helianthoides* (Asteraceae)', *Plant Biology*, 1(6) (1999), pp. 670–78.

temperature: C. J. van der Kooi et al., 'Functional optics of glossy buttercup flowers', *Journal of The Royal Society Interface*, 14(127) (2017): 20160933.

Alfred Döblin: 'Die Ermordung Einer Butterblume', *Der Sturm*, 1(28), 8 September 1910, pp. 220–21; *Der Sturm* 1(29), 15 September 1910, p. 229. This citation is from 8 September, p. 221.

31 MAY–5 JUNE: POPPIES POPPING

Robert Bridges: R. Bridges, *The Shorter Poems of Robert Bridges*. Oxford: Oxford University Press, 1890.

W. T. Fernie: W. T. Fernie, *Herbal Simples Approved for Modern Uses of Cure*. Bristol: John Wright, 1895.

Geoffrey Grigson: G. Grigson, *The Englishman's Flora*. London: Phoenix House, 1955.

glaucine: M. Asencio et al., 'Biochemical and behavioural effects of boldine and glaucine on dopamine systems', *Pharmacology Biochemistry and Behaviour*, 62 (1999), pp. 7–13.

6–10 JUNE: DANCING DRAGONFLIES

Francis Bacon: F. Bacon (W. Rawley ed.), *Sylva sylvarum, or, A natural history in ten centuries: together with the History natural and experimental of life and death, or of the prolongation of life: whereunto is added Articles of enquiry touching metals and minerals and the New Atlantis, with an alphabetical table of the* *principal things contained in the ten centuries*. London: Bennet Griffin, 1683. Pdf. https://www.loc.gov/item/95202443/ (accessed 20 October 2022).

etymology of 'dragonfly': B. Elwood Montgomery, 'Why snakefeeder? Why dragonfly? Some random observations on etymological entomology', *Proceedings of the Indiana Academy of Science*, 82 (1973), pp. 235–41; J. Ayto, *Word Origins*. London: A. & C. Black, 2009.

dragonfly movement: M. Mischiati et al., 'Internal models direct dragonfly interception steering', *Nature*, 517 (2015), pp. 333–8.

11–15 JUNE: OXEYE DAISIES TURN IN THE SUN

97 per cent meadowlands lost: A. Byfield, 'Oxeye Daisies', *The Guardian*, 28 June 2013.

16–20 JUNE: RAIN-SOAKED ROSES

Assyrian cuneiform tablets: R. Campbell Thomson, *A Dictionary of Assyrian Botany*. London: British Academy, 1949, pp 10, 23.

Song of Songs: Song of Solomon, Holy Bible (King James Version), chapter 4.

Roman de la Rose: G. de Lorris, *The Romance of the Rose*, trans. F. S. Ellis. London: J. M. Dent and Co., 1900, vol. 3, p. 205.

21–26 JUNE: THUNDERBUGS ON FIZZING ELDERFLOWER

ancient pollinators: I. Terry, 'Thrips: The primeval pollinators?', *Thrips and Tospoviruses: Proceedings of the 7th Annual Symposium on Thysanoptera*. Canberra: ANIC, 2001, pp. 157–62.

research on mutualism and pollination: A. S. Scott-Brown et al., 'Mechanisms in mutualisms: A chemically mediated thrips pollination strategy in common elder', *Planta*, 250 (2019), pp. 367–79.

27 JUNE–1 JULY: A MESSY RIOT

Hildegard of Bingen: M. Marder, *Green Mass: The Ecological Theology of St. Hildegard of Bingen*. Stanford: Stanford University Press, 2021.

'The Language of Flowers': G. Bataille, *Visions of Excess: Selected Writings, 1927–1939*. Minneapolis: University of Minnesota Press, 1985, pp. 10–14.

the legend of the Seven Sleepers: C. S. Krokus, 'The darkness is not death: Toward a Christian-Muslim comparative theological study of the Seven Sleepers of Ephesus', *Spiritus*, 17(1) (2017), pp. 40–59.

2–6 JULY: PURPLE KNAPWEED AGAINST THUNDEROUS SKIES

John Clare, 'May': *The Shepherd's Calendar*, 1827. The original version has 'knotweed' instead of 'knapweed', but we can presume that this was a local name for the same plant. The custom Clare describes is also mentioned in Grigson's *Englishman's Flora* in reference to knapweed.

one project in 2015: AgriLand and UK Insect Pollinators Initiative survey, 2014, https://www.agriland.leeds.ac.uk/news/documents/Stakeholderworkshopbooklet.pdf (accessed 9 September 2022).

images of thunder: A. Witze, 'Images expose thunder in exquisite detail', *Nature* (2015), https://www.nature.com/articles/nature.2015.17490 (accessed 10 September 2022).

7–11 JULY: YELLOW WAGTAILS COURTING

research on passerines: K. M. Wilson, M. Nguyen and N. T. Burley, 'Divorce rate varies with fluidity of passerine social environment', *Animal Behaviour*, 183 (2022), pp. 51–60.

the convergences between courtship and reproductive fighting: R. J. Andrew, 'The displays given by passerines in courtship and reproductive fighting: A review', *Ibis*, 103a(4) (1961), pp. 315–48.

'the drives': S. Freud, 'The ego and the id' (1923), *TACD Journal*, 17(1) (1989), pp. 5–22.

as the effects of climate change intensify, the aggressive behaviours of male birds escalate: J. M. Samplonius and C. Both, 'Climate change may affect fatal competition between two bird species', *Current Biology*, 29(2) (2019), pp. 327–31.

mid-season breeding dispersal in wetland and arable birds: R. A. Robinson, J. D. Wilson and H. Q. Crick, 'The importance of arable habitat for farmland birds in grassland landscapes', *Journal of Applied Ecology*, 38(5) (2001), pp. 1059–69.

12–16 JULY: PUFFS OF MEADOWSWEET

Hoffman: D. Jeffries, *Aspirin: The Remarkable Story of a Wonder Drug*. London: Bloomsbury, 2005.

Edward Stone: E. Stone, 'An account of the success of the bark of the willow in the cure of agues. In a letter to the Right Honourable George Earl of Macclesfield, President of R. S. from the Rev. Mr. Edmund Stone, of Chipping-Norton in Oxfordshire', *Philosophical Transactions*, 53 (1763), pp. 195–200.

fifty billion pills: A. Jones, *Chemistry: An Introduction for Medical and Health Sciences*. Chichester: John Wiley & Sons, 2005, p. 5.

Schmidt: for a translation of the lab note see Jeffries, *Aspirin*. A. Schmidt, *Die industrielle Chemie in ihrer Bedeutung im Weltbild und Erinnerungen an ihren Aufbau*. Berlin: De Greuter, 1934, p. 765 footnote.

Eichengrün: we are heavily indebted to the work of Walter Sneader for uncovering this story. W. Sneader, 'The discovery of aspirin: A reappraisal', *BMJ*, 321 (2000): 1591.

paper published in 1949: A. Eichengrün, '50 Jahre Aspirin', *Pharmazie*, 4 (1949), pp. 582–4.

IG Farben: P. Hayes, *Industry and Ideology: IG Farben in the Nazi Era*. Cambridge: Cambridge University Press, 1987; M. Spicka, 'The Devil's Chemists on Trial: The American Prosecution of IG Farben at Nuremberg', in J. Michalczyk (ed.), *Nazi Law: From Nuremberg to Nuremberg*. London: Bloomsbury, 2018.

press release: Bayer AG, 'Zum Vortrag von Dr. Walter Sneader über die Entwicklung der Acetylsalicylsäure', 1999. Available at https://web.archive.org/web/20070928132933/ http://pressearchiv-kubitschek.www.de/pharma-presse/ presseerklaerungen/texte/pharma_medikamente/bayer/bayer_ 110999.html (accessed 16 May 2023).

28 JULY–2 AUGUST: WORTS AND WEEDS FOR BEES

see plants differently: R. Mabey, *Weeds*. London: Profile Books, 2010.

3–7 AUGUST: BLACKBERRIES APPEAR

far from a wasteland: S. Mortimer et al., *The Nature Conservation Value of Scrub in Britain*. Peterborough: JNCC Report no. 308, 2000.

degraded grassland: Natural England, *The Biodiversity Metric 4.0* (2023), https://nepubprod.appspot.com/publication/ 6049804846366720 (accessed 16 May 2023).

'vegetable calendar': M. Spencer, *Murder Most Florid: Inside the Mind of a Forensic Botanist*. London: Quadrille Publishing, 2019.

several sets of chromosomes: P. Šarhanová et al., 'New insights into the variability of reproduction modes in European populations of Rubus subgen. Rubus: How sexual are polyploid brambles?', *Sexual Plant Reproduction*, 25(4) (2012), pp. 319–35.

Michaelmas: 29 September or 10 October, depending on whether you're working with a calendar from after the eleven-day shift of 1752 or before. For the English folklore see J. Simpson and S. Roud, *A Dictionary of English Folklore*. Oxford: Oxford University Press, 2003.

Halloween: see entry for 'puca' in T. P. Dolan, *A Dictionary of Hiberno-English*. Dublin: Gill and Macmillan, 1998.

'Blackberrying Black Woman': G. Nichols, *Passport to Here and There*. Hexham: Bloodaxe Books, 2020.

8–12 AUGUST:
GOLDFINCHES CHATTER ON THISTLES

swallow more per minute: E. Glück, 'Flock size and habitat-dependent food and energy intake of foraging goldfinches', *Oecologia*, 71(1) (1986), pp. 149–55.

Ted Hughes: T. Hughes, 'Autumn Nature Notes', *The Listener*, 26 September 1974.

1871: C. Darwin, *The Descent of Man, and Selection in Relation to Sex* (2 vols.), vol. 2. London: John Murray, 1871, pp. 39–40.

Ian Newton: I. Newton, 'The adaptive radiation and feeding ecology of some British finches', *Ibis*, 109(1) (1967), pp. 33–96.

parasite load of the bird: G. López and J. Figuerola, 'Carotenoid-based masks in the European goldfinch *Carduelis carduelis* reflect different information in males and females', *Ardea*, 96(2) (2008), pp. 233–42.

Herbert Friedmann: *The Symbolic Goldfinch: Its History and Significance in European Devotional Art*. Washington: Pantheon Books, 1946.

13–17 AUGUST: VIBRANT ROWAN BERRIES

these red berries were said to contain the regenerating force of the gods: G. Varner, *Mythic Forest, the Green Man and the Spirit of Nature*. New York: Algora Publishing, 2006.

in pre-modern medicine: D. Allen and G. Hatfield, *Medicinal Plants in Folk Tradition: An Ethnobotany of Britain and Ireland*. Portland, OR: Timber Press, 2004.

research carried out on the wider *Sorbus* family: V. Sarv, P. R. Venskutonis and R. Bhat, 'The *Sorbus* spp. – underutilised plants for foods and nutraceuticals: Review on polyphenolic phytochemicals and antioxidant potential', *Antioxidants*, 9(9) (2020), p. 813.

the undefined word 'aroint' in Early Modern English: A. Liberman, 'Shakespeare's Aroint thee, witch for the last time?', *Neuphilologische Mitteilungen*, 115(1) (2014), pp. 55–62.

18–22 AUGUST: SWALLOWS PREPARE TO LEAVE

fatten up: L. Coiffait et al., 'Fattening strategies of British & Irish Barn Swallows *Hirundo rustica* prior to autumn migration', *Ringing & Migration*, 26(1) (2011), pp. 15–23.

change speed or direction: D. R. Warrick, 'The turning- and linear-maneuvering performance of birds: The cost of efficiency for coursing insectivores', *Canadian Journal of Zoology*, 76 (1998), pp. 1063–79; D. R. Warrick et al., 'Foraging at the edge of the world: Low-altitude, high-speed manoeuvering in barn swallows', *Philosophical Transactions of the Royal Society B*, 371(1704) (2016): 20150391.

shorter-tailed males took four times as long: A. Møller, 'Female choice selects for male sexual tail ornaments in the monogamous swallow', *Nature*, 332 (1988), pp. 640–42.

longer female tails and reduced reproductive success: J. Cuervo, A. P. Møller and F. de Lope, 'Experimental manipulation of tail length in female barn swallows (*Hirundo rustica*) affects their future reproductive success', *Behavioral Ecology*, 14(4) (2003), pp. 451–6. It is worth noting that A. P. Møller's work has been accused of data irregularities; see A. Abbott, 'Prolific ecologist vows to fight Danish misconduct verdict', *Nature*, 427 (2004) p. 381.

significant energy costs: P. Pap et al., 'Sexual dimorphism and population differences in structural properties of barn swallow (*Hirundo rustica*) wing and tail feathers', *PLoS One* 10(6) (2015): e0130844; A. Muñoz, J. M. Aparicio and R. Bonal, 'Male barn swallows use different signalling rules to produce ornamental tail feathers', *Evolutionary Ecology*, 25 (2011), pp. 1217–30; K. Buchanan and M. Evans, 'The effect of tail streamer length on aerodynamic performance in the barn swallow', *Behavioral Ecology*, 11(2) (2000), pp. 228–38.

without stalling: R. Åke Norberg, 'Swallow tail streamer is a mechanical device for self deflection of tail leading edge, enhancing aerodynamic efficiency and flight manoeuvrability', *Proceedings: Biological Sciences*, 257(1350), (1994), pp. 227–33.

ground effect: J. Rayner, 'On the aerodynamics of animal flight in ground effect', *Philosophical Transactions: Biological Sciences*, 334(1269) (1991), pp. 119–28.

20 per cent of the time: J. Finn et al., 'Avoidance of headwinds or exploitation of ground effect – why do birds fly low?', *Journal of Field Ornithology*, 89(2) (2012), pp. 192–202.

'The Swallow': Charlotte Smith, *A Natural History of Birds Intended Chiefly for Young Persons*. London: J. Johnson, 1807, 2nd edn. 1819.

emerge again: the anatomist John Hunter had already proven that swallows could not survive either hibernation or submergence, but these theories lingered nonetheless.

6,000-mile trip: C. Mead, 'Barn Swallow', in C. Wernham et al., *The Migration Atlas: Movements of the Birds of Britain and Ireland*. London: T. & A. D. Poyser, 2002, pp. 462–4.

23–27 AUGUST: A SHOWER OF HAZELNUT HUSKS FROM FATTENING SQUIRRELS

tannins and squirrels: P. Smallwood and W. D. Peters, 'Grey squirrel food preferences: The effects of tannin and fat concentration', *Ecology*, 67(1) (1986), pp. 168–74.

squirrels take particular care to cache preferred nuts: L. Hopewell and L. Leaver, 'Evidence of social influences on cache-making by grey squirrels (*Sciurus carolinensis*)', *Ethology*, 114(11) (2008), pp. 1061–8.

'a wild female nutcracker': F. Kafka, *The Blue Octavo Notebooks*, 1917–19, in I. Bruce and R. March, *Kafka and Cultural Zionism: Dates in Palestine*. Madison, WI: University of Wisconsin Press, 2007.

28 AUGUST–1 SEPTEMBER: BROWN OAK GALLS

usually parasitic: for this definition of galls I'm indebted to M. Redfern, *Plant Galls*. London: Collins, 2011.

fifty different kinds: M. Chinery, *Britain's Plant Galls*. Old Basing: WildGuides, 2011.

Neuroterus quercusbaccarum: Chinery, *Britain's Plant Galls*.

very recent research: A. Korgaonkar et al., 'A novel family of secreted insect proteins linked to plant gall development', *Current Biology*, 31(9) (2021), pp. 1836–49.

Andricus kollari: M. Redfern and R. Askew, *Plant Galls*. Slough: Richmond Publishing, 1992.

1735: Redfern and Askew, *Plant Galls*.

stick to the paper: the website irongallink.org offers instructions.

corrosive effect: P. Garside and Z. Miller, 'Iron gall ink on paper: Saving the words that eat themselves', British Library Collection Care blog, https://blogs.bl.uk/collectioncare/ink/ (accessed 3 August 2022).

2–7 SEPTEMBER: PUHPOWEE, THE FORCE THAT MAKES MUSHROOMS POP UP OVERNIGHT

Kimmerer: R. Kimmerer, *Gathering Moss*. London: Penguin, 2021.

Frank: J. Sapp, *Evolution by Association: A History of Symbiosis*. Oxford: Oxford University Press, 1994.

Cage: I am deeply indebted to the brilliant work of Kingston Trinder in uncovering Cage's complex relationship with mushrooms. See *John Cage: A Mycological Foray*. Los Angeles: Atelier Editions, 2020.

8–12 SEPTEMBER: ARACHNIDS ASSEMBLE!

taxonomic controversy: G. Oxford and A. Bolzern, 'Molecules v. morphology – is *Eratigena atrica* (*Araneae*: *Agelenidae*) one species or three?', *Arachnology*, 17(7) (2018), pp. 337–57.

under a microscope: for an excellent field guide to spiders see L. Bee, G. Oxford and H. Smith, *Britain's Spiders: A Field Guide*. Princeton: Princeton University Press, 2nd edn. 2020.

Gleanings in Natural History: vol. 2, London: John Murray, 1832, p. 136. The identical text also appears in Pierce Egan's *Book of Sports, and Mirror of Life*. London: T. T. and J. Tegg, 1832.

not a drainpipe: W. Nentwig et al., *All You Need to Know About Spiders*. Cham: Springer, Association for the Promotion of Spider Research, 2022.

whirling: R. R. Jackson, R. J. Brassington and R. J. Rowe, 'Anti-predator defences of *Pholcus phalangioides* (*Araneae*, *Pholcidae*), a web-building and web-invading spider', *Journal of Zoology*, 220(4) (1990), pp. 543–52; B. A. Heuts et al., 'Long-duration whirling of *Pholcus phalangioides* (*Araneae*, *Pholcidae*) is specifically elicited by Salticid spiders', *Behavioural Processes*, 55(1) (2001), pp. 27–34.

mimics an insect: R. Jackson and R. Brassington, 'The biology of *Pholcus phalangioides (Araneae, Pholcidae)*: Predatory versatility, araneophagy and aggressive mimicry', *Journal of Zoology*, 211(2) (1987), pp. 227–38.

venom: Rainer Foelix, *Biology of Spiders*. New York: Oxford University Press, 3rd edn. 2011.

13–17 SEPTEMBER: DEW-DRENCHED COBWEBS

Arachne: for the story see Ovid, *Metamorphoses* (trans. F. J. Miller). Cambridge, MA: Harvard University Press, Loeb Classical Library, vol. 1, Book VI (1916).

metamorphosed: M. Vincent, 'Between Ovid and Barthes: "Ekphrasis", orality, textuality in Ovid's "Arachne"', *Arethusa*, 27(3) (1994), pp. 361–86.

Marx: K. Marx, *Capital*, trans. Ben Fowkes. London: Penguin, 2004, vol. 1, p. 284.

prosthetic extension: H. F. Japyassú and K. N. Laland, 'Extended spider cognition', *Animal Cognition*, 20(3) (2017), pp. 375–95.

scorpions: P. Brownell and R. D. Farley, 'Detection of vibrations in sand by tarsal sense organs of the nocturnal scorpion, *Paruroctonus mesaensis*', *Journal of Comparative Physiology*, 131(1) (1979), pp. 23–30; P. Brownell and R. D. Farley, 'Orientation to vibrations in sand by the nocturnal scorpion *Paruroctonus mesaensis*: Mechanism of target localization', *Journal of Comparative Physiology*, 131(1) (1979), pp. 31–8; P. Brownell and R. D. Farley, 'Prey-localizing behaviour of the nocturnal desert scorpion, *Paruroctonus mesaensis*: Orientation to substrate vibrations', *Animal Behaviour*, 27(1) (1979), pp. 185–93.

biotremology: P. S. Hill, 'How do animals use substrate-borne vibrations as an information source?', *The Science of Nature*, 96(12) (2009), pp. 1355–71.

features of their anatomy: R. Foelix, *Biology of Spiders*. New York: Oxford University Press, 3rd edn. 2011.

communicate proactively: W. Eberhard, *Spider Webs: Behaviour, Function and Evolution*. Chicago: University of Chicago Press, 2020.

not potential prey: S. Sivalinghem, 'Communication in the Black Widow Spider, *Latrodectus Hesperus (Araneae: Theridiidae)*', PhD thesis, University of Toronto.

across the species barrier: T. Saraceno, *Arachnid Orchestra Jam Sessions*. Singapore: NTU CCA, 2016.

18–22 SEPTEMBER: BEES CLING TO IVY

80 per cent of the nectar collected by honey bees: M. Garbuzov and F. L. W. Ratnieks, 'Ivy: An underappreciated key resource to flower-visiting insects in autumn', *Insect Conservation and Diversity*, 7(1) (2013), pp. 91–102.

23–27 SEPTEMBER: CACOPHONIES OF CONKERS

in a letter dated 26 July 1557: H. W. Lack, 'Lilac and horse chestnut: Discovery and rediscovery', *Curtis's Botanical Magazine*, 17 (2000), pp. 109–41.

imports of the horse chestnut into European gardens: E. Bellini and S. Nin, 'Horse chestnut: Cultivation for ornamental purposes and non-food crop production', *Journal of Herbs, Spices and Medicinal Plants*, 11(1–2) (2005), pp. 93–120.

Linnaeus encoded this into scientific 'knowledge' proper in his *Species Plantarum*: C. Linnaeus, *Species Plantarum: exhibentes plantas rite cognitas, ad genera relatas, cum differentiis specificis, nominibus trivialibus, synonymis selectis, locis natalibus, secundum systema sexuale digestas.* Stockholm: Impensis Laurentii Salvii, 1st edn. 1753.

the gentleman traveller John Hawkins: Lack, 'Lilac and horse chestnut'.

in modern medicine: C. Ulbricht et al., 'Horse chestnut', *Journal of Herbal Pharmacotherapy*, 2(1) (2002), pp. 71–85.

28 SEPTEMBER–2 OCTOBER: BEECH NUTS FALL

pollen in charcoal: H. A. Hyde, 'Pre-Roman beech charcoal in South Wales: A preliminary note', *New Phytologist*, 36 (1937), p. 184.

3–7 OCTOBER: THE SOUND OF MIGRATING GEESE AND SWANS

Exeter Book: P. F. Baum North (trans.), *Anglo-Saxon Riddles of the Exeter Book.* Durham, NC: Duke University Press, 1963.

Ride of the Valkyries: according to Ludwig Koch, cited in C. Higgins, *This New Noise: The Extraordinary Birth and Troubled Life of the BBC.* London: Faber, 2015.

small vortex: S. Portugal et al., 'Upwash exploitation and downwash avoidance by flap phasing in ibis formation flight', *Nature*, 505 (2014), pp. 399–402.

thirteen hours: C. Pennycuick et al., 'Response to weather and light conditions of migrating Whooper Swans *Cygnus cygnus* and flying height profiles, observed with the Argos satellite system', *Ibis*, 141(3) (1999), pp. 434–43.

syrinx: P. A. Johnsgard, *Swans: Their Biology and Natural History*. Lincoln, NE: Zea Books, 2016.

trachea: M. Brazil, *The Whooper Swan*. London: T. and A. D. Poyser, 2003.

in his diary: Jean Sibelius (Fabian Dahlstrom ed.), *Dagbok 1909–1944*. Helsinki: Svenska litteratursällskapet i Finland/ Stockholm: Atlantis, 2005. I am very grateful to the editor of this volume, Hedvig Rask, not only for permission to reproduce the extract but for help with my translation into English.

8–12 OCTOBER: OWLS DUET

ideal conditions: H. Hanmer et al., 'Large-scale citizen science survey of a common nocturnal raptor: Urbanization and weather conditions influence the occupancy and detectability of the tawny owl *Strix aluco*', *Bird Study*, 68(2) (2021), pp. 233–44; I. Zuberogoitia et al., 'Factors affecting spontaneous vocal activity of tawny owls *Strix aluco* and implications for surveying large areas', *Ibis*, 161(3) (2019), pp. 495–503.

establishing and advertising territory: M. Toms, *Owls*. London: Collins, New Naturalist Library, 2014.

according to The Sound Approach: M. Robb and The Sound Approach, *Undiscovered Owls: A Sound Approach Guide*. Poole: The Sound Approach, 2015.

of the caller: B. Appleby and S. Redpath, 'Indicators of male quality in the hoots of tawny owls', *Journal of Raptor Research*, 31(1) (1997), pp. 65–70; S. Redpath, B. Appleby and S. Petty, 'Do male hoots betray parasite loads in tawny owls?', *Journal of Avian Biology*, 31(4) (2000), pp. 457–62.

an aggressive response to intruders: P. Galeotti and G. Pavan, 'Differential responses of territorial tawny owls *Strix aluco* to the hooting of neighbours and strangers', *Ibis*, 135(3) (1993), pp. 300–04.

courtship feeding early in the year: B. Appleby et al., 'Sex-specific territorial responses in tawny owls *Strix aluco*', *Ibis*, 141(1) (1999), pp. 91–9.

open habitats: Robb et al., *Undiscovered Owls*.

13–17 OCTOBER: CHESTNUTS GLISTEN

a smell of roasted chestnuts: C. Dickens, *The Mystery of Edwin Drood: Reprinted Pieces, and Other Stories*. London: Chapman and Hall, 1892, p. 248.

***A Christmas Carol*:** C. Dickens, *A Christmas Carol*. London: Chapman and Hall, 1843, pp. 81, 95.

Rooke Church: R. Church, *An olde thrift newly revived: wherein is declared the manner of planting, preserving, and husbanding young trees of divers kindes for timber and fuell*. London: Richard Moore, 1612, p. 7.

a staple in the British diet: W. A. Scribonius (D. Widdowes and I. Wydowes contribs.), *Naturall philosophy, or, A description of the world, namely, of angels, of man, of the heauens, of the ayre, of the earth, of the water and of the creatures in the whole world*. London: I.D. for Iohn Bellamie [. . .], 1621.

18–22 OCTOBER: ACORN-CACHING, FOREST-PLANTING JAYS

larger nuts: J. Pons, and J. Pausas, 'Not only size matters: Acorn selection by the European jay (*Garrulus glandarius*)', *Acta Oecologica*, 31(3) (2007), pp. 353–60.

open areas with loose soil: F. Vera, *Grazing Ecology and Forest History*. Wallingford: CABI Publishing, 2000.

landmarks like bushes and rocks: A. Bennett, 'Spatial memory in a food storing corvid. 1. Near tall landmarks are primarily used', *Journal of Comparative Physiology A*, 173 (1993), pp. 193–207.

from April to August: I. Bossema, 'Jays and oaks: An eco-ethological study of a symbiosis', *Behaviour*, 70(1–2) (1979), pp. 1–117.

both sound and vision: R. Shaw and N. Clayton 'Pilfering Eurasian jays use visual and acoustic information to locate caches', *Animal Cognition*, 17(6) (2014), pp. 1281–8.

the more dominant the bird, the more aggressive its thieving: R. Shaw and N. Clayton, 'Eurasian jays, *Garrulus glandarius*, flexibly switch caching and pilfering tactics in response to social context', *Animal Behaviour*, 84 (2012), pp. 1191–200.

less discreet when they thought that they were unobserved: E. Legg and N. Clayton, 'Eurasian jays (*Garrulus glandarius*) conceal caches from onlookers', *Animal Cognition* 17(5) (2014), pp. 1223–6.

noise can give them away: R. Shaw and N. Clayton, 'Careful cachers and prying pilferers: Eurasian jays (*Garrulus glandarius*) limit auditory information available to competitors', *Proceedings of the Royal Society B*, 280(1752) (2013): 20122238. However, some of these findings have proven difficult to replicate; see P. Amodio et al., 'Little evidence that Eurasian jays protect their caches by responding to cues about a conspecific's desire and visual perspective', *eLife* 10:e69647, 2021.

a 'desire state': L. Ostojić et al., 'Evidence suggesting that desire-state attribution may govern food sharing in Eurasian jays', *PNAS*, 110(10) (2013), pp. 4123–8.

Plutarch: 'Whether Land or Sea Animals are Cleverer' in *Moralia Volume XII* (H. Cherniss and W. Helmbold trans.). Cambridge, MA: Harvard University Press, Loeb Classical Library, 1957.

23–27 OCTOBER: WIND SWIRLS THROUGH FALLEN LEAVES

'through leaves': V. Sackville-West, 'Walking through leaves', BBC Home Service, 1950.

2–6 NOVEMBER: FIRST FROSTS

iron-hard earth and stone-like water: C. Rossetti, 'A Christmas Carol', *Scribner's Monthly*, 3 (1872), p. 278.

later frosts: J. R. Lamichhane, 'Rising risks of late-spring frosts in a changing climate', *Nature Climate Change*, 11 (2021), pp. 554–5.

Central England Temperature record: https://www.metoffice.gov.uk/hadobs/hadcet/ (accessed 19 September 2022).

7–11 NOVEMBER: FOG, DRIZZLE AND MIST

modern English cities: C. L. Corton, *London Fog: The Biography*. Cambridge, MA: Harvard University Press, 2015.

12–16 NOVEMBER: THE SMELL OF DECAYING LEAVES

memory is effectively created: R. Khamsi, 'Unpicking the link between smell and memories', *Nature*, 606, (2022), pp. 2–4.

17–21 NOVEMBER: CHATTERING STARLINGS

size and duration increase when predators are nearby: A. Goodenough et al., 'Birds of a feather flock together: Insights into starling murmuration behaviour revealed using citizen science', *PLoS One*, 12(6) (2017): e0179277.

Recent research has studied the various shapes: R. Storms et al., 'Complex patterns of collective escape in starling flocks under predation', *Behavioural Ecology and Sociobiology*, 73(1) (2019):10.

Craig Reynolds: C. Reynolds, 'Flocks, herds, and schools: A distributed behavioral model', *Computer Graphics*, 21(4) (1987), pp. 25–34.

Batman Returns: L. Fisher, *The Perfect Swarm: The Science of Complexity in Everyday Life*. New York: Basic Books, 2009.

correlating their flight with other birds: M. Ballerini et al., 'Interaction ruling animal collective behavior depends on topological rather than metric distance: Evidence from a field study', *PNAS*, 105(4) (2008), pp. 1232–7.

something called 'criticality': A. Cavagna et al., 'Scale-free correlations in starling flocks', *PNAS*, 107(26) (2010), pp. 11865–70; W. Bialek et al., 'Social interactions dominate speed control in poising natural flocks near criticality', *PNAS*, 111(20) (2014), pp. 7212–7.

22–26 NOVEMBER: EVEN THE LIGHT GROWS COLD

seasonal changes in human colour perception: L. E. Welbourne, A. B. Morland and A. R. Wade, 'Human colour perception changes between seasons', *Current Biology*, 25(15) (2015), pp. R646–7.

27 NOVEMBER–1 DECEMBER: TEASEL BRUSH SILHOUETTES

teasel sound: M. Mouchemore, 'Shadows and Reflections', Caught by the River, 24 December 2020, https://www.caught bytheriver.net/2020/12/shadows-and-reflections-melissa-mouchemore/ (accessed 16 September 2022).

teasel carnivory: J. Schaefer, 'Dipsacus and Drosera: Frank's favourite carnivores', darwinproject.ac.uk (accessed 14 September 2022); J. J. Krupa and J. M. Thomas, 'Is the common teasel (*Dipsacus fullonum*) carnivorous or was Francis Darwin wrong?', *Botany*, 97(6) (2019), pp. 321–8; P. J. A. Shaw and K. Shackleton, 'Carnivory in the teasel *Dipsacus fullonum* – The effect of experimental feeding on growth and seed set', *PLoS One*, 6(3) (2011): e17935.

2–6 DECEMBER: ROBINS DEFEND
WINTER TERRITORIES

and it stuck: D. Lack, *Robin Redbreast*. Oxford: Clarendon Press, 1950, p. 44.

dummy robins: D. Chantrey and L. Workman, 'Song and plumage effects on aggressive display by the European Robin *Erithacus rubecula*', *Ibis*, 126(3) (1984), pp. 366–71.

rival's song: H. Schwabl and E. Kriner, 'Territorial aggression and song of male European robins (*Erithacus rubecula*) in autumn and spring: Effects of antiandrogen treatment', *Hormones and Behavior*, 25(2) (1991), pp. 180–94.

Richard Mabey: quoted in Andrew Lack, *Redbreast: The Robin in Life and Literature*, introduction. London: SMH Books, 2008.

low-light conditions: R. Thomas et al., 'Eye size in birds and the timing of song at dawn', *Proeedings of the Royal Society B*, 269(1493) (2002), pp. 831–7.

the basis for a highly sensitive compass: K. Schulten, C. Swenberg and A. Weller, 'A biomagnetic sensory mechanism based on magnetic field modulated coherent electron spin motion', *Zeitschrift für Physikalische Chemie*, 111(1) (1978), pp. 1–5. I am deeply indebted to the admirably lucid account provided by Peter Hore in P. Hore and H. Mouritsen, 'The radical-pair mechanism of magnetoreception', *Annual Review of Biophysics*, 45 (2016), pp. 299–344.

Caged robins: T. Ritz et al., 'Magnetic compass of birds is based on a molecule with optimal directional sensitivity', *Biophysical Journal*, 96(8) (2009), pp. 3451–7

cryptochrome: R. Wiltschko and W. Wiltschko, 'Sensing magnetic directions in birds: Radical pair processes involving cryptochrome', *Biosensors*, 4(3) (2014), pp. 221–42; J. Xu et al., 'Magnetic sensitivity of cryptochrome 4 from a migratory songbird', *Nature*, 594 (2021), pp. 535–40.

7–11 DECEMBER: MISTLETOE BOUGHS
DRIP FROM BRANCHES

viscin uses: N. Horbelt, P. Fratzl and M. J. Harrington, 'Mistletoe viscin: A hygro- and mechano-responsive cellulose-based adhesive for diverse materials applications', *PNAS*, 1(1) (2022):pgac026.

uses in HIV+ patients: R. W. Gorter et al., 'Tolerability of an extract of European mistletoe among immunocompromised and healthy individuals', *Alternative Therapies in Health and Medicine*, 5(6) (1999), pp. 37–8.

12–16 DECEMBER: THE BLACK MONTH DEEPENS

in the Celtic tradition, the 'black month' is the polar opposite of early spring: Dafydd ap Gwilym, 'Mis Mai a Mis Tachwedd'. Welsh Department, Swansea University and the Centre for Advanced Welsh and Celtic Studies. https://dafyddapgwilym. net/AnaServer?dafydd+75787+compareNotesCymEng. anv+edEl=75158&localEl=75787&titleEl=75146 (accessed 1 July 2022).

a tradition of tales of hags or Cailleacha: E. Hull, 'Legends and traditions of the Cailleach Bheara or Old Woman (Hag) of Beare', *Folklore*, 38(3) (1927), pp. 225–54.

the botanist Richard Bradley's 1718 tract: R. Bradley, *The Gentleman and Gardeners Kalendar: Directing What Is Necessary to Be Done Every Month, in the Kitchen-Garden, Fruit-Garden, Nursery, Management of Forest-Trees, Green-House and Flower-Garden. With Directions for the Making and Ordering Hop-Grounds*. London: W. Mears, 1718.

his book titled *A philosophical enquiry into the late severe winter, the scarcity and dearness of provisions, and the occasion of the distemper raging in several remote parts of England*: R. Bradley, *A Philosophical Enquiry into the late Severe Winter, the scarcity and dearness of provisions, and the occasion of the distemper raging in several remote parts of England: with letters from many eminent physicians in the country, etc.* London: J. Roberts; R. Montagu, 1729.

earthworms push deeper into the ground: M. Holmstrup and K. E. Zachariassen, 'Physiology of cold hardiness in earthworms', *Comparative Biochemistry and Physiology Part A: Physiology*, 1996, 115(2), pp.91–101.

meteorologists have discovered that it is possible to predict cold weather: https://www.nsf.gov/news/special_reports/ autumnwinter/index.jsp (accessed 1 August 2022).

seas in the Outer Hebrides, where the Cailleach's washtub is situated, are stimulated by low-pressure systems: S. P. Neill et al., 'The wave and tidal resource of Scotland', *Renewable Energy*, 114, Part A (2017), pp. 3–17.

17–21 DECEMBER:
DARKNESS AND LIGHT HOLD HANDS

the 'planet tilts': A. Dillard, *The Abundance*. Edinburgh: Canongate, 2016.

'The sun never knew': Louis Kahn quoted by C. Moore in the introduction to J. Tanizaki's *In Praise of Shadows*. London: Vintage, 2001.

shadows in art: W. C. Sharpe, *Grasping Shadows: The Dark Side of Literature, Painting, Photography and Film*. Oxford: Oxford University Press, 2017.

22–26 DECEMBER: JOLLY HOLLY

researchers in Spain: C. Herrera and P. Bazaga, 'Epigenetic correlates of plant phenotypic plasticity: DNA methylation differs between prickly and nonprickly leaves in heterophyllous *Ilex aquifolium (Aquifoliaceae)* trees', *Botanical Journal of the Linnean Society*, 171 (2013), pp. 441–52.

important winter feed: J. Radley, 'Holly as a winter feed', *The Agricultural History Review*, 9(2) (1961), pp. 89–92.

Lyarde: T. Wright and J. Halliwell (eds.), *Reliquiae Antiquae: Scraps from ancient manuscripts, illustrating chiefly early English literature and the English language*. London: John Russell Smith, 1845, vol. 2, p. 280.

Thomas West commented: cited in M. Spray, 'Holly as a fodder in England', *The Agricultural History Review*, 29(2) (1981), pp. 97–110, p. 100.

27–31 DECEMBER: TREE SKELETONS AND SKY

Anna Botsford Comstock: *Trees at Leisure*. Ithaca, NY: Comstock Publishing Co., 1916.

Robin Wall Kimmerer: 'White Pine', in J. C. Ryan, P. Viera and M. Galiano, *The Mind of Plants: Narratives of Vegetal Intelligence*. Santa Fe: Synergetic Press, 2021.

'not collections of isolated organisms': R. Schiffman, ' "Mother Trees" are intelligent: They learn and remember', *Scientific American*, 4 May 2021.

being like a forest: ' "The trees knotted their branches and": A conversation with Ross Gay', YouTube, 6 February 2021 (accessed 21 September 2022).

Acknowledgements

KIERA

Serendipity is always important in creativity, but no project in my life has been as brimful of chance and good fortune as this one. The chances of meeting strangers online who not only share one's passion for nature, but with whom one can work creatively, are very small. And yet that has been my good fortune. Over the past few years, Rebecca, Rowan and Lulah have filled me with job, inspiration, encouragement and fellow-feeling on a daily basis, their sheer vitality off-setting a time of climate, nature and pandemic emergency. Special thanks also to Nicola Headlam, who was involved in our project in its earlier stages.

When writing this book, I was overwhelmed by the sheer kindness and generosity of a whole community of scientists, artists and writers. A huge number of individuals were kind enough to spare the time to read, comment, check and offer constructive criticism on drafts of these essays.

Writers, editors, researchers and librarians: David Higgins offered insightful editorial comment and advice on the question of how to handle climate change without driving readers to despair, providing a welcome counter to my doom-laden first drafts. Wendy Pratt, editor of the brilliant *Spelt* magazine, allowed me to reproduce part of an essay I'd written for her publication as the basis for the introduction to this volume. Dr Jeremy Brown of the Wellcome Collection helped me when I was at the end of my tether trying to find a copy of Eichengrün's 1949 article for the essay on meadowsweet. Hedvig Rask kindly helped me translate the Swedish quote from Sibelius's diary about migrating swans. Above all, huge thanks go to Laura Barber of Granta for her incredible editorial skill, her diplomacy, her wit and her patience as she wrangled our sentences into order and sharpened our sensory noticings. Thanks also to our copy-editor, Linden Lawson, and proofreader, Jack Alexander, for their sharp eyes and patience with my footnotes. And special gratitude to Christine Lo, our Production Editor, whose generous, painstaking and detailed work really improved the book.

Scientists, ecologists and species specialists: Grant Bigg kindly checked my work on ENSO and helped me to understand the contribution of meteorology to the seasons. Leading arachnologist Geoff Oxford was incredibly generous with his time, reading and commenting on the two essays on spiders and teaching me about the evolutionary origins of arachnophobia. Will Peach of the RSPB shared insights from his work on sparrows and alerted me to an unfortunately worded sentence in which I had inadvertently blamed the entire COVID-19 pandemic on them (!); leading flight researcher Tyson Hedrick looked over my writing on the delicate movements of swallows and enriched my understanding of the ground effect. Mark Powell checked my lichen science and rescued me from errors about haustoria; Margaret Redfern, queen of the plant galls, taught me about the tannin content of different species. Entomologist extraordinaire Dave Goulson looked through my essay on bumblebees and offered solidarity on saving them. Will Shepherd and Joanna Watts helped me with my first draft on starlings, and Andrea Cavagna took time out of his busy schedules to help me to understand criticality. Peter Hore, himself a brilliant scientist and scientific communicator, assisted me in understanding and explaining the quantum robin.

Artists: Hubert Fenzl shared insights into his lichen reliefs and his working process, particularly the colours red and gold, and provided me with much-needed emotional relief with a series of wonderful emails filled with ideas and inspiration.

I'm also indebted to the Department of Urban Studies and Planning at the University of Sheffield for funding a trip to the British Library, which was pivotal in checking my footnotes, and especially to Liz Sharp, my very patient boss. Most of all, I'm grateful to my husband, Malcolm Tait, for putting up with me while I was writing this book (and frequently stressed and grumpy). He read every single draft and cheered me on, while offering tactful advice about how I could improve things (and a glass of wine when necessary). Also to my Mum and Dad, who encouraged me, and who gave me my love of nature in the first place: a gift for which I wasn't nearly as grateful as I should have been as a child.

LULAH

This book evolved organically out of a connection between four strangers, and I want to thank my fellow Noticers, Kiera, Rowan and Rebecca, for all their wisdom, wit and support as we grew our project and created a new form for our words. Huge thanks also to our editor, Laura Barber, whose eye for sharpening a sentence and shrewd questions have made my sections so much better. Thanks to the wonderful team at Granta, who have imagined, enthused and laboured to make this beautiful book the best it could be. Thanks to our agent Natalie Galustian for corralling and encouraging.

Thanks to our Twitter community, who have filled the past year with joyful observations and shared their immense expertise. I have learned so much.

And finally, thanks to my family for tolerating my nature-based anecdotes and fact-sharing at the kitchen table and on soggy walks. I hope that somewhere I have planted the seeds of a lifelong connection with the natural world. And I'm sorry that my generation have failed so miserably to protect it.

REBECCA

I would like to thank my co-authors, Kiera, Lulah and Rowan, for their constant enthusiasm and sparkling ideas during the writing of this book. In bringing their unique views and insights to our project, they have opened my eyes to different ways of noticing nature, making this a truly collaborative volume. I am deeply grateful to Laura Barber at Granta, who developed our essays into a fluent whole with such kindness; to Clare Skeats, who has set my drawings into the text with a sure eye, and to our agent Natalie Galustian for her help and support. I have – as ever – leaned on my brother, Philip Warren, for his advice on matters biological, but owe my greatest thanks to Paul Brown for his relentless cheerfulness and support and for the many dinners he cooked while I buried myself in the intricacies of illustrating *Nature's Calendar* at the end of the working day.

ROWAN

This book emerged at a strange point in my life, between the end of my doctoral research and the start of my academic career in the Department of Geography at the University of Sheffield. I want to thank my fellow authors, Lulah, Kiera and Rebecca, for supporting me and filling my days with friendship and the reminder to look beyond the bounds of my thesis to a world teeming with life. Thanks also to the team at Granta, I'm particularly grateful for Laura Barber's deft edits as well as her enthusiasm and support. I also want to thank my colleagues in the Department of Geography, especially Jessica Dubow, Eric Olund and Richard Phillips, for encouraging my curiosity, developing my writing and researching practice and inspiring me.

I owe so much to my friendship with Ian Sharman, whose botanical knowledge and critical eye have delighted and excited me for nearly twenty years now. I also recognise my debt to Chief, Phoebe and Astrid, who taught me that noticing nature could be something more than a scholarly endeavour. Woof.

I am endlessly grateful to my husband, Thom Sullivan, who invited me into his world in the Peak District and showed me how to read it like a book and dive into it like an enchanted pool. He also put up with me working messily and endlessly at the kitchen table during this process and offered his ear, edits and reading recommendations. Finally, thank you to my grandfather, Neil Schooling, who taught me that nature is a friend, and that it is only polite to say good day to the trees as you pass under their branches.

Index